James Quinter

A Vindication of Trine Immersion as the Apostolic form of Christian Baptism

James Quinter

A Vindication of Trine Immersion as the Apostolic form of Christian Baptism

ISBN/EAN: 9783337403140

Printed in Europe, USA, Canada, Australia, Japan

Cover: Foto ©Lupo / pixelio.de

More available books at **www.hansebooks.com**

A VINDICATION

OF

TRINE IMMERSION

AS THE

APOSTOLIC FORM

OF

CHRISTIAN BAPTISM.

BY JAMES QUINTER.

"*And I saw, and behold, the Lamb standing on the mount Zion, and with him a hundred and forty and four thousand, having his name, and the name of his Father, written on their foreheads.*"—*Rev. xiv, 1.* (*Revised version.*)

HUNTINGDON, PA.:
THE BRETHREN'S PUBLISHING COMPANY.
1886.

Entered, according to Act of Congress, in the year 1886, by
JAMES QUINTER,
in the Office of the Librarian of Congress, at Washington.

DEDICATION.

To the Christian Fraternity of Brethren or German Baptists, the people by whom, under God, the writer was brought to a knowledge of the truth as it "is in Jesus," and who have, not only maintained the apostolic form of immersion, but who have also maintained against the influence of compromising forms of Christianity in the world, the faith and practice of the Apostolic Church, in their simplicity and integrity; and to all who desire to "obtain like precious faith," is this volume gratefully and affectionately inscribed by

THE AUTHOR.

Prefatory and Introductory.

The reason that has induced us to add another to the already large amount of works on Christian baptism that we have, is a strong conviction of the necessity of something of the kind that we have attempted to produce, to meet an existing want. We shall not affirm that we have fully met that want. But we indulge the hope that our humble contribution will help to supply it.

Christian baptism has been extensively and ably discussed under several of its aspects. That immersion is the proper action of baptism, and a believer, the proper subject, are propositions that have been so clearly proved by the cumulative amount of testimony produced in the baptismal controversy, as to leave no reasonable doubt. But there is an aspect of baptism, that has not, comparatively speaking, had much attention given to it. We refer to the *mode* of immersion—to the question, should that mode be a single or trine immersion?

It is a fact that trine immersion was the prevailing mode of immersion from the end of the second to the close of the twelfth century. It is a fact that the Greek church with all its branches, and with its millions of communicants, and existing in the country in which Christianity was founded by its divine Author, and using the language in which the Scriptures were originally written, has always practiced trine immersion. It is a fact that the ancient Greek and Latin Fathers practiced trine immersion. It is a fact that many eminent scholars and reformers, who were impartial judges, John Wesley among them, conceded to trine immersion an Apostolic origin. It is a fact that Ecclesiastical historians and Christian writers, furnish data from which trine immersion can be traced to the Apostolic age of the Christian church. And though the foregoing facts in themselves do not prove that trine immersion was the mode of immersion established by Christ in His church, they form a strong presumption that it was the mode of immersion that He appointed. And they at least constitute an argument in its favor entitling it to a candid investigation by all professing

Christians, especially by all Baptists. But this it has not had. There has existed a strong prejudice against it, as is manifested by the disparaging manner in which it has been spoken of.

In entering upon a Christian life, we accepted trine immersion as the Scriptural form of immersion. And believing that trine immersion was the Scriptural mode of immersion, we were not a little surprised to find so much prejudice existing against it as we found. When, however, we considered that it was not the popular mode of immersion in America, nor in that part of Europe with which we of America are most familiar, and that there was not much literature besides the Scriptures upon the subject accessible to people generally, our surprise was somewhat diminished. But we could not but think that the subject of trine immersion had not had justice done it in the discussion of Christian baptism. And our conviction was greatly strengthened as we further studied the subject, and found so much testimony as we did to prove the Apostolic and primitive form of baptism was that mode of immersion.

And perceiving that trine immersion had been placed under disadvantageous circumstances, our early attention in our Christian life, and especially in our ministerial life, was directed to the gathering of information, and in using it to subserve the promotion of the true knowledge of a Christian ordinance which in an important feature was not understood.

Our position as editor of the *Gospel Visitor* made it necessary for us to review some works which involved the subject of trine immersion. In our reviews we gave to the brotherhood and to the world some of the fruits of our humble labors. The public discussion we held with Eld. N. A. M'Connell, in Linn Co., Iowa, in 1867, was published, and trine immersion being one of the subjects discussed, we gave considerable of the results of our study and reading upon the subject of trine immersion, in that published discussion.

As we have said, there has much prejudice existed against trine immersion. And this prejudice has been increased by a misinterpretation of a passage in the writings of Tertullian. This ancient Christian Father has been represented as saying, that trine immersion is "somewhat more than the Lord prescribed in the Gospel," and that it had tradition and that alone for its origin. And living so near the Apostolic age as Tertullian did, and possessing the influence that he did, such a declaration from him would have an effect. And after the misrepresentation alluded to was started, it was repeated, and we find it in many of the works written on baptism. Single immersionists have used it freely against trine immersion. We have shown that the construction put upon Tertullian's language making him speak disparagingly of trine immersion, is a wrong construction, and that he bears the most decided testimony to the Scriptural authority of it. And as Tertullian and other ancient Fathers are represented by single immersionists as claiming no authority but tradition for trine immersion, we have clearly shown that such a representation does great injustice to both trine immersion and those ancient Fathers.

The historical aspect of trine immersion has been pretty thoroughly examined, and history is clear and decided in its testimony as we have shown, that that form of immersion was the primitive and apostolic form of baptism.

But we have given special attention to the baptismal formula, regarding that as the most reliable source from which information is to be obtained to settle the form of immersion that is to be practiced in the Christian Church. We have given it a searching and extensive analysis, and examination, and shown that when its grammatical construction is complete, it contains a form of construction that requires trine immersion, and a form that single immersionists admit justifies a trine immersion.

To lay a plain and permanent basis for our course of argument, we have introduced the recognized principles of Scriptural interpretation, and applied them to the discussion of our subject. And in thus applying these principles, we have maintained the position that as the literal and primary meaning of the word baptize or *baptidzo*, should, according to the ground usually assumed by immersionists, decide the action of baptism, so the grammatical and literal meaning of the baptismal formula should decide the proper form of immersion.

The import of " name " in the baptismal formula, and the import of the baptismal formula itself, have been considered, not only because of their bearing upon our subject, but because there is a rich vein of suggestive gospel truth contained in the baptismal formula when understood, that is not, apparently appreciated as it should be.

We have reviewed a few works on baptism as they seem to have been written with the ostensible object of repudiating trine immersion, or do repudiate it in references made in them. And while there is much pretence to truth and logic, a careful examination of the reasoning will show a considerable want of both.

And we have felt that fidelity to the truth required a notice of the works to which allusion has been made, and a reply to their arguments against trine immersion.

We have not exhausted the subject upon which we have written, though we have discussed it under many of its aspects. We have endeavored to show the fallacy of much that has been written against trine immersion. This seemed to be necessary on account of the prejudice which such writing has created against it. And we entertain the hope that our humble production will, if properly used, be a help to those who are anxious to ascertain the true form of Christian immersion, and a confirmation of those who have accepted trine immersion as that form.

We have endeavored to avoid the use of harsh and denunciatory language. We have felt grieved at the manner in which trine immersion has been spoken of by different writers, but we have felt no inclination to retaliate by replying in the same style. We have written with the consciousness of a great responsibility resting upon us. We have not intentionally misstated any fact, nor misquoted any author. Our authorities have been carefully examined, and reference made to the works, and the places in those works in which the passages referred to, may be found.

We have given our work much time, prayerful thought, and study, and have consulted a considerable number of authors as our references will show. And while we trust that we have kept truth in view in our researches and reasoning, and have based our sentiments and positions upon the truth, we would, therefore, offer no apology for them. But we are very sensible that the style and composition of our work are far from being faultless.

In sending out our book on its mission to promote Christian truth, we ask for it a careful reading and a candid examination. And we commend it to the Lord, and pray Him to bless it, and to make it a blessing to our erring race.

J. QUINTER.

Huntingdon, Pa.

CONTENTS.

PREFATORY AND INTRODUCTORY.

CHAPTER I.
The Baptismal Formula of the Church.................. 1

CHAPTER II.
The Correct Rendering of the Baptismal Formula........ 17

CHAPTER III.
Principles of Interpretation........................... 24

CHAPTER IV.
What we have in the Baptismal Formula................ 33

CHAPTER V.
The Import of Name in the Baptismal Formula.......... 53

CHAPTER VI.
The Practical Import of the Baptismal Formula......... 63

CHAPTER VII.
The Introduction of Single Immersion into the Church... 81

CHAPTER VIII.
The Elliptical and Full Form of the Baptismal Formula.. 121

CHAPTER IX.
An Application of the Principles contained in the Baptismal Formula.. 152

CHAPTER X.
A Common Error Refuted............................. 187

CHAPTER XI.
Trine Immersion in its Historical Aspect.................. 198

CHAPTER XII.
The Testimony of Reformers, Theologians, and Literary Men in favor of Trine Immersion..................... 214

CHAPTER XIII.
The Churches that have Practiced Trine Immersion........ 223

CHAPTER XIV.
Objections to Trine Immersion Answered................ 234

CHAPTER XV.
Trine Immersion an Important Support to Immersion..... 243

CHAPTER XVI.
The Posture of the Body in Baptism.................... 254

CHAPTER XVII.
A Review of Dr. Forney............................. 363

CHAPTER XVIII.
A Review of Dr. Cathcart........................... 327

CHAPTER XIX.
A Review of F. M. Bowman.......................... 342

CHAPTER XX.
Conclusion... 357

TRINE IMMERSION.

CHAPTER I.

THE BAPTISMAL FORMULA OF THE CHURCH.

BAPTIZING them into the name of the Father, and of the Son, and of the Holy Ghost." This part of the great Commission of our Lord, is called, *The Formula of Baptism;* and the meaning of this is, that it contains the prescribed form of words that was to be used in administering this Christian ordinance. And the question is, Did Christ design that that form of words should constitute a permanent rule in His Church for the administration of baptism? And it seems altogether proper that we should, in the discussion of our subject, give some attention to this question.

1. That He intended it for a permanent rule, will appear evident from the following considerations and testimonies: 1. In looking at the formula of baptism as given by Christ, its binding authority is very manifest. Our Lord directs his apostles to do several things. (*a*) They are to teach the nations; (*b*) They are to baptize believers, or those that

would receive their word; (*c*) They are to teach those they baptize to observe or do what he, their Lord and Master had commanded; (*d*) They are not only commanded to baptize believers, but the *manner* in which they are to baptize them was prescribed; they are to baptize "them into the name of the Father, and of the Son, and of the Holy Ghost." Now as this part of the commission pertaining to the *manner* of baptizing is as imperatively given as is the command itself to baptize, or as is any one of the commands in the great Commission, it would then be as much of a violation of the command of our Lord to change the formula given by him for baptizing, as it would to do something else instead of baptizing, or as it would to fail to teach the baptized after their baptism, or before it. It would appear then that strict obedience to the commands of Christ contained in the commission, requires believers to be baptized according to the formula that he gave for the administering of baptism, for he gave it as he gave all the commands in the commission, under circumstances solemn and impressive. "*All power is given unto me in heaven and on earth.*" These words constitute Christ's introduction to his last and great commission to His apostles, and they are impressive and appropriate. Then following in the commission after such an introduction as does the formula for administering baptism, "*baptizing them into the name of the Father, and of the Son and of the Holy Spirit,*" who would be so presumptuous as to attempt to make any improvement upon it, or any change in it?

2. From an occurrence we have narrated in the 19th chapter of the Acts of the Apostles it would seem that they understood, that the formula for baptizing given by Christ was to be observed by them. The apostle Paul in his travels came to Ephesus, where he found "certain disciples." Prompted by some feeling, and no doubt it was a proper one, he addressed a question to them which drew from them an answer which seems to have surprised the apostle. The following is a part of the conversation that passed between the apostle and those disciples: "Have ye received the Holy Ghost since ye believed? And they said unto him, we have not so much as heard whether there be any Holy Ghost. And he said unto them, unto what then were ye baptized? And they said, unto John's baptism." The importance of the Holy Spirit in Christian life and experience is plainly recognized in apostolic teaching. And whether Paul saw something in the

conduct of those twelve disciples that indicated a want of the Holy Spirit's influence over their lives and actions that led him to put the question to them that he did, or whether it was from some other consideration, we cannot tell. However the question, "Have ye received the Holy Ghost since ye believed?" was put to them. And they answered as we have seen, "We have not so much as heard whether there be any Holy Ghost." And when Paul saw that they knew nothing about the Holy Ghost, he seemed surprised, and said to them, "Unto what then were ye baptized?"

It appears that Paul took it for granted that these believers were baptized, as it was the practice of the apostolic church to baptize those that believed. But whence the propriety of the apostle's question, "Unto what then were ye baptized?" The propriety of the question is seen in the circumstance that baptism had the Holy Spirit associated with it, since Christ had commanded the apostles to baptize "into the name of the Father, and of the Son, and of the Holy Spirit." And as Paul associated baptism with these disciples, as it was common for disciples to be baptized, so it would seem that he associated the Holy Spirit with baptism, as it was so associated in the baptismal formula as given by

Christ. In bringing out what seems to be the meaning of Paul's language in the question, and the propriety of the question, "Unto what then were ye baptized?" we may paraphrase his language thus: I am somewhat surprised that you know nothing of the Holy Spirit. Were you not baptized into the name of the Holy Spirit, as well as into the name of the Father, and of the Son, when you were baptized? Or unto what or into what were you baptized? Some translations read *into* instead of *unto*. In looking at the subject in this way, the propriety of Paul's question is apparent. He certainly thought that they ought to know something about the Holy Spirit from their baptism. And is it not reasonable to suppose it was because the name of the Holy Spirit was in the baptismal formula? We believe it is, and we therefore regard Paul's language in his interview with the twelve disciples at Ephesus, as affording evidence that the baptismal formula given by Christ to his apostles was observed by them.

It seems altogether probable that the twelve disciples that Paul met at Ephesus had been Gentiles, and that they had not been baptized by John, nor properly unto his baptism, though they said they had been. Had they been Jews, or the disciples of

John, they would have known something about the Holy Spirit, for something was to be learned about him both from John and from the Jewish prophets. But as they did not know whether there was any Holy Spirit, it is most likely they were Gentiles, and had been baptized by some one, who without authority, used John's baptism. John probably had no authority to authorize any to baptize, though some took the authority to administer his baptism.

3. As in the age immediately succeeding the apostolic age, the formula given by Christ to his apostles was used in baptizing, it would seem that the apostles used it, and that their successors obtained it from them. It is very evident from the writings of the ancient Christian Fathers that the formula given by Christ for baptizing was strictly observed. Justin Martyr, the first authentic uninspired writer upon the subject of baptism that we have, and who lived in the early part of the second century of the Christian era, and within about sixty years of the apostles, in giving an sccount of the manner in which persons who became Christians, dedicated themselves to God, says, "As many as are persuaded and believe that what we teach and say is true, and undertake to live accordingly, are instructed to pray and entreat God with fasting, for the remission of their sins that

are past, we praying and fasting with them. Then they are brought by us where there is water, and are regenerated in the same manner in which we were ourselves regenerated. For, in the name of God, the Father and Lord of the universe, and of our Saviour Jesus Christ, and of the Holy Spirit, they then receive the washing with water."—*Justin Martyr's Works, page 79.* It is evident from the above that, in the time of Justin, the formula of baptism as given by Christ was used. In referring to the divine names used in baptizing, he calls the second person in the Godhead by the name of Jesus Christ instead of Son. But he no doubt had reference to the order of baptizing given by Christ, wherein are recognized the three distinct persons, Father, Son, and Holy Spirit. Bingham in maintaining the idea that Justin had reference to the baptismal formula given by Christ, though there is a little difference between his language and that occurring in the formula, quotes Vossius as saying, "Justin Martyr is only giving a paraphrastical explication of the words used in baptism for the instruction of the heathens, to whom he is writing, when he tells them how the Christians baptized in the name of the Father of all things, who was Lord and God, and in the name of Jesus Christ our Lord, and of the Holy Ghost."

—*Bingham's Antiquities of the Christian Church, Book XI, Chap. III, Sect. 12.* Bingham and his author Vossius quoted by him, both believed that Justin had the baptismal formula in his mind when he described the manner in which Christians baptized.

Mr. Alexander Campbell gives the following version of Justin Martyr's abridged description of the manner of baptizing in his time. It will be noticed that according to this reading, Justin gives the names, Father, Son, and Holy Spirit as they occur in the baptismal formula.

"I will declare unto you how we offer up ourselves to God, after that we are received through Christ: Those among us instructed in the faith, are *brought to the water*, then they are baptized therein, in the name of the Father, and of the Son, and of the Holy Ghost. Then we bring the person thus baptized or washed to the brethren, where the assembled are, that we may pray both for ourselves, and the new illuminated person; that we may be found by doctrine and good works, worthy observers and keepers of the commandments. Then bread and wine being brought to the *chief brother*, he taketh it and offereth praise and thanksgiving to the Father, in the name of the Son, and the Holy Ghost. After prayer and thanksgiving the whole assembly saith *Amen.* When thanksgiving is ended by the *chief guide* and consent of the whole people, the Deacons (as we call them) give to every one present, part of the bread and wine, over which thanks is given; this we call the *Eucharist,* to which no man is admitted but he that believeth the truth of the doctrine, and lives as Christ has taught."—*Campbell and Walker's Debate, Enlarged Edition, page 265.*

Tertullian lived some time after Justin Martyr. That the baptismal formula as given by Christ was observed in his day, is very evident. In his work on baptism, he says, "For the *law* of baptizing has been *imposed,* and the formula prescribed: 'Go,' saith [Christ], 'teach the nations, baptizing them into the name of the Father, and of the Son, and of the Holy Spirit.'"—*The Writings of Tertullian, Vol. I, page 248.*

The Seventh Council of Carthage took place in A. D. 256. The re-baptism of heretics was discussed in that council which was composed of eighty-seven bishops. Monnulus, one of the bishops said, "The true doctrine of our Holy Mother the catholic church, hath always my brethren, been with us, and doth yet abide with us, and especially in the article of baptism, and the trine immersion wherewith it is celebrated; our Lord having said: *Go ye, and baptize the Gentiles, in the name of the Father, and of the Son, and of the Holy Ghost.*" *Cyprian's Works, Marshall's Translation, Part I, page 241.* Here we have the baptismal formula as given by Christ recognized, and trine immersion connected with it. And Monnulus claims that these had always been with them. This was as early as A. D. 256.

The fiftieth canon of *The Apostolical Constitutions*, a work that contains many of the doctrines and practices of the Ancient Church, is plain and positive in its teaching upon the importance of the baptismal formula. "If any bishop or presbyter do not perform three immersions of one initiation, but one immersion which is given into the death of Christ, let him be deposed; for the Lord did not say, *baptize into my death; but, Go ye, make disciples of all nations, baptizing them into the name of the Father, and of the Son and of the Holy Ghost.* Do ye, therefore, O Bishops, baptize thrice into one Father, and Son, and Holy Ghost, according to the will of Christ and our constitution by the Spirit."— *Dr. Chase's Edition, page 252.*

In the ancient manuscript discovered and published recently by Bishop Bryennios of the Greek church, called *Teaching of the Twelve Apostles*, a work supposed to have been written very early in the Christian era, even as early as the second century by some, is given a number of the practices of the Christians of the time in which it was written. In it we have a plain recognition of the fact that the formula of baptism as given by Christ was then strictly observed. The following are the directions for baptizing in this ancient work: "Baptize into the name of the Father, and of the Son, and of the Holy Spirit, in running water. But if thou hast not running water, baptize in other water; and if thou canst not in cold, then in warm. But if thou hast neither, pour water upon the head thrice, in the name of Father, and Son and Holy Spirit."—*Edition of Drs. Hitchcock and Brown, page 15.*

Dr. Shedd in his *History of Christian Doctrine, Vol. I, page 330,* in discussing the nature or divinity of Christ, makes reference to the ancient church, in regard to the importance it attributed to the baptismal formula as follows: "In the controversy respecting the validity of heretical baptism, the Church came to the decision that baptism in the name of Christ is not valid. It must be administered according to the Scriptural formula in the name of the Eternal Three. But if baptism in the name of the God-man solely, is not justifiable; still less would it be proper to baptize in the name of the 'Son,' if that term denoted a merely temporal and transitory distinction and relationship."

Bingham, the author of an extensive and popular work on *Christian Antiquities*, having given considerable attention and research to the subject we are examining, after referring to many authors in different ages of the church, remarks as follows: "Indeed among all the writings of the ancients I have never yet met with any but two, that plainly and directly allow or approve of any other form of baptism save that which was appointed by Christ at the institution."—*Bingham's Antiquities, Vol. 1, page 483.* We thus perceive that among the ancients, the baptismal formula as given by Christ, was almost universally accepted. And among modern professing Christians, there is the same general acceptance of the baptismal formula as there was among the ancient Christians. All the Christian denominations of modern times, that practice Christian baptism do it according to the baptismal formula, or if there are any exceptions, they are very few. It would appear then that the baptismal formula given by Christ was designed for all ages of the Christian Church, and for all who would accept the Christian faith.

4. But there have been a few from a very early age among Christian believers who have not regarded the common formula for administering baptism as essential to the validity of the ordinance. And they have been led to look favorably upon another form because they have thought that after the time of Christ, some of the baptisms recorded in the Acts of the Apostles were not performed according to the baptismal formula. But they have been misled in forming their views of the manner in which those baptisms were performed. While we have no record in the Acts of the Apostles of the baptismal formula given by Christ being used when baptism was administered, we should not conclude that it was not used because it is not mentioned. There is merely an allusion made to those cases of baptism when they are mentioned. The inspired writers did not deem it necessary to explain the performance in full after Christ had given the form, for it was to be understood that it was performed according to the formula which he had given unto his apostles. In Acts 20: 7, it is said, "And on the first day of the week when the disciples came together to break bread," etc. Here reference is no doubt made to the whole communion, both bread and wine, though

nothing but the breaking of bread is mentioned. So, no doubt it was in baptism. The formula was used, though the Lord Jesus alone is named, and he is named because of the relation in which he stands to the great work of redemption, into connection with which believers are brought by baptism.

5. We shall give a couple of extracts from reputable authors, containing testimony in regard to the apparent discrepancy between the baptismal formula given by Christ and some of the cases of baptism recorded in the Acts of the Apostles. Their testimony is plain and positive, and agrees with our own view upon the subject as stated above. Dr. Wm. Smith, in his unabridged *Dictionary of the Bible*, under the head of Baptism, and under the 11th division of the subject, which he calls *The Formula of Baptism*, has the following: "It should seem from our Lord's own direction (Matt. 28:19) that the words made use of in the administration of baptism should be those which the church has generally retained, 'I baptize thee in the name of the Father, and of the Son, and of the Holy Ghost;' yet wherever baptism is mentioned in the Acts of the Apostles, it is only mentioned as in the name of the Lord Jesus,' or 'in the name of the Lord.' (Acts 2: 38;

8:16; 10:48; 19:5). The custom of the primitive church as far as we can learn from the primitive Fathers, was always to baptize in the names of the three Persons of the Trinity (see Suicer s. v. Baptize); and there is little doubt that the expressions in the Book of Acts mean only that those who were baptized with Christian baptism were baptized into the faith of Christ, into the death of Christ, not that the form of words was different from that enjoined by our Lord in St. Matthew." Dr. Scott, the Commentator, in commenting upon the formula of baptism as given by our Lord, says, "There can be no reasonable doubt that the Apostles and Primitive Christians always administered baptism in this very form; and it would be strange to infer their disobedience to so express a command of Christ, from the brevity with which matters of this nature are recorded in the Acts of the Apostles. Indeed it would be a most daring presumption in any man to alter it, as if he knew better than the Lord himself in what manner to administer this sacrament."

As there seems to be a tendency in the Christian world to depart from the baptismal formula as given by Christ, or at least a tendency to depreciate its importance, we have extended our argument for its observance as we have done. And perhaps the propriety of doing so will appear, when we shall refer again to the subject of this chapter, as we shall have occasion to do hereafter.

CHAPTER II.

THE CORRECT RENDERING OF THE BAPTISMAL FORMULA.

WHAT the true rendering of the baptismal formula is, demands some consideration. We mean by this, shall the formula be read, "Baptizing them *in* the name of the Father, and of the Son, and of the Holy Spirit," or "*into* the name of the Father, and of the Son, and of the Holy Spirit?" Upon the first thought, to some the difference between the two readings may appear to be very small. But there is a considerable difference—more than those who have not carefully and critically examined the subject, would be likely to perceive in reading the two forms above given.

The question which we are considering, and which involves the choice of one of the two prepositions, *in* and *into*, resolves itself into the following form: Did our Lord in directing his apostles to baptize *in the name of the Father, and of the Son, and of the Holy Spirit*, mean that they should baptize in or by the authority of all three of the Divine Persons named? This is the idea conveyed by the reading of the formula as we have it in our common English version, with *in* in the text.

That the formula read as given in our common English version conveys the idea of authority as above attributed to it, will appear from the following considerations: When anything is said to be done in the name of another, it is understood that it is done by the authority of the person in whose name it is done. When there was a plot laid to destroy King Ahasuerus, and Mordecai discovered it, he revealed it to Esther, and it is written, "The thing was known to Mordecai, who told it unto Esther the queen, and Esther certified the king thereof in Mordecai's name."—*Esther 2:22*. By the authority of Mordecai, Esther informed the king of what he had learned concerning the design against the king's life. And it is written that Jezebel "wrote letters in Ahab's name, and sealed them with his seal."—*1 Kings 21:8*. She wrote and did what she did by the authority of Ahab, as she acted in his name. And in the cure of the cripple who lay at the gate of the temple, we have the same idea attached to the phrase, "in the name of." Peter said to the lame man, "In the name of Jesus

Christ of Nazareth, rise up and walk."—*Acts 3:6.* Peter had previously said in speaking to the Jews, "God hath made that same Jesus, whom ye have crucified, both Lord and Christ."—*Acts 2:36.* Now as Christ was thus exalted, and as Peter was preaching and acting under his authority, he said to the lame man, "in the name of Jesus Christ," meaning by the authority of Jesus Christ, "rise up and walk." Christ interposed his power and the lame man walked.

But did the Lord mean that the converts made to him by the teaching of the apostles were to be baptized by the authority of the Father, and of the Son, and of the Holy Spirit, as the formula according to our English version would seem to imply? It is not at all probable that he did. In his introduction to the *Formula of Baptism,* he said to his apostles, "All power is given unto *me* in heaven and in earth."—*Matt. 28:18.* Then as all power is invested in Christ in his mediatorial character, in which he has been acting since His ascension, it was under His authority that the apostles taught and baptized, and under His authority that believers were to be baptized, and not directly under the authority of the Father, and of the Holy Spirit. Peter therefore said to the penitent Jews, "Repent, and be baptized, every one of you, in the name of Jesus Christ for the remission of sins."—*Acts 2:38.* In the name of Jesus Christ here means by the authority of Jesus Christ. In the original, the preposition is not *eis* but *epi*; and *epi* means not into but upon or on. The import of it here seems to be that Peter commanded them to be baptized upon or on the authority of Jesus Christ. And this seems to be a judicious and proper direction of the apostle. The Jews had denied the Messiahship and authority of Christ; and by this denial they had destroyed themselves and their nation. They must be humbled and own the authority of Christ before they can obtain pardon and salvation. Hence Peter's command to them requiring of them a recognition of the authority of Christ whom they had denied. They were required to be baptized in the name of or under the authority of Christ whom they had rejected. This agrees with Dr. Lange's explanation. In referring to Peter's command to the penitent Jews, he says, "He prescribes a two-fold duty, and promises a two-fold gift. He *demands* that these persons should (1) change their minds (their whole moral state should undergo a change, *metanoeite,* reform,) and (2) be baptized in the name of Jesus (epi to honomati *Ieesou Kristou* (upon the name

of Jesus Christ), as an expression of their faith in Jesus, or a recognition of him, and as a pledge of their submission to him as the Lord Messiah)."
—*Lange's Exegetical and Critical Notes on Acts 2:38.* The Greek preposition that is translated into is *eis*, and *into* is the first or primary meaning of this word, while *en* is the preposition that is translated in; and as *eis* and not *en* occurs in the baptismal formula, it should read, "Baptizing them into the name of the Father, and of the Son, and of the Holy Spirit." Dean Alford of England, an eminent Biblical Scholar, remarks as follows in reference to this subject: "It is unfortunate again here that our English Bibles do not give us the force of this *eis*. It should have been *into* (as in Gal. 3:27, et al.) both here and in 1 Cor. 10:2, and wherever the expression is used." Dr. Whately, a well-known author and one of acknowledged ability, in having occasion to refer to the baptismal formula, says, "*eis to honoma*, 'into the name,' not 'in the name.'"—*Whately's Logic, page 360.* Dr. Dwight, an eminent Presbyterian minister, and at one time President of Yale College, thus expresses himself upon the point in the baptismal formula, which we are explaining: "All persons are baptized not *in* but *into* the name of the Father, and of the Son, and of

the Holy Ghost; that is, they are in this ordinance publicly and solemnly introduced into the family and entitled in a peculiar manner to the name of God. Accordingly they are called godly; Christians; Spiritual; sons and daughters of God; and children of God, throughout the Scriptures. That this is the true construction of the passage just quoted is, I think, obvious from the Greek phraseology, *eis to honoma*, the proper English of which is, *into the name*. Accordingly it is customarily rendered in this manner, by the translators of our Bible in those passages where the same subject is mentioned. Thus, Rom. 6: 3-4, St. Paul asks, *Know ye not, that so many of us as were baptized* INTO *Jesus Christ were baptized* INTO *his death? Therefore we are buried with him by Baptism into death.*—1 Cor. 12: 13; *For by one Spirit we were all baptized* INTO *one body.* —Gal. 3: 27; *As many of you as have been baptized* INTO *Christ have put on Christ.* In all these instances the phraseology is the same with that first quoted, and from analogy, teaches us, that it ought, there also, to have been rendered in the same manner: *into*, being the original and proper meaning of the preposition; and *in* being a meaning so uncommon as heretofore to have been resolved into a *Hebraism*. Several of these passages also directly de-

clare that those who are baptized, are baptized into Christ; that is, into the Church, or Body of Christ."
—*Dwight's Theology, Vol. IV, page 318.*

We could multiply authorities high in literary attainments, and in Biblical knowledge, confirming the view of the reading of the baptismal formula we have given as the preferable and proper reading, but we do not consider it necessary nor advisable. We will, however, yet add that the reading *into* instead of *in*, in the baptismal formula, is almost universally accepted by modern Biblical critics and translators. The following English versions all have the reading *into* instead of *in*, in the baptismal formula: *The Revised Version*, *The Version published by Alexander Campbell*, *Anderson's Version and Kneeland's*. We name these as we have them in our library. And commentators generally agree with the above English versions, in accepting *into* instead of *in*, in the baptismal formula.

CHAPTER III.

PRINCIPLES OF INTERPRETATION.

THE Bible contains the will or law of God for the use and government of man. The divine law was once written upon man's heart. But sin has erased or so far obliterated it, that it cannot now be relied upon. Hence the necessity of the divine law coming to us from without, as we can no longer read it from within. The Scriptures are a revelation and a communication from God to man to make known to him not simply the will or law of God, but also the remedial scheme of redemption, that man may be redeemed from guilt, and be restored to the honorable position in the universe of God, that he occupied before his apostasy.

The Bible is then a revelation to reveal to man, all things that "pertain to life and godliness." And it is mainly a revelation of the revealed things of God to man through the medium of human language. This divine revelation was originally communicated to man in different languages, but it has been translated from one language into another that the different nations of the earth might have it and read it in their vernacular or native tongue. And when it is translated into any language, the divine utterances of the Spirit of God become clothed or embodied in the words common to that language, and the meaning of the Spirit must be ascertained in the same way that the utterances or speech of the people using that language, are to be ascertained in their communications with one another. And while human language if properly appreciated, will be highly valued as a means of men's communicating with one another, the fact that it is the medium through which God communicates his thoughts or ideas to man, will add greatly to its value. And the circumstance that God speaks to us through his word translated into our language in our vernacular tongue, should be a great incentive to us to study our language and become acquainted with it, that we may the more readily and the more correctly understand Him as He speaks to us. There is no doubt that in receiving the word of God as we do through translations, we receive it under some disadvantages. But such disadvantages do not materially detract from the value or plainness of the divine oracles. And they have been translated into many languages.

In the English language we have several excellent translations.

From the benevolent character of the Divine Author of the Bible and from the ignorance and stupidity of man, the creature that is to be taught, we would reasonably suppose that he would communicate his will to man in a manner no less intelligible than men communicate their thoughts to one another. That he has done so, appears from what he has declared in his word. The prophet speaking of the way of holiness revealed in the word of God, says of its plainness, "wayfaring men, though fools shall not err therein."—Isaiah 35:8. And Paul says, "we use great plainness of speech."—2 Cor. 3:12.

We have made the foregoing remarks preparatory to our introduction of some of the recognized principles of biblical interpretation that may be applied to advantage in explaining many passages of Scripture as well as that which contains the baptismal formula. But as the meaning of this is now the subject of our investigation, it is to this that we desire a candid and intelligent application made of the recognized principles that we shall introduce. Language is to be explained and understood by rules. There is an implied understanding between readers and the authors they read. It is understood that authors use the words and phrases they do, with such meaning attached to them as obtains in general literature. And it is also to be understood that readers will do the authors the justice of interpreting their language according to the common use of the words and phrases which they employ to convey their ideas.

Dr. Fairbairns, professor of divinity in the Free Church College, Glasgow, and author of several popular works, in that called the *Hermeneutical Manual, pp. 83, 84,* in stating rules and principles to be followed in interpreting the Scriptures, says, "And we, therefore, lay it down as another principle to be sacredly maintained in Scriptural interpretations, that *nothing should be elicited from the text but what is yielded by the fair and grammatical explanation of the language.* The import of each word, and phrase, and passage, must be investigated in a manner perfectly accordant with the laws of language, and with the actual circumstances of the writers. Not what we may think they should have said, or might possibly wish they *had* said, but simply what, as far as we are able to ascertain, they *did say*—this must be the sole object of our pursuit, and the more there is of perfect honesty and discriminating tact in our efforts to arrive at this, the more certain is our success. For in the words of Bengel: 'It is better to run all lengths with Scripture truth in a natural and open manner, than to shift, and twist, and accommodate. Straight-forward conduct may draw against us bitterness and rancour for a time, but sweetness will come out of it. Every single truth is a light of itself, and every error, however minute, is darkness as far as it goes.'"

Alexander Campbell has the following just and truthful remarks: "If we have a revelation from God in human language, the words of that volume must be intelligible by the common usage of language; they must be precise and determinate in signification, and that signification must be philologically ascertained—that is, as the words and sentences of other books are ascertained by the use of the dictionary and grammar. Were it otherwise, and did men require a new dictionary and grammar to understand the Book of God,—then without that divine dictionary and grammar, we could have no revelation from God, for a revelation that needs to be revealed is no revelation at all."—*Campbell on Baptism, page 54.*

From the principles Mr. Campbell enunciates, he draws several rules; among them is the following: "To understand the meaning of what is commanded, promised, taught, &c., the same philological principles, deduced from the nature of language, or the same laws of interpretation which are applied to the language of other books, are to be applied to the language of the Bible."—*Ibid, page 61.*

In *Horne's Introduction to the Critical Study and Knowledge of the Holy Scriptures, Vol. I, page 326*, we have the following rule: "Of any particular passage the most simple sense—or that which most readily suggests itself to an attentive and intelligent reader, possessing competent knowledge,—is in all probability the genuine sense or meaning."

In a work called, *The Bible and Its Study*, made up of articles that had been written by different writers for *The Sunday-School Times*, we have the following observations in an article written by Prof. M. B. Riddle, D. D. "The light of private judgment for which Protestantism contends, is neither the right to doubt nor the right to think as we please. It is the right to listen to God when God speaks to us, and the right to receive that direct teaching of the Spirit of God which is one of the noblest prerogatives that Christ confers on all that believe in Him. (Dale, Protestantism, pp. 42, 43.) As applied to the interpretation of Scripture, this position assumes that the Bible is a human book;

that, however its human authors were inspired they wrote or spoke so as to be understood, using words, whether literally or figuratively, in the sense in which general usage employs them. For if this principle of interpretation were not correct, there could be no duty of private judgment. A cabalistic meaning is known only by those who have learned the key to the cipher. On the other hand this position implies that there is an illuminating influence of the Holy Ghost bestowed upon the individual believer who prayerfully studies his Bible. These two principles are based upon the character of the sacred Scriptures as constituting one divine-human book, revealing a divine-human person, Jesus Christ our Lord. . . . . . The Bible is to be interpreted in accordance with the plain historical sense of its words, as determined by the ordinary laws of language. This is the general principle, accepted by all Protestants in theory, at least. As already intimated, if this were not correct, there would be no right or duty of private judgment. Indeed any other position makes the Bible a dishonest book. Of course, the measure of knowledge will differ in different readers; but a denial of this theory, which puts before the interpreter the single aim of exactly ascertaining and establishing on due grounds *the purely historical sense of Scripture* (Meyer), makes the Bible a sealed book, both to the philologist and to the ordinary reader. The greatest scholar and the well-nigh illiterate Christian may make common cause against every other theory of interpretation. On the face of it, this theory is best adapted to the contents of the Bible; a very much larger half of both Testaments being simple, historical narrative." pp. 40, 41.

Mr. Milligan in speaking of positive law, says, "It depends for its existence and all that pertains to it, wholly and exclusively, on the will of the law-giver. And hence the necessity that *every positive law should be expressed in the most clear, definite and specific terms possible:* and furthermore, that *it should be interpreted and obeyed according to the strict letter and conventional meaning of the terms used to express it.*"—*The Great Commission, page 89.*

Such principles and rules laid down by authors when giving rules for a proper and safe explanation of the Scriptures—principles and rules that cannot fail from their truthfulness and reasonableness to commend themselves to every candid and intelligent mind, could be greatly multiplied, but we have quoted sufficient to remind our readers of the commonly accepted principles which are to govern us in so construing the language of the Scriptures that we may obtain from them the precise meaning that God intended to be conveyed to us by the words he used in the revelation he has given us. By the foregoing rules we shall explain the baptismal formula, and the reader should keep them in mind.

CHAPTER IV.

WHAT WE HAVE IN THE BAPTISMAL FORMULA.

WHAT we have in the baptismal formula, "baptizing them into the name of the Father, and of the Son, and of the Holy Spirit." 1. We have a plurality of personal subjects. 2. We have a distinction of personal subjects. 3. We have a plurality of names.

SECTION I.

1. We have a plurality of personal subjects, distinguished by the names, Father, Son, and Holy Spirit. And as these have personal attributes attributed to all of them in the Scriptures, they have been called Persons, their personality bearing some analogy to human personality.

The three-fold plurality of Father, Son, and Holy Spirit, that we have in the baptismal formula, we have in several passages in the New Testament. We have it in the baptism of Christ. The Father was in heaven, the Son was in Jordan submitting to baptism by John, and the Holy Spirit in the form of a dove came down from heaven upon the Son.—*Matt. 3 : 13-17*. Here as in the baptismal formula, the threefold plurality of the Father, Son, and Holy Spirit was most clearly and impressively manifested.

2. We have also the three-fold plurality of the same divine Persons in the apostolic benediction: "The grace of the Lord Jesus Christ, and the love of God, and the communion of the Holy Ghost be with you all."—2 Cor. 13 : 14.

3. We have another example of the same kind in the apostle John's salutation to the seven churches of Asia: "John to the seven churches in Asia, grace unto you and peace, from Him who is, and who was, and who is to come, and from the Seven Spirits which are before the throne, and from Jesus Christ, the Faithful Witness, the First-born from the dead, and the prince of the kings of the earth."—Rev. 1 : 4, 5. Accepting the prevailing view that the seven spirits represent the Holy Spirit with the perfection of its character, the completeness of its gifts and offices as the correct view of the seven spirits in this passage as it probably is, it presents to us the same three divine Persons that we have in the baptismal formula.

We shall next offer the testimony of several authors of reputation to confirm our position that there is a three-fold plurality of Persons in the baptismal formula. The first testimony that we shall offer is that of Dr. Halley, an English author of reputation. In his work called *The Sacraments*, Part I, page 231, and in a lecture on *The Mode of Christian Baptism*, he says: "Two inquiries are suggested: the one, are we bound by the terms of the commission to administer baptism according to the form of words there prescribed; that is, in the name of the Father, and of the Son, and of the Holy Ghost? The other, is immersion the only proper mode of administering this ordinance?

As to the former inquiry, the command of our Lord seems so clear and absolute, as to admit of no exception. I do not see how any person can baptize into the name of the Father, and of the Son, and of the Holy Ghost, without mentioning the three names of these Divine Persons; by an act of invocation, imploring their blessing; or by an act of of authority, administering by their commission; or by an act of dedication devoting the person to their service." Here the plurality of persons is recognized.

We shall next give the testimony of Dr. Bethune,

of the *Reformed Dutch Church.* In a course of lectures on the Heidelberg Catechism, Vol. II, page 33, in a lecture on "The Divinity, Personality, and Work of the Holy Ghost," he says: "Again in the divinely prescribed form of baptism: 'In the name of the Father, and of the Son, and of the Holy Ghost,' (the three present at the baptism of our Head.) Nothing but the extremest prejudice could bring one to believe that these several names belong to only a single person, and do not intend three distinct persons in the Godhead." Here again we have the plurality of persons, and a three-fold plurality recognized.

Our next witness is Alexander Campbell, well known in the Christian world as a scholar and as an author. In alluding to the language of the formula for administering baptism, he says: "No language could more clearly indicate a change of state than the phrase just now read. The prominent design of baptism is thus fully expressed by the transition spoken of in the words, 'baptizing into the name.' The subject is here represented as in some way entering *into the name* or *into the persons*, represented by the Father, Son, and Holy Spirit."—*Campbell and Rice Debate, page 441.* Here Mr. Campbell teaches a plurality of persons in the baptismal formula and that it is into this three-fold plurality of persons that the subject of baptism is baptized.

We will next hear Dr. Waterland of the Episcopal Church. He was an eminent minister in that church and a popular author. In a sermon on the commission of Christ to his Apostles, and on Christ's Divinity, he has the following: "And now since Christ himself had undertaken to draw all men unto him, the first and principal thing which all the nations of the world were to have notice of, was the obligation they lay under to three Persons, of *high* character and distinction, and *related* to each other, called by the names of *Father, Son,* and *Holy Ghost.*"—*Waterland's Works, Vol. II, pp. 171, 172.*

We have in the above language of Dr. Waterland, a three-fold plurality recognized in the baptismal formula.

SECTION II.

We have in the baptismal formula a distinction of persons. The names Father, Son, and Holy Ghost, occurring in the baptismal formula, have been applied to but one person, or understood to constitute but one person. Sabellius, the leader and founder of a sect in the ancient church, held and taught that the Father, Son, and Holy Spirit were not three persons, but one only—one person with three names. He held that as Creator of the world, this one person was called Father; as the Redeemer of the world he was called Son; and as the Sanctifier of the world he was called Holy Spirit. But the Scriptures plainly teach a distinction in the three-fold plurality of the persons in the Godhead. And that distinction is taught and represented in the baptismal formula. The names Father, Son, and Holy Spirit, represent, three personal subjects or Persons. This distinction is also taught in other passages of Scripture. It is taught in those passages to which we referred in the first part of this chapter, which teach the three-fold plurality of persons in the baptismal formula. But we shall present a few other passages in which the distinction under consideration is taught. The following are examples:

1. In the 5th chapter of Revelation we have a scene that shows very clearly the distinction between the Father and the Son. The scene occurred in heaven. John, the inspired writer, saw the Father upon the throne with a book in his hand; John wept because no one at first appeared to open the book. But finally a Lamb appears to open the seals. "And he came and took the book out of the right hand of him that sat upon the throne." How

plainly and distinctly are the Father and Son presented to us in that scene! The one that occupied the throne was no doubt the Father, and the Lamb represented the Son. But we also have the Holy Spirit presented to us in the vision of John. The Lamb had seven eyes which are declared to be "the seven Spirits of God." These seven Spirits represent the Holy Spirit. This was sent forth by the Saviour into all the earth, as a help to his Apostles, and as a seal to all believers.

2. In Revelation 14: 1 we have a very important illustration of the distinction between the Father and the Son. We give the passage as we have it in the *Revised Version*. The distinction is here brought out very fully. "And I saw and, behold, the Lamb standing on the Mount Zion, and with him a hundred and forty and four thousand, having his name, and the name of his Father written on their foreheads." How naturally does this passage thus rendered, associate it with the baptismal formula in which we have the Father's, the Son's, and the Holy Spirit's name presented to us!

We shall now give the authority of some Christian writers concerning what we have said in regard to the *distinction* of persons in the baptismal formula.

1. Our first authority will be Dr. A. Clark, a well

known commentator. In his notes on the baptismal formula, "Baptizing them into the name of the Father, and of the Son, and of the Holy Spirit," he says, "Is it possible for words to convey a plainer sense than these do? And do they not direct every reader to consider the Father, the Son, and the Holy Spirit, as three distinct persons?" Here plurality and distinction are affirmed by Dr. Clark of the persons named in the baptismal formula.

2. Our next authority will be Alexander Campbell. Mr. Campbell, in speaking of the divinity of the Godhead, says, "For the divine nature may be communicated or imparted in some sense; and, indeed, while it is essentially and necessarily singular, it is certainly plural in its personal manifestations. Hence we have the Father, Son, and Holy Spirit equally divine, though personally distinct from each other. We have, in fact, but one God, one Lord, one Holy Spirit; yet these are equally possessed of one and the same divine nature."—*The Christian System, page 20.*

3. We had Dr. Bethune's testimony upon the plurality of Persons in the baptismal formula; we shall now give it in regard to the distinction. He gives the following: "When we say that there is this distinction of three in the Godhead, we mean that this

distinction is real and not merely nominal; that is, these names are not several names of the Godhead, as Caius Julius Cæsar are names of one man; nor are they used separately of the Godhead in reference to the several operations of the divine will, as that God is called the Father, in reference to the creation; the Son in reference to the Redemption; the Holy Ghost, in reference to the sanctification of man; but that, as the Scriptures teach, these three are so distinct from each other as to have relations to each other. It is absurd to speak of a being having relations to himself, because relativeness implies distinctiveness between those spoken of as related."—*Bethune's Lectures on the Catechism, Vol. I, page 202.*

4. Dr. Waterland gives the following strong testimony to the distinction we are explaining, in A Familiar Discourse upon the Doctrine of the Holy Trinity. After noticing the nature of the Divine Persons, he says, "I may next consider their *distinction*. They are constantly represented in Scripture as distinct from each other: the Father is not the Son, nor is the Holy Ghost either of the other two. They are described, as any other distinct persons are by different characters and offices. This is so plain through every page almost of the New Testament,

that it were needless to instance in particulars. The Father is said to *send*, the Son to be *sent*, and the Holy Ghost to proceed or go forth. The Father is represented as *one witness*, and the Son as *another* witness: the Son as *one Comforter*, the Holy Ghost as *another* comforter, not both one comforter. The Father is introduced as speaking to the Son, and the Son, as speaking to the Father, and the Holy Ghost as delivering commands from both. These and a multitude of other particulars plainly prove their distinction one from another; which being analogous to, and nearly resembling the distinction among men, or angels, or other rational creatures, we therefore presume to call it a *personal* distinction, and to call the three three persons."—*Waterland's Works, Vol. V, page 349.*

5. J. C. Ryle, the author of *Expository Thoughts on the Gospels*, a work that possesses some merit as a commentary, in his exposition of the baptismal formula, says, "This is one of those great plain texts which directly teach the mighty doctrine of the Trinity. It speaks of Father, Son, and Holy Ghost as three distinct persons, and speaks of all three as co-equal. Such as the Father is, such is the Son, and such is the Holy Ghost. And yet these three are one." The distinction is here clearly affirmed.

6. We shall yet give the strong testimony of Bishop Sherlock. As quoted by Dr. Terry, he says, "The distinction of persons can not be more truly and aptly represented than by the distinction between three men; for Father, Son, and Holy Ghost are as really distinct persons as Peter, James and John."—*Biblical Hermeneutics, page 590.*

SECTION III.

We have also in the baptismal formula, "baptizing them in the name of the Father, and of the Son, and of the Holy Spirit," a plurality of names. If there are a plurality of Persons and a distinction of Persons, in the baptismal formula, as we have seen there are, it would seem to follow as a necessary consequence, that there must also be a plurality of names, as one name would not be likely to to be applied to the three distinct Persons; and therefore it might seem unnecessary for us to make the plurality of names a special part of our subject, and to offer any proof that there is a plurality of names in the baptismal formula. But strange as it may seem, while a plurality of Persons and a distinction of Persons are recognized in the baptismal formula, there is not that proper and full appreciation of the plurality of names in every respect that there should be in order to bring out the practical doctrine and action that the formula is designed to teach. This will appear more fully hereafter. And as there is a want of a full understanding of the word "name" as it stands connected with "Father" in the baptismal formula, something upon the plurality of names seems to be necessary in our work. Hence this division of our subject. The materials here collected will hereafter be more fully applied. We shall now proceed to show how fully a plurality of names is admitted.

1. Our first example will be that of Bishop Beveridge, an eminent scholar and theologian in the Episcopal Church. In referring to the baptismal formula he says: "In which words we observe: *First*, 'A Trinity of Persons,' into whose names we are baptized, the 'Father, Son, and Holy Ghost.'" —*Beveridge's Works, Vol. VIII, page 336.* This writer recognizes three names in the baptismal formula, and declares that it is into these names that we are baptized.

2. Mr. Isaac Errett, the able editor of *The Christian Standard*, and an eminent minister of the Disciple Church, in referring to baptism and the form of administering it, says, "It is the only act with which are associated the names of Father, Son, and Holy

Spirit. The glory and the benediction of the Godhead rest on this ordinance as on no other—for in the peculiar place it occupies, it brings us face to face with Deity in the three-fold manifestations of Father, Son, and Spirit, and establishes new and permanent relations with the Father as *our* Father, with the Son as *our* brother and Redeemer, with the Holy Spirit as our Comforter, the earnest of *our* inheritance."—*First Principles: or the Elements of the Gospel, page 108.* The plurality of names is here plainly recognized.

3. W. H. Hopson, a Disciple minister, says: "Is it not strange, passing strange, that the Protestant parties in the land consider the acknowledgment of the Trinity an *essential* element of an orthodox faith, and an *essential* qualification for admission into an orthodox Church; yet will treat as a matter of inferior moment (speaking of it as a *non-essential*) a commandment of Jesus the Christ, which is a clear revelation of his will concerning our duty, and the only one in all the Bible commanded to be done in or into the *names* of Father, Son, and Holy Spirit?" *The Living Pulpit of the Christian Church, page 301.*

4. In the same work there is a sermon by O. A. Burges, also a Disciple minister, and in that sermon there is a division under the head, "*Immersion into*

the name of the Father, Son and Holy Spirit." And in referring to these he says, "The ordinance, therefore, must not only be immersion, but immersion into these three names."—*Ibid, page 176.*

5. Hervey D. Ganse of the Protestant Reformed Dutch Church, New York, preached a sermon on the Trinity, from Matt. 28:19, "Go ye therefore, and teach all nations, baptizing them in the name of the Father, and of the Son, and of the Holy Ghost." He says, "This text embraces three names, which the New Testament, especially, has made very familiar to us. Our work to-night is to inquire to whom these names belong. What are we to understand by 'the Father?' and what by 'the Son?' and what by 'the Hoiy Ghost?'"—*South Church Lectures, page 241.*

Mr. Ganse understands that the three names in the baptismal formula are to be applied to three Persons, "Father," "Son," and "Holy Ghost." The following language also occurs in his introductory remarks: "The first question will not detain us for a moment; for all the readers of the Bible will admit that the Father is represented to be God supreme and infinite." According to this language, the author of it understood God and Father to be interchangeable terms and expressive of the same divine Person. This will be generally if not universally admitted. This the Scriptures teach. But more of this hereafter.

6. We next give the order of baptizing in the Roman Catholic church. After the proper question is put and answered, the order is thus prescribed: "Then the godfather and godmother both holding or touching their godchild, the priest pours, or where the custom is to dip, dips three times, saying at the same time these words: '*N*. I baptize thee in the name of the Father, and of the Son, and of the Holy Ghost.' Which words are pronounced in such a manner that the three pourings of the water concur with the pronouncing of the three names of the divine Persons. For the form is to be pronounced but once."—*The Catholic Christian Instructed, page 39.*

7. In *Lard's Quarterly*, a periodical of the Christian or Disciple church, Vol. IV, No. 2, there is an article on "The Commission," the design of the writer being to prove the necessisy of adhering strictly to the order of words containing a divine command. He, having referred to that part of the commission containing the baptismal formula as given by Matthew, and also to that part of the commission given by Mark, says: "Putting both of

these passages of Scripture together, we understand that the gospel is first to be preached; second, to be believed; and third, to be obeyed. We understand that our Lord, in naming the persons (yes, the divine persons) into whose names baptism was to be performed, followed the order of nature, and therefore he said, first, Father; second, Son; and third, Holy Spirit. Therefore we are not at liberty to change this order. Nor would the apostles have obeyed the Saviour, if, in baptizing, they had said: 'I baptize you,' or 'you are baptized' into the name of the Son, and of the Holy Spirit, and of the Father; nor in adopting any other order of pronouncing these names than that uttered by the Lord Jesus, as recorded by his apostle Matthew." The writer of the above recognizes both a plurality of persons, and also of names in the baptismal formula. He also expresses the idea that it was into those names that believers were to be baptized.

And his logical reasoning upon the necessity of adhering to the order of words given by Christ, in order to fulfil the divine command, suggested to our mind, when reading it, the question, does not the principle contended for, require "name" as used before "Father" confined to him and name to be added to "the Son" and to "the Holy Spirit," mentally when it is read, to complete the constructive language of the baptismal formula, as this would seem to be the natural order of the words in the phraseology, and the natural deduction of the human mind? We believe it does and then a plurality of immersions or trine immersion would be required to strictly obey the command, as we shall hereafter see.

It is well known, we presume, that the baptismal formula has occupied a very prominent place in the Trinitarian controversy that commenced at an early age of the church, and has continued until the present time. It has not, however, been exclusively used by one side of the controversy, though the Trinitarians perhaps have sought to make the most use of it. John H. Morrison, in his *Disquisitions and Notes on the Gospels*, when commenting on the words, "Go ye, and make disciples of all nations, baptizing them into the name of the Father, and of the Son, and of the Holy Ghost," says, "Sectarian writers generally maintain that *their* peculiar views of the Trinity, whatever they may be, and they are many and various, are taught in this formula." There is a good deal of truth in these remarks. But to confine the broad and deep meaning of the baptismal formula to the controversial aspect of it as in the Trinitarian controversy, is to deprive Christians of much spiritual nourishment, and the text itself of much of its usefulness.

Dr. Meyer, the great German commentator and scholar, in explaining the passage containing the baptismal formula, in his commentary, after defending the propriety of using name before Father, in the singular number, and in repeating it before Son, and also before Holy Ghost, making the baptismal formula read, "baptizing them into the name of the Father, and into the name of the Son, and into the name of the Holy Ghost," says, "We must beware of making any such *dogmatic* use of the singular as to employ it as an argument either *for* (Basilides, Jerome, Theophylact) or *against* (the Sabellians) the orthodox doctrine of the Trinity." This popular commentator and theologian, though himself a Trinitarian, did not think there was anything in the baptismal formula that would give either side in the Trinitarian controversy any special advantage over the other. And the explanation and use we are making of the baptismal formula, cannot materially be effected by its being looked at from either side of the controversy to which we have alluded. Though there may be some difference of judgment in regard to the character of the personal subjects named in it, there will probably be no difference in regard to the *number* of personal subjects, their distinction, and the number of names contained in it.

We shall have occasion to allude in our work to the supposed connection between trine immersion and the doctrine of the Trinity, but that will be done at a future stage of our work. In this connection we may also remark that in quoting the various authorities we do, it is not with any reference to their views of the Trinity that we quote them. With those views we are not particularly concerned. We quote them more as scholars than as theologians—more to obtain an expression of their judgment upon the literal construction or meaning of the baptismal formula, than to astertain their view of its doctrinal teaching. The literal meaning of Scriptural terms and phraseology should be first ascertained before their spiritual or doctrinal import is settled. This course we are endeavoring to pursue in the investigation and elucidation of our subject. And we hope the propriety of our course, and of the authorities we are quoting will be seen as our plan and work are developed.

We have clearly showed both from the Scriptures and from writers of acknowledged reputation as scholars and theologians, that there are in the baptismal formula a three-fold plurality of persons, a distinction of persons, and a plurality of names. And this being the case, it seems to follow as a necessary consequence, that there is in the baptismal formula all that is necessary to give it that form or character that we claim it should have in its complete construction, namely, this: baptizing them into the name of the Father, and into the name of the Son, and into the name of the Holy Spirit. Our object, in quoting the authorities we have quoted in this chapter, is to show that when there is nothing to bias the mind of the candid and intelligent reader in reading the baptismal formula, it will be read in its natural order, and according to its literary meaning. And this is the way in which it should be read whatever application is made of it in proving the mode of Christian immersion, or anything else it is supposed to contain. We yet remark that both Arians and Trinitarians have practiced trine immersion. *See Bingham's Antiquities of the Christian Church, Book XI, Chapter XI.* Showing there is nothing in this form of immersion, that will "emphasize" or favor the views of one of these bodies, more than those of the other, concerning the Godhead.

CHAPTER V.

THE IMPORT OF NAME IN THE BAPTISMAL FORMULA.

BAPTIZING them into the name of the Father, and of the Son, and of the Holy Spirit."

A clear understanding of *name* as it occurs in the baptismal formula will materially help to understand our subject in its further development. We shall therefore examine the import of *name* as it stands connected with each one of the persons designated in the formula.

In referring to the use of *name* as it occurs in Scripture, and as it is applied to the persons in the Godhead, it will be seen that it means those persons themselves. The following are some such references: "O magnify the Lord with me, and let us exalt his name together."—Ps. 34: 3; "Give unto the Lord the glory due unto his name."—Ps. 29: 2; "The name of the Lord is a strong tower."—Pv. 18: 10; "Who is among you that feareth the Lord, that obeyeth the voice of his servant, that walketh in darkness, and hath no light? Let him trust in the name of the Lord, and stay upon his God."—Isa. 50:10. Name here stands for the Lord himself. "But unto the place which the Lord your God shall choose out of all the tribes to put his *name* there, even unto his habitation shall ye seek, and hither shalt thou come."—Deut. 12:5. Here the place where He would put His name, means the place where He would dwell, and where His people could find Him, when they desired to meet Him. "Praise his name, for his name alone is excellent."—Ps. 148:13. Name stands in all the above passages for the Lord himself, as in the last example. Praise the Lord for He alone is excellent; this is equivalent to "Praise his *name*, for his *name* alone is excellent."

In the following passages in the New Testament, name refers to Christ, and is equivalent to Christ himself. "He came unto his own and his own received him not. But as many as received him, to them gave he power to become the sons of God, even to them that believe on his name."—John 1:11, 12. Here believing on the name of Christ, plainly means believing on Christ himself. The following are similar passages: "But these are written that ye might believe that Jesus is the Christ, the

Son of God; and that believing, ye might have life through his name."—John 20:31; "And in his name thall the Gentiles trust."—Matt. 12:21. Any number of texts similar to the above, could be quoted. But enough have been quoted to show that in the Scriptures, when the names of the divine Persons occur, those divine Persons themselves are generally to be understood.

The following reputable testimony will confirm what we have said, and further illustrate the subject: Mr. Bate in his *Cyclopædia of Illustrations*, under the word *name* has the following: "A name is generally the synonym of a thing, a place or a person; or, in other words, to make mention by name of a certain thing, or place, or person, is to call up before the mind all those things which we know to belong to each respectively. Hence when you utter the name of some things, that name includes the characteristics of those things so far as known by those that hear the name."

Dr. Fairbairn, in his *Hermeneutical Manual* and under the head of *The Characteristics of New Testament Greek, pp. 44, 45,* has the following: "In like manner in the use of the word *honoma* (name) in a great variety of expressions, such as, 'calling upon the name,' or doing anything in the name of another, 'hallowing God's name,' 'believing on the name of Christ,' 'trusting in the name of the Lord,' and such like—while the *honoma* (name) precisely corresponds to the *sham* (name) in Hebrew, and *name* in English to both, it is still only through the Hebrew usage that we can get at the proper import of the expressions. The Hebrews were wont to regard the name of an individual, as, what it doubtless originally was, the index to the nature; and when the primary name failed properly to do this, they very commonly superseded it by another, which yielded a more significant or fitting expression of the individual properties. Hence, with them the *name* was very much identified with the *person*, as on the other side the person was very often contemplated in the light of the name. Among the Greeks the significance of names never assumed the same place that it did among the Hebrews; they were regarded more as arbitrary signs, having their chief use in distinguishing one person or one object from another; and consequently the same identification did not prevail in the ordinary Greek usage, as in the Hebrew, between the name, and the person or properties of the individual. In dealing with such expressions, therefore, as those specified above, we must have recourse to the Hebrew in order to arrive at the proper import."

Dr. Doddridge, in his explanation of the phrase, *believed in his name*, in John 2:23, translates it *believed in him*. And he has the following remarks containing his reason for so translating it: "It is in the original, *believe in his name*: a Hebraism which it did not seem necessary to retain. Nothing is more common than to put the *name* of a person for the person himself. Compare John 1:12; 20:31; Ps. 75:1; Acts 1:15; and Rev. 3:4."

We shall yet add a few testimonies from the ancient Fathers to show that they understood *name* in the baptismal formula to import what we have explained it to mean. Tertullian, in referring to the faith delivered by Christ to his apostles, says, "Accordingly, after one of these had been struck off, he commanded the eleven others, on his departure to the Father, to 'go and teach [all] nations, who were to be baptized into the Father, and into the Son, and into the Holy Ghost.'"—*Tertullian's Works, Vol. II, pp. 22, 23.* Let it be observed that this writer does not use the *name* of the Father, and of the Son, and of the Holy Ghost, as something that believers are to be baptized into, but he gives the

Father, Son, and Spirit themselves as the proper objects into which believers are to be baptized. And he repeats the same idea on page 395 of the same volume.

In the apostolic constitutions we have the following: "If any Bishop or Presbyter do not baptize according to the Lord's constitutions, into the Father, and the Son, and the Holy Ghost, but into three beings without beginning, or into three Sons, or into three comforters, let him be deposed."—*Chase's Constitutions and Canons of the Church, page 252.* According to the above Canon, the 49th, the ancients that formed this Canon, understood that the candidates for baptism were baptized into the Father, and into the Son, and into the Holy Ghost, and not simply into their names. The same idea is presented in the 50th Canon.

"Great, indeed, and all-powerful in gifts, and wonderful, is the Holy Ghost; wonderful in truth is that SPIRIT, holy and good; and fittingly were we baptized into FATHER, SON, AND HOLY GHOST."— St. Cyril in *Suggestive Thoughts on Religious Subjects*, Art. Holy Spirit.

While the idea seems to have been common among the Ancient Fathers that it is into the Father, and into the Son, and into the Holy Spirit that we are baptized, when we are baptized according to the baptismal formula, it probably is the idea that all candid, sincere, and intelligent minds will receive upon reading the baptismal formula. Modern writers have expressed themselves as the Ancient Fathers did. Mr. Milligan in his *Great Commission*, a work already referred to, after attempting to explain the word "name" in the baptismal formula says, "The passage may, therefore, without violence, be rendered into the English idiom as follows: 'Go ye, therefore, and make disciples of all the nations, immersing them into the Father, and the Son, and the Holy Spirit,' the one God revealed in the Holy Scriptures."—Page 139.

We are to understand, then, that when we are baptized into the name of the Father, and of the Son, and of the Holy Spirit, we are baptized into the three glorious and divine Persons, that those three names in the baptismal formula represent. The correctness of this idea is further proved from the fact that Christians are represented as being in the Father, and in the Son, and in the Holy Spirit. That they are so represented will appear from the following passages in Scripture: "If that which ye have heard from the beginning shall remain in you, ye also shall continue in the Son and in the Father."

—1 John 2:24. This language implies that the Christians to whom the apostle wrote had been brought into the Son, and into the Father, and he instructs them how to live that they might continue in them. That which they had heard from the beginning, namely, the living, quickening, and sanctifying truth was to continue in them. To that they were to hold fast. By doing so they would continue to dwell where they were put by their baptism, namely in the Father and in the Son. The Holy Spirit was not mentioned in connection with the Father and Son, by John, but it was common to mention only a part of an experience or work where the whole was implied. And though John does not represent Christians as being in the Holy Spirit, when he represents them as being in the Father and in the Son, they are represented as being in the third person in the Godhead, as well as in the first and second. Paul thus addresses the Galatian brethren: "If we live in the Spirit, let us also walk in the Spirit."—Gal. 5:25. From this language we may infer the Galatian brethren professed to live in the Spirit. And as they made such a profession, and did not always live it out, the apostle kindly admonished them to walk in the Spirit as they professed to live in it. It was another way of saying,

Let us be consistent. They might very properly profess to live in the Spirit, as they had been baptized into it.

And in accordance with the view we have given of Christians, in regard to their relation to the Father, and the Son, and the Holy Spirit, is the view which the apostle Paul presents of the church of the Thessalonians. In both of his letters to that church he represents it as being "in God the Father, and in the Lord Jesus Christ."—1 Thess. 1:1.

We have also reference in the following passage to the manner in which Christians are brought into the divine Beings in whom they are represented to be: "For as many of you as have been baptized into Christ have put on Christ."—Gal. 3:7. Here believers are represented as being brought into Christ by baptism. And we may justly infer that they were brought into the Father, and into the Holy Spirit in the same way that they were brought into Christ or into the Son.

Then as Christians are represented as being in the Father, and in the Son, and in the Holy Spirit, and as it appears that they were brought into them by baptism; we have thus in the experience or spiritual state of Christians, as given by the apostles in their writings, a strong confirmation of the idea that the names of Father, and Son, and Holy Spirit, stand for and represent those divine persons themselves.

And how distinguished and how glorious is the state into which believers are brought upon a sincere and effectual acceptance of Christianity, in being brought into the Father, and into the Son, and into the Holy Spirit! It is a state of honor, of safety, and of the highest enjoyment.

CHAPTER VI.

THE PRACTICAL IMPORT OF THE BAPTISMAL FORMULA.

WE have considered the import of *name* as it occurs in the baptismal formula, and we found that, occurring as it does in the Scripiures, in such a manner as it occurs in the baptismal formula, it usually stands for the person it represents, and that it does so in the form of words to be used in administering baptism. And it seems proper that we should now give some attention to the import of the Persons themselves, who bear the impressive names of Father, and Son, and Holy Spirit. The embodying of the divine Persons that constitute the Godhead, in the baptismal formula, and the relation that those Persons stand in to believers, and the relation that believers stand in to them, give to those Persons an importance that can not be overestimated. And their practical import should be well studied. There is a great depth of meaning in them, and though that depth may not be fathomed, as one of the wells of salvation, refreshing draughts of spiritual water may be drawn from it.

Baptizing them into the name of the Father, and of the Son, and of the Holy Spirit. "Here is wisdom, let him that readeth understand." And reverence and humility will become the student of the Bible. This phraseology presents the Godhead in a three-fold manifestation. In the former dispensation when polytheism and idolatry were so common, and the people of God were exposed to their corrupting influence, the unity of the Godhead was asserted distinctly and authoritatively. "Hear, O Israel; the Lord our God is one Lord."—Deut. 6: 4.

But as the world under the teaching and power of Christianity, or such in the world as hear the teaching and yield to the claims of Christianity, are to be presumed capable of appreciating a higher and fuller development of the Godhead, as well as all kinds of spiritual truth, we now have the Godhead presented to us in a three-fold manifestation. Consequently the attention of all who make the good confession is directed to the consideration of the divine Persons, the Father, Son, and Holy Spirit, into whom they are baptized. Upon the connection of believers with these divine Persons, and the spiritual power derived therefrom, depend their spiritual growth and

Christian character. With access to such sources, from which may be obtained all "that pertain to life and godliness," believers may go on to perfection.

As it is in Christianity that we have the Godhead manifested so fully and in a manner so well adapted to meet man's wants, we have in that form of religion a divine power that can renew man, and develop all his numerous and various powers, and restore him to his primeval state of holiness, glory, usefulness, and enjoyment. And it is the peculiar manifestation of the Godhead in three Persons, Father, Son, and Holy Spirit, that gives to Christianity its distinctive character, and its redeeming, restoring, and perfecting power over fallen and ruined humanity.

Though the manifestation of all the Persons in the Godhead in their expressive names, Father, Son, and Holy Spirit, and their relations to one another, and to men, was not fully revealed until the introduction of the Christian dispensation, they had all been previously known by some names and by some representations. But they were known by comparatively very few. Those, however, that had some knowledge of them, enjoyed that knowledge and valued it highly; with the foretaste they had of it, they anxiously desired more, as we learn from the words of our Lord, "For, verily, I say unto you, that many prophets and righteous men have desired to see those things which ye see, and have not seen them; and to hear those things which ye hear and have not heard them."—Matt. 13:17.

We have said that the divine Persons of whom we have such a full and interesting manifestation in the Christian dispensation, and in the baptismal formula, had been previously known in some degree, and by some names and representations. They had all been known in the work of creation and in the work of providence as well, but especially in the work of creation.

"In the beginning God created the heaven and the earth. And the earth was without form and void; and darkness was upon the face of the deep. And the Spirit of God moved upon the face of the waters."—Gen, 1:1, 2. Here we have God and His Spirit performing their respective work in creation. "In the beginning was the Word, and the Word was with God, and the Word was God. The same was in the beginning with God. All things were made by him; and without him was not anything made, that was made."—John 1:1-3. Here we have the Word which afterwards was more commonly known by the name of the "Son of God," or "Son of Man," performing his part in the great work of creation. And so we have the three divine Persons in the Godhead performing their work in creation. These are the same divine Persons that we have in the baptismal formula connected with redemption which work they performed as well as that of creation.

But we have them presented to us in the baptismal formula, and in the Gospel in a somewhat different manner to that in which we have them presented in the former dispensation. First, we have them all presented together, as in the manner of baptizing and in various cases. Secondly, we have them presented under different names; and it is with the import of those names that we are now particularly concerned.

First, we have the name, Father. The Christian at the very beginning of his Christian life recognizes God in the character of Father. In this representation of God, the gospel abounds. It is worthy of remark that, very frequently, when the name of God occurs, it stands immediately connected with the name of Father. We have noticed this in a previous part of our work, as there seemed to be a necessity of showing that the name of God and the name of Father, each was used to represent the first Person in the Godhead. We now simply refer to it again, not so much to show that both of these names represent the same divine Person—the first in the Godhead—as to show that they are used when occurring together, as explanatory one of the other, as, "For him hath God the Father sealed."—John 6: 27; "But to us there is but one God, the Father, of whom are all things, and we in him."—1 Cor. 8: 6. In such cases, it seems that Father is added to God, to show that in the Christian dispensation, and to Christians, all that God is and all that he contains are possessed by him that bears the name of Father.

It seems that the frail children of humanity subject to all the infirmities, and all the fears and sorrows that sin has brought upon them, need an objective representation, and the personal manifestation of God, to give them confidence in him, and to open the way for their return to him, and for that knowledge of him and that familiarity with him, that are necessary to give to man the rest and assurance of immortality that his higher nature so earnestly desires. Man cannot comprehend the essence of God; he therefore wants some name that will express the qualities of the character of God, and that will so present the divine Being to him, as to attract him. Man wants such a representation of the Supreme Being who is regarded as the Great

First Cause of all things as will commend him to his feeble intellect, weak conscience, and to the slumbering affections of his heart. All these wants found expression in the language of the apostle Philip, when he exclaimed, "Lord, shew us the Father, and it sufficeth us."—John 14:8. This is the cry of humanity. And it was to supply this deep and common want of man that Christ came into the world. And he has done all that was necessary to be done in order that man might see the Father. The invisible spirit of man is observed in his works. And the divine Father was seen through the works and person of his Son. Hence the reply of Jesus to Philip, "He that hath seen me, hath seen the Father."—John 14:9.

We then have God presented to us in the baptismal formula and in the gospel, not in the mysterious language of the "Triune God," not in "his essence," in the abstract; these would be views of Deity that might be presented if angels or even the adepts in the Christian faith were the disciples that were to be taught, or those to whom spiritual food was to be ministered. But as babes in Christ were the disciples that were to be taught and those that were to be fed, and that with the sincere milk of the word, simple and plain language would seem to be best adapted to the character of the learners. And as we have seen, the cry is, "show us the Father," God is presented not in a name full of mystery, nor yet in such dazzling light as would blind the eye upon beholding Him, but in the endearing name, "*Father*"; "baptizing them into the name of the Father." It is upon the very threshold of the Christian life and profession, that the disciples of Christ receive their baptism. And to receive that baptism intelligently—and this is necessary to obtain from it the greatest possible amount of good—it is very desirable that it be presented to the believing heart of the childlike disciple, in the simplest form of speech. And we cannot but believe that the great Christian Teacher so presented it. Hence we think it highly improbable that "name" before Father in the baptismal formula should be referred to "the Triune God" as the person to whom it belongs, or to "the essence of God." Such an idea seems to be too deep for those about being initiated into the Christian faith to receive. But apply it to "Father," to whom it belongs according to the structure of the language, and the acknowledged principles of Biblical interpretation, and the idea of a Father with all its pleasant associations, will be accepted by the initiated to their great joy and profit.

Secondly, we have the name, "Son." In the three-fold plurality of the Godhead, the Son is the second person. His relation to the Father is recognized. It is probable that as the first person in the Godhead is called Father, the second is called Son. In the apostolic benediction, where the first Person is called God, the second Person is called the Lord Jesus Christ. See 2 Cor. 13: 14. Our Lord is called the "Son of God" and the "Son of man." But he is also called simply "the Son." In the baptismal formula he is called simply "the Son." And as he is called simply "the Son," we are left so to connect him that we may read either "the Son of God," or "the Son of man," or both. We believe that in contemplating the divine character that is presented to us in the baptismal formula by the name of the Son, we should look at him as the Son of God, and as the Son of man. We shall then have him presented to us, both in his divine, and in his human nature. This is the broad and gospel view that we are to take of him. In this two-fold nature we are to believe in him and receive him, and in giving ourselves up to him, we are to feel that such is the Saviour to whom we consecrate ourselves.

In applying the name "Son" in the baptismal formula to our Redeemer in his relation to man, and in his relation to God, or to both his human and divine nature, we must regard him as *the* Son of God, and *the* Son of man, as there are many sons of God, and many sons of man. While our Lord has some things in common with all the sons of God, he differs so much from them all, that he may justly be called, "the only begotten of the Father," John 1:14, and "the only begotten Son," John 3:18. "Being made so much better than the angels, as he hath by inheritance obtained a more excellent name than they. For unto which of the angels said he at any time, thou art my son, this day have I begotten thee? And again, I will be to him a Father, and he shall be to me a Son? And again, when he bringeth the first-begotten into the world, he saith, and let all the angels of God worship him. And of the angels he saith, who maketh his angels spirits, and his ministers a flame of fire. But unto the Son he saith, thy throne, O God, is for ever and ever; a sceptre of righteousness is the sceptre of thy kingdom."—Heb. 1:4-8. So much greater is *the* Son of God than all the other sons of God.

And while the name "the Son of man" indicates

that our Redeemer possesses enough of all the distinctive elements of human nature, to give him a claim to that name; the title *the* Son of man in contrast with *a* son of man, shows that he possesses a character and qualifications which make him excel all other men. It is highly probable that not only in his mental culture and discipline, and in his spiritual attainments, but also in his physical development, he greatly excelled the sons of men. No doubt there might be less difference in all these between Christ and his brethren, were greater efforts made on their part to rise higher in every department of their nature. But with all our Lord's superiority over the sons of men, he was closely related to our nature, for "the Word was made flesh."—John 1 : 14. "For verily he took not on him the nature of angels; but he took on him the seed of Abraham. Wherefore in all things it behooved him to be made like unto his brethren; that he might be a merciful and faithful high priest, in things pertaining to God, to make reconciliation for the sins of the people."—Heb. 2 : 16-17.

Thirdly, The third person in the Godhead that we have in the baptismal formula, is the Holy Spirit. He was known by this name by some in the former dispensation. But the number that knew anything by experience about him, was limited. And the power and gifts of the Spirit were likewise limited. But our Lord having so successfully completed the work He came to do, and having all power in heaven and on earth given unto him, upon his ascension to heaven, sent down the Holy Spirit to his church, and has made it available to all that believe on Him and receive Him as their Lord and Master. Hence the Holy Spirit stands associated with the Father and the Son, in the baptismal formula, and believers are baptized into His name, as well as into the name of the Father and of the Son.

Such is a brief view of a few of the ideas suggested by the divine Persons named in the baptismal formula. We have merely opened the caskets, and taken a glance at the precious gems within. There are three of these caskets, and they are all filled with precious jewels. Into the possession of these, believers are brought by the exercise of a living, active faith.

The subject of the Godhead is looked upon by many as a very mysterious subject. It is mysterious if we attempt to understand or explain the nature of the union that exists between the three divine Persons of whom it consists. Their essence and other things pertaining to them that are not revealed in the Scriptures, and which with our present capacity for knowledge we can not understand, and which we need not understand, as a knowledge of what is not revealed and what we can not understand, are not essential to our salvation. But if we accept the simple facts and statements concerning the manifestations of the Godhead as we have them presented in the Father, Son, and Holy Spirit, not perplexing our minds in studying them in their metaphysical aspect, or in their essence; but simply regarding what their three names express according to the revelation and explanation that are given of them in the Gospel, we shall readily understand enough of them to make them worthy of our confidence and our love.

When the precious names Father, Son, and Holy Spirit are received in their simple form, and with the meaning and sense associated with them in the Scriptures, we shall not only understand them sufficiently to justify us in believing in them with a Christian faith, and in offering our bodies unto them as living sacrifices, learning from the knowledge we obtain of them that it is our reasonable service to do so, Rom. 12:1, but we shall do all this with delight, "our rejoicing being this, the testimony of our conscience."—2 Cor. 1:12. There is a consciousness of safety, as well as of moral rectitude, when we are baptized into the name of the Father, and of the Son, and of the Holy Spirit. This is entering by the door into the sheep-fold, and we "shall be saved and shall go in and out, and find pasture."—John 10: 19. And being in the Father, and in the Son, and in the Holy Spirit, none "shall pluck us out" of their hands.—John 10: 28, 29. "Who shall separate us from the love of Christ? Shall tribulation, or distress, or persecution, or famine, or nakedness, or peril or sword? (As it is written, for thy sake we are killed all the day long; we are accounted as sheep for the slaughter.) Nay, in all these things we are more than conquerors, through Him that loved us. For I am persuaded that neither death, nor life, nor angels, nor principalities, nor powers, nor things present, nor things to come, nor height, nor depth, nor any other creature shall be able to separate us from the love of God, which is in Christ Jesus our Lord."—Rom. 8: 35-39.

By the ordinance of baptism, which is the initiatory rite into the Christian faith, and when it is administered according to the formula given by our Lord, Christians are introduced into the name of the Father, and of the Son, and of the Holy Spirit.

And from the character of the ordinance of baptism, and of the Christian profession which Christians make by being baptized, they become devoted to the divine Persons into whose names they are baptized. And therefore they are represented as having the names of those Persons to whom they are devoted and whose they are, written upon their foreheads. Hence the following language: "And I saw, and behold, the Lamb standing on the Mount Zion, and with him a hundred and forty and four thousand, having his name and the name of his Father written in their foreheads."—Rev. 14: 1. *Revised Version.* They have not only one name, but they have a plurality of names written upon them.

According to the foregoing passage of Scripture, Christians are represented as bearing with them into the future state, evidences of the distinction in the Godhead. Indeed, the distinction in the Godhead, which the baptismal formula shows, and which it was designed to show according to its own peculiar form and structure, and according to the views entertained by authorities that we have already introduced, seems to have been considered a matter of no little importance. Each Person in the Godhead having his part to perform in the great work of redemption, the distinction of the three Persons was to be preserved and indicated in baptism. This is done in the formula of baptism, and in the trine immersion which is in complete harmony with the formula.

It seems to be a principle in the Divine method of appointing ordinances to have them represent the distinction that there is in what those ordinances symbolically or otherwise are designed to represent. Hence, when our Lord appointed an ordinance to represent himself in his sacrificial and atoning character, he did not only take bread, and say of it alone, "take, eat; this is my body," and "this is my blood of the New Testament, which is shed for many for the remission of sins."—Matt. 26: 26-28. As the blood is contained in the body, he might might have said so. But to present plainly the distinction between his body or his flesh and blood, which it appears he desired to do, he selected a plurality of symbols; bread and wine, the bread to represent his body, and the wine to represent his blood. This distinction was observed in the communion. So in the ordinance of baptism. The baptismal formula and the ordinance performed according to it, plainly show the distinction of Persons in the Godhead, which it appears was to be shown in the ordinance of baptism. It is not into the name of the Godhead, or into the name of "the Triune God," that believers are to be baptized, but into the three personal manifestations of the Godhead, or into the Father, and into the Son, and into the Holy Spirit,

The baptismal formula then plainly shows that there is a plurality of Persons in the Godhead, the Father, Son, and Holy Spirit, and that there is a distinction as well as a plurality. It also shows that believers are bought by baptism into each one of the divine Persons, and, consequently, into possession of what each one has already done objectively in the work of redemption, and by holy faith and hope to anticipate what each one will do subjectively, in making them the personal and experienced subjects of redemption in its progressive stages until it is completed in them, and they can adoringly and joyfully exclaim, "Thanks be to God which giveth us the victory through our Lord Jesus Christ."

In the meantime, Christians being brought into such a relation to all the Divine Persons in the Godhead that their baptism brings them into if they experience its designed effects, have access to the very "fountain of life." And being favored with such opportunities for holiness and happiness, their obligations are correspondingly great. They, therefore, should go forth with the Divine names upon iheir foreheads, and the love of God shed abroad in their hearts, the living witnesses to the excellency of that system of reforming, regenerating, and saving truth, that originated with the Father, that was finished by the Son, and revealed and applied by the Holy Spirit through the word.

CHAPTER VII.

THE INTRODUCTION OF SINGLE IMMERSION INTO THE CHURCH.

THOSE immersionists who baptize by a single immersion may be divided into two classes. They may be distinguished by the different times in which they have lived, and by the difference in the form of words used by them in administering baptism.

SECTION I.

Single immersion in ancient times. It appears that those who practiced single immersion in ancient times did not generally, if at all, use the baptismal formula given by Christ to his disciples. During the first ages of the church, when trine immersion was the mode of immersion practiced by Christians, the baptismal formula given by Christ was the form of administering baptism universally used, or nearly so. There may have been a few at a very early age who departed from the use of the form given by Christ, but there were not many who did so, as we have seen in the chapter of our work, in which we considered the binding authority of the baptismal formula.

But when some abandoned trine immersion, and adopted the single, they seem also to have abandoned the form of words given by Christ for administering baptism and to have adopted some other form. It would seem that single immersion was not thought to agree with the baptismal formula given by Christ, and hence it was not performed according to that formula, but another form was used. Hence those who are charged with having introduced single immersion, are also charged with having departed from the form given by our Lord. Theodoret, the author of an ecclesiastical History, and other works, and who lived in the early part of the fourth century, has the following testimony in regard to the change in the mode of immersion, and the form of words used in administering it: "He (Eunomius) subverted the law of holy baptism, which had been handed down from the beginning from the Lord and the apostles, and made a contrary law, asserting that it is not necessary to immerse the candidate for baptism thrice, nor to mention the names of the Trinity, but to immerse once only into the death of Christ."—*Chrystal's History of the Modes of Bap-*

tism, page 78. Socrates, in his Ecclesiastical History, p. 296, in speaking of the Eunomians, says, "I shall merely observe that they adulterated baptism; for, instead of baptizing in the name of the Trinity, they baptize into the death of Christ."

The 50th Apostolic Canon declares, "If any bishop or presbyter do not perform three immersions of one initiation, but one immersion which is given into the death of Christ, let him be deposed; for the Lord did not say, 'Baptize into my death;' but, 'Go ye, and make disciples of all nations, baptizing them into the name of the Father, and of the Son, and of the Holy Ghost.' Do ye, therefore, O bishops, immerse thrice into one Father, and Son, and Holy Ghost, according to the will of Christ and our constitution by the Spirit."—*Constitutions and Canons of the Church, by Dr. Chase, page 252.*

Pelagius, bishop of Rome, living in the 6th century, says, "There are many who say that they baptize in the name of Christ alone, and by a single immersion, But the gospel command, which was given by God himself, and our Lord and Saviour Jesus Christ, reminds us that we should administer holy baptism to every one, in the name of the Trinity and by trine immersion, for our Lord said to his disciples, 'Go, baptize all nations in the name of the Father, and of the Son, and of the Holy Ghost.'"—*Chrystal's Modes of Baptism, page 80.*

According to the testimony of the writers above quoted, single immersion when first practiced was not done according to the baptismal formula, but in the name of Christ, or into his death. And as there was but one subject into which believers were to be baptized, one action or one immersion was considered sufficient. But when baptism was performed according to the formula instituted by our Lord, "into the name of the Father, and of the Son, and of the Holy Ghost," it was done by trine immersion. It appears, however, that the single immersion did not prevail to any great extent, as Dr. Cathcart, a Baptist author, says, "Trine immersion was the general practice of Christians from the end of the second till the close of the twelfth century. The proof of this statement is overwhelming."—*Baptism of the Ages, page 15.* And Henry in his *Christian Antiquities, page 129,* bears the following testimony to its prevalence: "Strabo considers it (trine immersion) to have been the prevalent practice of the church till the seventh century; and Vossius speaks of trine immersion, or what corresponds to it—the trine aspersion, being the general practice of the modern church." And Dr. Wall has the following concerning the practice of single and trine immersion: "The school-men among the papists, though they say that either way may do, yet speak of trine immersion, where immersion is used, as much the more fitting. And for the Protestants, Vossius says, 'What son of the church will not willingly hold to that custom which the ancient church practiced all over the world, except Spain? &c. Besides, at present the trine immersion is used in all countries; so that the custom cannot be changed withont an affectation of novelty, and scandal given to the weak.' He means all countries where immersion is used."—*History of Infant Baptism, Vol. II, page 424.*

SECTION II.

Single immersion in modern times. Those immersionists of the present age of the world who practice the single immersion, use the baptismal formula as given by Christ, as do those who practice trine immersion. But the single immersionists of ancient times baptized into the death of Christ or into the name of Christ as we have seen in the testimonies given. We may also remark that those in ancient times who practiced affusion, did it by a trine affusion, as is testified by Vossius in his testimony above given. But while those of modern times who practiced baptism by single immersion and those who do it by aspersion or affusion, use the baptismal formula, many recognize but one name in the formula into which believers are to be baptized. And this seems to be the reason why but one action is used in administering the ordinance by those who perform it by single immersion and a single aspersion. Those who practice trine immersion recognize three names in the formula into which believers are to be baptized. And upon the different views entertained of the baptismal formula, are founded our different modes of immersion.

We shall offer some testimony to prove that many recognize but one name in the baptismal formula. Dr. Ray, a well known Baptist minister and writer, in his debate with J. W. Stein, says, "We repeat that the Bible commission demands '*one* baptism in the *one name of the Triune God.*'"—*Stein and Ray Debate, page 51.* Mr. F. M. Bowman, a Baptist minister, and the author of a pamphlet bearing the imposing name, *Trine Immersion Weighed in the Balances and Found Wanting*, seems to supply the name of Jesus as the one name, from the following language: "By one faith we enter the one ineffable name JESUS, the LORD JESUS CHRIST, who by one death and one resurrection, procured our redemption, sanctification, and justification; whose complete redemption work we set forth in our one immersion for his one burial and our one emersion for his one resurrection."—Page 32 of the pamphlet above named. "Baptizing them in the name of the Father, of the Son, and of the Holy Ghost.' The Father, Son, and Holy Ghost; there are three distinct persons; in the name, not names; there is one essence."—*Homiletic Encyclopædia, Art. Trinity, by Adams.* The catechism of the council of Trent, a Roman Catholic work, has the following in regard to the baptismal formula: "The word 'name' is here referred not to the persons, but to the divine essence, virtue, and power, which are one and the same in the three persons."

In a Baptist publication we find the following under the head of *Special Subjects:* "The four Baptist principles; their bearing and practical application. Sin and danger of compromising any part of Christ's truth. The work and claims of our publication so-society. Colportage. Trine immersion wrong; 'name' not names."—*Baptist Advanced Quarterly, October-December, 1882.*

Trine immersion in the above is pronounced wrong because we have "name' and not names in the baptismal formula. The formula was read by the writer with the common misapprehension of it. We have in it a plurality of names. This has been testified by several of the authors we have quoted. We have the name of the Father, and the name of the Son, and the name of the Holy Spirit. Hence we plainly have names. It seems to be implied in the above quotation, that if there is a plurality of names in the formula, trine immersion would not be wrong, as the wrong seems to be attributed to a want of plurality of names. Let the reader keep this in mind.

"Our Lord instituted but two ordinances—baptism and the Lord's supper; he erected but two monumental pillars—one without, and the other within, the church; on the first of these—that which fronts the world—he inscribed the great name of the Triune God; and, as if to render the inscription more impressive, he made it his last act. Baptism is the vestibule, or entrance, to his spiritual temple, the church; so that, before his disciples can cross the threshold, he requires them to receive the print of the Sacred Name; and by making that one ceremony final, he reminds them that the holy signature is indellible."—*The Great Teacher, page 151.*

There is in the above such reference to "the Triune God," and "sacred name," that we would suppose, did we not know better, that the baptismal formula contained such language. But there is no such language in it. There is a misconception of our Lord's words. We have three sacred names, instead of but one, the name of the Father, and the name of the Son, and the name of the Holy Spirit.

Dr. Olshauson, in his remarks upon the baptismal formula in his Commentary on the New Testament, says, "The sublime object to which baptism binds, consists of Father, Son, and Holy Ghost." He also gives *name* in the Greek language, and also in the Hebrew, and says of "name" as it occurs in the formula, "it signifies the very essence of God himself."

The above does not seem to be satisfactory. Are we not bound in baptism to three objects, to the Father, and Son, and the Holy Spirit? We surely are. And whatever "name" may express in some of its connections, it cannot express the essence of God as it occurs in the baptismal formula, for the Godhead is expressed in the three names, Father, Son, and Holy Spirit.

Mr. R. Milligan, a prominent minister in the community of Christians called Disciples, president of one of their colleges, and the author of several works of reputation, and deservedly so, wrote a book called *The Great Commission.* As its name indicates, it is written on the commission of Christ to his apostles. The subject is presented under different aspects, and there is a section under the following head: "*Into the name of the Father, and of the Son, and of the Holy Spirit.*" After some remarks in justification of the reading, "*into* the name of the Father," etc., instead of *in* the name, and some other preliminary remarks, he says: "In the Hebrew and Hellenistic dialects, the word *name* often implies more than a mere abstract designation of the person represented. *Very frequently it means the person himself, as he is revealed to us in the Scriptures.* Thus, for instance, in the Old Testament, the name of God is very often equivalent to God himself, as he is therein revealed to us." He then proceeds to prove the correctness of his position in regard to *name* as stated above, and this he does successfully in our judgment, we having maintained the same position in the earlier part of our work. After having proved his position as above stated in regard to name, in the course of his remarks that follow, he uses the following language: "This then is manifestly the meaning of the word *name*, as it occurs in the Commission. It is in the singular number, and does not mean any particular title or literary designation of the Father, and of the Son, and of the Holy Spirit taken either separately or conjointly; but it means simply the Father, and the Son, and the Holy Spirit themselves, revealed to us in the Holy Bible, as the one eternal and immutable *Eloheem Jehovah;* the creator, preserver, and upholder of all things: to whom be honor and glory, for ever and ever. Amen.

"The passage may, therefore, without violence, be rendered into the English idiom as follows: Go ye, therefore, and make disciples of all the nations, immersing them into the Father, and the Son, and the Holy Spirit; the one God revealed in the Holy Scriptures."—*The Great Commission, pp. 138, 139.* We must dissent from some of Mr. Milligan's views of the commission as they are expressed in the above quotation from his work named. And we must confess that his attempt at the explanation of the commission as given above, reminds us of, and to us seems very much like the explanations that are often given by the advocates of aspersion, of the meaning of baptism, to sustain their position that aspersion is the action of baptism. There is in Mr. Milligan's explanation a departure from the ordinary construction of language, and use of words, that is not sanctioned by sound principles of Biblical exegesis and explanation. What these principles are, we have already shown. In referring to name as it occurs before Father, in the commission, Mr. Milligan says: "It is in the singular number, and does not mean any particular title or literary designation of the Father, and of the Son, and of the Holy Spirit, taken either separately or conjointly; but it means simply the Father, and the Son, and the Holy Spirit themselves," etc. It is true it is in the singular number, because it belongs to but one person or object, and that person is the Father,—*in the name of the Father.* And is not *name* as it occurs before Father, the "particular title or literary designation of the Father?" It surely is according to the ordinary use of language occurring in such forms of construction. And it is remarkably strange that Mr. Milligan should declare it is not, belonging as he does to a body of professing Christians, that has strongly repudiated any theory of Biblical interpretation that does not give to Scriptural words and phrases explanatory of human duty, their common force and meaning. And while *name* before Father is the title or literary designation of the first person of the three that occur in the commission, *name* understood before Son is the title and literary designation of the second of the three Persons that are named, while *name* understood before Holy Spirit is the title or literary designation of the third of the three that are named. The idea of referring name in the singular number to three persons, is not in harmony with the principles of the English language or of the grammar of our language.

It does seem to us that Mr. Milligan forgot when he made the foregoing explanation of name in the baptismal formula, the principles that he himself has laid down for the interpretation of the Scriptures. In referring to positive law, he says, "It depends for its existence and all that pertains to it, wholly and exclusively, on the will of the law giver. And hence the necessity that *every positive law should be expressed in the most clear, definite, and specific terms possible:* and, furthermore, that *it should be interpreted and obeyed according to the strict letter and conventional meaning of the terms used to express it.*"—*The Great Commission, page 89.* And we here give again a rule laid down by Mr. Campbell: "To understand the meaning of what is commanded, promised, taught, &c., the same philological principles, deduced from the nature of language, or the same laws of interpretation which are applied to the language of other books, are to be applied to the language of the Bible."—*Campbell on Baptism, page 61.* Now if the above principles are kept in view and applied in explaining the baptismal formula, and "name" as it occurs in it, surely Mr. Milligan could not say with propriety, or correctness, that "name" "does not mean any particular title or literary designation of the Father, and of the Son, and of the Holy Spirit, taken either separately or conjointly; but it means simply the Father, and the Son, and the Holy Spirit themselves," &c, It does seem very strange, that accepting such principles as the foregoing, Mr. Milligan would make the explanation he has of "name" in the formula. What would be the idea that would be likely to present itself to the humble and teachable mind of the attentive reader, with an ordinary degree of intelligence, entirely free from prejudice, when reading the baptismal formula, "baptizing them into the name of the Father, and of the Son, and of the Holy Spirit?" Would it not be that "name" belongs to "Father?" It surely would. The baptismal formula to be properly understood, should be looked at as the word *baptize*, a word occurring in it should be looked at to get its first and proper meaning. The word baptize should be looked at in its primary and literal meaning. And the baptismal formula should be looked at in its literary character and structure to ascertain its true and proper meaning.

Dr. Scott, the well known commentator, in his *Essays*, has one *On the Personality and Deity of the Holy Spirit; with some thoughts on the Doctrine of the Sacred Trinity.* In this essay he says, "When our Lord was baptized, the Father by a voice from heaven, declared him to be his beloved Son, and publicly sealed his appointment to the mediatorial office; of which he solemnly accepted, and on which he then entered; and the Holy Spirit descending visibly, under the emblematic representation of a dove lighted upon him; as through him to be communicated to all his true disciples. Thus the Three Persons, in the sacred Trinity, evidently acted according to the parts sustained by them, in the great work of man's salvation. But the appointed form of Christian baptism is far more conclusive: 'Baptizing them *into the name*' (not *names*) 'of the Father, and of the Son, and of the Holy Ghost.' By baptism we declare our dependence and devotedness to Him in whose name we are baptized." *p. 199.* This writer fully recognizes three Persons in the Godhead, the Father, and the Son, and the Holy Spirit, and yet speaks of baptizing according to the formula of baptism in the *name* of Him to whom we are devoted. Now, we are surely devoted to the three, and we are baptized into the three.

The same popular commentator has the following remarks upon the baptismal formula, in his Commentary: "The apostles and preachers of the gospel were ordered to baptize those who embraced the gospel, into the *name* (not *names*) 'of the Father, and of the Son, and of the Holy Ghost.' (Note Numbers 6: 24-27.) This is a most irrefragable proof of the doctrine of the Trinity; that is, of the Deity of the Son, and of the distinct personality and Deity of the Holy Spirit; for it would be absurd to suppose that a mere man, or creature, or a mere *modus*, or quality of God, should be joined with the Father in the one 'name' into which all Christians are baptized."

Dr. Scott sees but one name in the baptismal formula into which believers were to be baptized, though there are evidently three according to a fair and just interpretation of the formula, and according to many authors who express the idea of a plurality of names in the formula, when looking at its simple literary construction, and having nothing to bias their minds.

Dr. Sumner, an English Bishop, and one of our Commentators, in his explanation of the passage containing the baptismal formula, after quoting the passage and making some explanation of it, says, "Instruct them that there is one God and Father of all; and that 'he is a rewarder of them that diligently seek him.' Instruct them that there is one 'Mediator between God and man.' He is 'the way, the truth, and the life;' 'no man cometh to the Father but by him.' Instruct them, that the Holy Spirit, proceeding from the Father and Son, will purify the hearts of all who come to God through Christ Jesus, and will enable them to 'live righteously, soberly, and godly,' as becometh those who are looking for a heavenly kingdom. In the name of this Triune God baptize them; that they may be born again of water and of the Holy Ghost, and, being cleansed from their sins, may be renewed in the spirit of their minds." Now this writer and commentator after representing the three divine Persons engaged in the work of our redemption, and after assigning to each his work, says, "In the name of this Triune God baptize them." Where does he get the name of the Triune God in the form of Christian baptism, since there is no name occurring therein but the names of Father, Son, and Holy Ghost? Why did he not say into these names, or into the name of the Father, and of the Son, and of the Holy Ghost, baptize them, as there are evidently three names in the baptismal formula.

We next quote from Matthew Henry's popular Commentary. After some explanatory remarks on the words of the commission containing the baptismal formula, he says, "We are baptized not into the *names*, but into the *name*, of Father, Son, and Spirit, which plainly intimates that these Three are One, and their name one. The distinct mentioning of the *Three Persons* in the Trinity, both in the *Christian baptism* here, and in the Christian blessing, (2 Cor. 13:13,) as it is a full proof of the doctrine of the Trinity, so it has done much toward the preserving of it pure and entire through all ages of the church; for nothing is more great and awful in *Christian assemblies* than these two. . . (1) It is into the name of *the Father*, believing him to be the *Father of our Lord Jesus Christ*, (for that is principally intended here,) by *eternal generation*, and our *Father*, as our Creator, Preserver, and Benefactor, to whom we therefore resign ourselves as our absolute *Owner* and *Proprietor*, to act us, and dispose of us; as our supreme *Rector* and *Governor*, to rule us, as free agents by his law; and as our *chief Good* and *highest End*. (2.) It is into the name of *the Son*, the *Lord Jesus Christ*, the *Son of God*, and correlate to the Father. Baptism was in a particular manner administered *in the name of the Lord Jesus,* Acts 8:16; 19:5. In baptism we *assert,* as Peter did, *Thou art Christ,* the Son of the living God, (chap. 16:16,) and *consent,* as Thomas did, *My Lord and my God,* John 20:28. We take Christ to be our Prophet, Priest, and King, and give up ourselves to be taught, and saved by him. (3) It is into the name of *the Holy Ghost.* Believing the Godhead of the Holy Spirit, and his agency in carrying on our redemption, we give up ourselves to his conduct and operation, as our Sanctifier, Teacher, Guide, and Comforter." Here we have as express a recognition of baptizing into the three names, Father, Son, and Holy Spirit as we possibly could have, notwithstanding Mr. Henry had previously said, "We are baptized not into the *names,* but into the *name* of Father, Son, and Spirit." When he came to make a plain and direct application of the words of the baptismal formula, it appears he could not do otherwise than recognize three names, and the fact that believers are baptized into them. There does seem to be a plain contradiction in writing and explaining the baptismal formula in this way; first saying it is "not into names," and then declaring that it is "into the name of the Father," and "into the name of the Son," and "into the name of the Holy Ghost." He was either wrong when he declared it was "not into names," or when he aftewards explained that it was into names. For he declares they were baptized into the name of the Father, and into the name of the Son, and into the name of the Holy Ghost. Here are three names. And into them all he declares they were baptized. Therefore they were baptized into names. And he was evidently wrong when he said, "not into names," according to his own explanation which he afterwards made. Failing to apply "name" to Father, to whom it justly belongs, his explanation is confused, and not consistent with itself.

Elder Adamson, of the Disciple church, is the author of a pamphlet entitled *Treatise on Trine Immersion*. It is against trine immersion. He attempts an analysis of the baptismal formula, and in his analysis he has the following: "'Father,' 'Son,' and 'Ghost,' are adjective modifiers of the noun 'name'."—*p. 8*. Here Elder Adamson recognizes but one name. But instead of applying that "name" to the "divine essence," to "the Triune God," or to "Jesus," as others have done, as we have observed, he very improperly applies it to all of the three persons, Father, Son, and Holy Ghost presented in the formula of baptism. We say improperly, for if Father, Son, and Holy Ghost are all joined together by the conjunction *and*, as Elder Adamson maintains they are, name should be in the plural according to a principle of English grammar contained in the following rule: "Two or more nouns, etc., in the singular number, joined together by a copulative conjunction expressed or understood, must have verbs, nouns, and pronouns agreeing with them in the plural number."—*Murray's Grammar, p. 143.*

"*Of the Father, and of the Son, and of the Holy Ghost.* Observe it is in the *name* of these three persons as ONE GOD, not in their NAMES as though they were three Gods. The same phraseology is used, when speaking of any *one being*, as 1 Cor. 1:13, were ye baptized in the name of Paul? This language therefore gives the NAME of God—three persons in one Godhead."—*Jacobs on the New Testament.*

"*Which was to be done in the name of the Father, and of the Son, and of the Holy Ghost;* by the authority of these three divine Persons, who all appeared and testified their approbation of the administration of this ordinance, at the baptism of Christ; and as they are to be invocated in it, so the persons baptized not only profess faith in each divine person, but are devoted to their service, and worship, and are laid under obligations to obedience to them. Hence as a confirmation of the doctrine of the Trinity, there are three persons, but one name, but one God, into which believers are baptized."—*Gill, on Matt. 28:19.*

From the examples we have given, it will be perceived that the baptismal formula is so read and explained by a large number of writers and expositors, as to convey the idea that there is but one name in it as that into which believers are to be baptized. This we hold to be a wrong view of it, and our reasons for our view which differs from the view of those writers quoted, will be given at length hereafter. But, however foreign to the true meaning of the baptismal formula the explanation of it as given by the writers we have quoted may be, such an explanation seems to be the ground upon which single immersionists justify their mode of immersion. That is, they justify their mode of immersion on the ground that there is, as they maintain, but the one "name" contained in the baptismal formula. And from the implied concessions of the single immersionists, they concede the ground that if there is a plurality of names in the baptismal formula, trine immersion is taught in it. That we are correct in what we say in regard to the ground upon which those who practice single immersion do so, and also in regard to their concession in reference to trine immersion, will appear evident from the testimony we shall offer.

Dr. Conant one of the most prominent, learned, and influential ministers of the Baptist church in America, and perhaps in the world, was one of the scholars who executed the Revision of the Scriptures by the American Bible Union. He translated the Gospel by Matthew, and before it was accepted by the final examining committee, he published it with critical notes. In a note on the baptismal formula, he says, "The practice was adopted at an early period, of immersing at the utterance of each name. But this is clearly contrary to the terms of the command. To justify such a practice, the form should have been either, *in the names of*, or *in the name of the Father, and in the name of the Son, and in the name of the Holy Spirit.*" Dr. Conant's language in his note clearly implies that a plurality of names in the baptismal formula would make a plurality of actions or of immersions necessary to meet its requirements. But he does not accept the idea that there is a plurality of names in it. And though he does not directly say so, his language plainly implies that he believes there is but one name in it, and he therefore maintains single immersion, and rejects the trine, and thus virtually makes the one name the ground of single immersion.

We invite the reader's careful, candid, and serious attention to the foregoing quotations that we have given concerning the meaning of the baptismal formula. The writers quoted are a part of a class of expositors that explain the baptismal formula as including but one name. Some of the writers quoted speak of the essence of God. If name alone expresses the essence of God, how are we to know any thing about his essence from that name? We know nothing of the essence of things in the abstract. It is only by the manifestations of the properties of things that we know anything about them. We know nothing about the essence of matter. We only know its properties. So we know nothing about the essence of the Godhead or of Divinity only as it is revealed to us through certain manifestations. And these manifestations are the Father, Son, and Holy Spirit.

The Father is the manifestation of the Godhead in his parental care and fatherly love for all nations. "Have we not all one Father? Hath not one God created us?"—Mal. 2: 10. To these questions we must give an affirmative answer. Our Lord taught the love and kindness of our heavenly Father when he said, "He maketh his sun to rise on the evil and on the good, he sendeth rain on the just and on the unjust."—Matt. 5: 45. In the parable of the lost son, we have the fatherly character of the Godhead most beautifully and impressively portrayed.

The Son is the manifestation of the Godhead as a merciful Redeemer of his guilty race and a lost world. He left the ninety and nine and went into the mountains to seek that which had gone astray. "Behold how he loved him!"—John 11: 36.

The Holy Spirit is the manifestation of the Godhead in his all pervading presence to enlighten, and to comfort. He is called the Comforter. And how full of meaning, and of practical and plain meaning is this term. He is also called an Advocate, and this is another very expressive term used to describe him. But all these manifestations of the Godhead, that we have called by such expressive and suggestive names as are contained in the baptismal formula, the names, Father, Son, and Holy Spirit, present to us the Godhead and Divinity in a manner that is adapted to our wants, and that we can understand in a considerable degree.

Again; "Into the name of this Triune God baptize them," says Bishop Sumner. So says Dr. Ray.

And it is not uncommon for writers when referring to the baptismal formula, and to "name" as it occurs before "Father," to apply it to God, meaning by God the entire Godhead. But of such a disposition or application of "name" we cannot accept for the following reasons: 1. The title or name of God is applied to the first person in the Godhead, in the Scriptures, and either God or Father may be used, as in the following passages: "But to us there is but one God, the Father, of whom are all things, and we in him; and one Lord Jesus Christ, by whom are all things and we by him."—1 Cor. 8:8. "Grace be to you; and peace from God the Father, and from our Lord Jesus Chaist, who gave himself for our sins, that he might deliver us from this present evil world, according to the will of God, and our Father."—Gal. 1:34. "There is one body and one Spirit, even as ye are called in one hope of your calling; one Lord, one faith, one baptism, one God and Father of all, who is above all, and through all and in you all."—Eph.

4 : 4-6. Here the three persons in the Godhead are all referred to, and the names God and Father are both applied to the first. "Paul and Silvanus, and Timotheus, unto the church of the Thessalonians, which is in God the Father, and in the Lord Jesus Christ; grace be unto you, and peace, from God our Father, and the Lord Jesus Christ."—2 Thess. 1 : 1-2. Here we have the church in both God and the Father, as well as in Christ. The same person is evidently referred to by God and Father. 2. The apostolic benediction, "The grace of the Lord Jesus Christ, and the love of God, and the communion of the Holy Ghost, be with you all,"—2 Cor. 13 : 14, contains the three persons of the Godhead, and it is often put along with the baptismal formula, as teaching with that the doctrine of the Trinity. But in the apostolic benediction, God occupies the place that Father does in the baptismal formula. And may we not, and should we not, understand that Father expresses as much in the baptismal formula, as God expresses in the apostolic benediction? We certainly should. Then if the baptismal formula would read, "baptizing them into the name of God, and of the Son, and of the Holy Spirit," would a candid and intelligent reader think of referring "name" as it occurs in the formula to any of

the persons mentioned but to God? He would not. Indeed he could not with any propriety or consistency do so. Let the principles of interpretation that we have given be referred to, and then the testimonies that we have given from a number of authors of different churches, proving that there is a plurality of names contained in the baptismal formula, and "name" coming before, and belonging to Father, can with no propriety or justice be applied to any other person but to the Father.

To apply "name" before "Father" to the "Triune God," or to the "essence of God," is to obscure the meaning of the baptismal formula, and to mystify it. Surely the simplest meaning that can be put upon the words of the formula should be accepted as the true meaning, for the ordinance of baptism is designed for the young convert, that needs "milk" and not "strong meat" for his spiritual food. But to talk about "the Triune God," and "the essence of God," to the young convert would not be likely to be very satisfactory. But Father, and Son, and Holy Spirit, are terms that are presented to us in the Gospel so frequently and in such a way, that with a little help, the young disciple can readily comprehend enough of them to cause him to believe in them, and to put his trust in them.

The mystified and irregular explanation of the baptismal formula in which "name" before "Father" instead of being applied to him, to whom it so evidently belongs, is applied to "the Triune God," or "the essence of God," is, we believe, owing to the fact that the baptismal formula has been so commonly associated with the Trinitarian controversy. And as the doctrine of the Trinity is acknowledged to be more or less mysterious by all, associating that doctrine with the formula of Christian baptism, the mysterious and uncommon explanations above alluded to have been made of it, and an idea conceived of its meaning which a plain and literal explanation of the language used, does not by any means convey.

When the baptismal formula is read and explained altogether independent of the Trinitarian controversy, and the mind is free from any prejudice arising from that controversy or anything else, it will be explained as other similarly constructed sentences are explained, and instead of "name" being applied to something else than the Father, it will be applied to him, and name understood will be applied to each of the other persons, to the Son, and to the Holy Spirit. And the baptismal formula will then read as we shall hereafter see, "baptizing them into the name of the Father, and into the name of the Son, and into the name of the Holy Spirit."

The doctrine of the Trinity under none of its controversial aspects, should influence the mind or views of any in reading or explaining the baptismal formula. It should be explained by the commonly recognized principles of biblical interpretation, without any reference to any denominational view of the Trinity.

Then from what we have said, and from what the authors that we have quoted have said, and especially Dr. Conant in his note which we have quoted, it would appear that single immersion as practiced by its advocates in modern times is founded upon that construction and interpretation of the baptismal formula which recognizes but one name in it, or which applies the word "name" occurring before "Father," to the Father, and Son, and Holy Spirit, or to the "Triune God," or to something else not directly contained in it. Whereas "name" occurring before Father, should be applied to Father only, while name understood should be applied to the Son and to the Holy Spirit. Hence single immersion is founded upon what we cannot but regard

INTRODUCTION OF SINGLE IMMERSION.

as a misapprehension of the baptismal formula. For there are evidently three names in it, and not one only.

In referring to our fourth chapter, the reader will find that we have clearly showed that there are in the baptismal formula, a plurality of persons, and a plurality of names. We have given Bishop Beveridge's decided testimony. In speaking of the form of words to be used in administering baptism, he says, "In which words we observe: *First*, A trinity of Persons, into whose names we are to be baptized, the 'Father, Son, and Holy Ghost.'" Mr. Errett says, "It is the only act with which are associated the names of Father, Son, and Holy Spirit." Mr. W. H. Hopson, in referring to the command of Christ to baptize, says, "The only one in all the Bible commanded to be done in or into the names of Father, Son, and Holy Spirit." The language of Mr. Burgess when alluding to the baptismal formula is, "The ordinance, therefore, must not only be immersion, but immersion into these three names."

We have given a few examples of writers who, when writing upon the baptismal formula, which reads, "baptizing them into the name of the Father, and of the Son, and of the Holy Spirit," take the position, that as name is in the singular, it is only into one name that believers are baptized. And "name" is applied by such writers as we have referred to, to the "Triune God," to "the essence of God," and even to all the persons, named, to the Father, and Son, and Holy Ghost. On the contrary, we maintain that "name" belongs to Father, and to Father only, according to the principles of our language. This will be shown in our next chapter. Although the present chapter contains a repetition of some things previously stated, we think it best to repeat them as we have done, to have them appear in connection with what we desire to introduce yet in connection with the subject of this chapter.

While, as we have stated above, the position is taken that believers when baptized according to the baptismal formula, are baptized into but one name, this position is in plain conflict with other positions that are taken when a practical explanation of the baptismal formula is made. We have seen in our quotation from Henry's Commentary, that there is a conflict between the different parts of his explanation of the baptismal formula. He first takes the position that believers are baptized into "name." He then, in explaining the important relation that the persons baptized stand in to the Father, Son, and Holy Spirit, affirms that they are baptized into the three names—into the name of the Father, and into the name of the Son, and into the name of the Holy Ghost. Now, while the position is taken by some that it is "name" in the singular number into which believers are baptized, yet it is a fact, that when the baptismal formula is looked at under some aspects and explained, a baptism into a plurality of names—into the name of the Father, and into the name of the Son, and into the name of the Holy Spirit is fully recognized.

1. We present a passage from the works of Prof. Curtis, a Baptist writer. In a work called *The Progress of Baptist Principles, in Book II, Chapter II, and Section II.*, under the head of *The Teaching and Profession of Christian Baptism Important*, we have the following: "The commission inserts the creed of the Church, the rock upon which it was founded. And short as the words are, there is couched under these three mysterious names, as here used, all that is essential in Christianity; so that every one who rightly and in his heart receives and embraces them, has therein all the elements of the Christian religion, and is fit for church membership; while no one not thus receiving them is wor-

thy. Mere assent to the words is nothing one way or the other, but the vital assent of the heart is the essence of Christianity.

"What is it, for instance to be baptized into the name of the Father! and why is this made the first requisite of the heavenly system? Because as the realization of the Fatherly character of God is the greatest requisite of all true piety; so the avowal of this realization by that living faith which gives alone *vitality* to all the teachings of natural religion, is made the first part of the Christian profession. When a man can lay his hand upon his heart and say, 'Now I believe—now I feel that God is my Father, and that I am His child—from Him I have derived a new and holy life—He has breathed into me the filial spirit—I commune with Him through prayer as my great Father in heaven—I love and look up to Him, depending on Him in all things, and being governed by His will and pleasure supremely; and I know that He loves and watches over me—that His providence is disciplining me, and His hand guiding all my affairs—that man has rightly learned this first article of the Christian creed; this portion of the great mystery of the Godhead. He believes in the doctrine of the Father."

Dr. Curtis, after explaining what it is to be baptized "into the name of the Father," as we have seen he does, he then proceeds to explain the relation the believer stands in to Christ when he properly accepts him as his Saviour. And though he does not say directly that the believer is baptized "into the name of the Son," that was evidently in his mind when he wrote as he did upon the relation of the believer to the Son of God, when that relation was all that it should be. He explains at length what it is to receive and enjoy Christ, as the believer is brought into connection with him in baptism. The theme of the section from which we are quoting is the importance of baptism when properly performed. And he shows that baptism brings the believer into such a relation to all the persons in the Godhead, the Father, Son, and Holy Spirit, as secures to him the help and blessing of all.

After plainly representing the believer as being baptized "into the name of the Father," and showing the fruits of such a baptism, and after plainly indicating that he is also baptized into the name of the Son, he comes to notice the name of the Holy Spirit, the third person in the Godhead, and the believer's relation to him, and says:

"What is it, then, that a man professes to believe in being baptized in the name of the Holy Ghost in

Certainly not less than that a Divine Spiritual Power operates consciously and directly upon his soul; and while he recognizes as distinct from all other impressions produced by the Father and the Son; a power which enlightens and elevates him, makes dark things light and difficult duties easy, instructs and keeps him in the way of holiness, gives him energy in feebleness, and comfort in sorrow; causes him to know what he could not know without, to love what he hated, and to hate what he loved: a power which thus changes his nature, restoring the soul, in its ultimate and perfect way, to its original image of God."

In *The Christian Review* of October, 1858, a Baptist periodical, there is an article written by Dr. Irah Chase, having the following title: *Basil the Great, an important witness respecting Baptism in the Fourth Century.* Dr. Chase wrote the article to show that Basil's writings indicate that he recognized no infant baptism in the Church in his time.

On page 586 of the *Review*, occurs the following language as a quotation from Basil, by Dr. Chase: "That the baptism in fire convinces of all badness, but receives what is right according to Christ, and introduces hatred of badness and love of virtue;

't through faith, we have been purified by the

blood of Christ from all sin ; that, baptized in water, into the death of the Lord, we have, as it were, deposited a written profession of having become dead to sin and to the world, and of being alive to righteousness; that thus, baptized into the name of the Holy Spirit, we have been generated anew; and having been so generated, and in the name of the Son baptized, we have put on Christ; and having put on the new man created according to God, we have been baptized in the name of the Father, and have been proclaimed children of God."

It is plain from the testimony of Basil, that he recognized three names in the baptismal formula, and not one only, and that into the three names, the name of the Father, and the name of the Son, and the name of the Holy Ghost, believers are baptized. Basil advocated and practiced trine immersion. But we have not referred to him as an advocate of trine immersion, but to show how he understood the language of the baptismal formula. He was a Greek, and a learned man. Dr. Chase in some remarks introductory to his article, speaks thus of Basil: "As a man of eloquence, and of rare intellectual endowments, as well as of uncommon piety, wisdom, laboriousness and self-denial, he acquired great celebrity in the stormy times in which he lived; and since his death, he has been honored by the Greek church, as one of her most illustrious saints."

When the baptismal formula is read without any doctrinal point in view to be sustained, or without any bias of mind to conceal the simplicity and common meaning of the language used, and the phraseology, "baptizing them into the name of the Father, and of the Son, and of the Holy Spirit," carefully considered, there being three persons—three distinct persons, and these having three names, the idea received will be that "name" before Father belongs to Father only, and there being two other persons, the Son, and the Holy Spirit, name will come before each of them as it comes before Father, and then there will plainly be three names, the name of the Father, and the name of the Son, and the name of the Holy Spirit.

In closing our chapter upon the introduction of single immersion into the church, and the ground upon which it is practiced by single immersionists of modern times, we make the reference we do to the contents of the fourth chapter of our work. We have there given the quotations more at length and have given the places in the works of the authors quoted where our quotations may be found. We want the reader to understand and remember that a plurality of persons and of names is recognized in the baptismal formula. And such a plurality of persons and names being recognized, the position that there is but one name in the baptismal formula, and that believers are baptized into but one name when they are baptized according to the formula, is surely a position that is not sustained by the authority of Christian authors when explaining the formula according to the plain principles of philology.

All immersionists contend for the necessity of interpreting and understanding the word baptize or *baptidzo*, the word used to express the ordinance of Christian baptism, in its primary and literal sense or meaning, if we would do justise to the subject in seeking the proper action of baptism. From whatever other sources we draw our arguments for immersion as the proper action of baptism, we regard the primary meaning of the word as it occurs in the Greek language, and as it is defined by Greek lexicographers, as affording the strongest argument for immersion.

The difference between single and trine immersionists in regard to the mode of immersion, is owing to the different views they hold in regard to the literal meaning of the phraseology of the baptismal formula, as the different views of Baptists and Pedo-baptists are owing to their different views of the literal meaning of the word baptize or *baptidzo*.

Single immersionists depart from the literal meaning of the baptismal formula, and put another meaning upon it than that which its literary and philological structure teaches, to sustain their mode of immersion. And by so doing they depart from the principle which they apply to the word *baptidzo*, in maintaining the action of baptism to be immersion. In maintaining immersion they justly contend for the literal meaning of baptize or *baptidzo*. But the trine immersionists adhere to the literal meaning of the phraseology of the baptismal formula which expresses the mode of immersion, as all Baptists do in regard to the meaning of the word baptize, that expresses the action of baptism. In other words, they who practice trine immersion, are more Baptistic, if we may use the expression, than those who practice single immersion, as they carry out more fully the great Baptist principle of adhering to the literal and primary meaning of the language of Scripture, when interpreting the divine laws of the kingdom of heaven. Trine immersionists adhere to the literal meaning of the baptismal formula as well as to the literal meaning of baptize.

CHAPTER VIII.

THE ELLIPTICAL AND THE FULL FORM OF THE BAPTISMAL FORMULA.

SECTION I.

AN *explanation of the ellipsis.* "Baptizing them into the name of the Father, and of the Son, and of the Holy Spirit."

There occurs in this form of the baptismal formula the figure of syntax called "Ellipsis." That is, there is an omission of certain words—the omission of "in the name" before "the Son," and also before the "Holy Spirit." And when these omissions are supplied, the baptismal formula will read, *Baptizing them into the name of the Father, and into the name of the Son, and into the name of the Holy Spirit.*

There is another theory of language, which would make the baptismal formula still more elliptical than we have made it. It is expressed by Prof. Latham, thus: "Whenever there is a conjunction, there are two subjects, two copulas, and two predicates: i. e., two propositions in all their parts."—*Handbook of the English Language, page 357.* According to this theory the baptismal formula would read, *Baptizing them into the name of the Father, amd baptizing them into the name of the Son, and baptizing them into the name of the Holy Spirit.* But as the supplying of *name* before "the Son," and before "the Holy Spirit," is sufficient to give it a form that requires trine immersion to fulfill its requirements, we shall only maintain its elliptical character in regard to the omission of name before "the Son," and before the "Holy Spirit," making it read when the ellipses are supplied, as already said, *Baptizing them into the name of the Father, and into the name of the Son, and into the name of the Holy Spirit.* That the elliptical character of the baptismal formula, and the propriety of supplying the ellipses as we shall do, may be understood and appreciated, we shall give an explanation of the ellipsis, and its use.

The ellipsis in grammar is thus explained by Webster: "Omission; a figure of syntax by which one or more words are omitted; as, the heroic virtues I admire, for, the heroic virtues which I admire."

"*Ellipsis* is the omission of a word, phrase, or clause, which is necessary to complete the construction. It should be understood that the words omitted by this figure as truly belong to the sentence, grammatically considered, as those which are expressed. They are omitted for rhetorical effect, that is, to render the sentence more agreeable and forcible."—*Greene's Elements of English Grammar, page 198.*

"An ellipsis is the omission of some word or words in construction. Such words are said to be understood. They are as much a part of the sentence, as if they were expressed. A full construction requires them: the meaning should be evident without them."—*Covell's Grammar, page 180.*

The reader will notice that both Greene and Covell declare that words omitted by the ellipsis are to be considered part of the sentence.

This figure of syntax occurs in all kinds of writing. It frequently occurs in the Scriptures. Dr. Terry in his *Biblical Hermeneutics, page 101,* in speaking of the Hebrew language as we have it in the Scriptures, says, "There are, again, many passages where a notable ellipsis enhances the impression."

In the introduction to *The Life and Epistles of St. Paul by Conybear and Howson, page 20,* the following statement is made in regard to the elliptical character of Paul's writings: "St. Paul's style is extremely elliptical, and the gaps must be filled up."

Mr. R. Milligan in his work entitled, *Reason and Revelation, page 315*, in giving rules for *Ascertaining the Meaning of Sentences*, has among the rules given, the following:

Be careful to ascertain its right construction. This requires attention,

1. To its ellipsis.
2. To its subject and predicate, with all their primary and secondary adjuncts.
3. To its punctuation."

SECTION II.

The Use of the Ellipsis. We notice from the foregoing remarks relating to the occurrence of the ellipsis in the Scriptures, that it does not occur in common writing or composition alone, but that it also occurs in the literary composition of the sacred writings.

Greene says in his remarks on the ellipsis that we have already quoted, in alluding to words omitted by this figure, "They are omitted for rhetorical effect, that is, to render the sentence more agreeable and forcible." Hence Hart has the following observations in his *Composition and Rhetoric:* "A sentence is made stronger by leaving out redundant words. It may be taken for granted that whatever does not add to the meaning enfeebles it. Every redundant word is so much dead weight."—page 31. In *Blair's Rhetoric, page 123*, we have the following: "The first rule which I give for promoting the strength of a sentence, is, to divest it of all redundant words. These may, sometimes, be consistent with a considerable degree both of clearness and unity; but they are always enfeebling. They make the sentence move along tardy and encumbered. It is a general maxim that any words which do not add some importance to the meaning of a sentence, always spoil it. They cannot be superfluous without being hurtful. All that can be easily supplied in the mind, is better left out in the expression."

"The vigorous conciseness and compression of a writer's manner should always be retained, even at the risk of requiring more attention and thought on the part of the reader. Diluted paraphrase does great injustice to any writer who thinks and expresses himself with brevity and point. One would rather not be understood than be diluted to what is not worth understanding."—*Dr. Conant's Introduction to his Translation of Matthew, page 7.*

SECTION III.

The standard of correct speaking and writing is the practice of literary men.

We shall now proceed to show that the baptismal formula is elliptical, and that the ellipses should be supplied in a full grammatical construction of it, and that when they are supplied, it will read "*baptizing them into the name of the Father, and into the name of the Son, and into the name of the Holy Spirit.*" There are two ways by which the elliptical character of the baptismal formula may be proved. First, we may analyze or parse it, according to the rules of English grammar, and prove by so doing that a full construction of it, according to the recognized principles of our language, requires name before "the Son," and before "the Holy Spirit," as well as before "the Father." Secondly, we may go back of the grammar of our language to that upon which it is founded, namely, the usage of our best speakers and writers in their conversation and writing. And as some of our readers may not be sufficiently acquainted with English grammar, to understand and appreciate grammatical analysis in its more intricate rules, and as others may have no taste for grammatical criticism, we shall pursue the second method above named, and go to the usages of men of literary reputation to prove the elliptical character of the baptismal formula. This method all can understand.

That the propriety and correctness of the course we design pursuing may be apparent to our readers, we shall make some explanation in regard to the foundation and origin of grammatical rules. It may not be known to all our readers that the principles and rules of the grammar of our language are derived from the usages of leading literary men. But such is the case. Dr. Carson says, "Use is the sole arbiter of language; and whatever is agreeable to this authority, stands justified beyond impeachment."—*Carson on Baptism, page 46.*

Dr. Hart in his *Manual of Composition and Rhetoric,* a work of authority in our schools and colleges, has a long quotation from Campbell's Essay on Use as the Law of Language. Dr. Campbell says: "Only let us rest on these fixed principles, that USE or the custom of speaking, is the sole original standard of conversation as far as regards the expression, and the custom of writing is the sole standard of style; that the latter comprehends the former, and something more; that to the tribunal of *use* as the supreme authority, and, consequently, in every grammatical or verbal controversy, the last resort, we are entitled to appeal from the laws and the decisions of grammarians; and that this order of subordination ought never on any account to be reversed."

Dr. Hart has also the following on page 76 of the work to which we have already alluded:

"*The Dictum of Horace.*—The dictum of Horace to this effect has received, I believe, the general assent of the critics, and it may now be considered as a part of the undisputed creed of the learned, namely, that *use is the law of language*, whether for single words, grammatical forms, or grammatical construction."

Dr. Jamieson says, "Use or *the custom of speaking* is, then, the sole original standard of conversation, as far as respects the expression; and the custom of writing is the chief standard of style. In every grammatical controversy, we are, consequently, as a last resort, entitled to appeal from the laws and decisions of the grammarians to THE TRIBUNAL of use, as the supreme authority. The conduct of our ablest grammarians proves that this order of subordination ought never on any account to be reversed."—*Jamieson's Rhetoric, p. 51.* After dwelling still further upon use as the standard of language, he deduces from what he had said, several principles, among which are the following:

I. That *use* is the sole mistress of language.

II. That her essential attributes are *reputable, national*, and *present*.

III. That grammar and criticism are but her ministers; and though like other ministers, they would sometimes impose upon the people, the dictates of their own humor as the commands of their sovereign, they are not so often successful in such attempts, as to encourage the frequent repetition of them."—*Ibid, page 55.*

In accordance with the principles above expressed in regard to reputable use constituting the standard of style in speaking and writing, many writers think that the best way to obtain a correct practical knowledge of language, is to closely observe, and imitate the example of our literary men of acknowledged reputation. James Freeman Clarke, a popular lecturer and writer, in his work on *Self Culture, page 84,* says "Locke in his treatise on education, advises that, in teaching Latin, no grammar be used at all, but to have a teacher able to teach Latin by conversation, without the perplexity of rules, just as a child learns his own language." Mr. Clarke in the same work, page 85, has also the following from Locke: "I would fain have one name to me that tongue that any one can learn or speak as he should do, by the rules of grammar. Languages were made not by rules of art, but by accident, and the common use of the people. And he that speaks them well has no other rule but that." Mr. Clarke expresses his own sentiments as follows, on page 86, of his work above named: "We do not learn to write and speak correctly by committing to memory unintelligible definitions and rules, but by reading well-written books and conversing with educated speakers." The following appeared some time ago in the *Buffalo Express:* "Cincinnati has made a new departure and a real reform in educational methods by throwing out the study of grammar from the curriculum, substituting therefor elementary lessons from the English and American writers most noted for their simplicity and purity of style. The children will probably learn less and understand more under the new system. There is absolutely but one rule in English composition and that is good use—the usage of the best writers. That is what the fortunate Cincinnati children are now to be taught."

Now as the language used by our speakers and writers of reputation is the basis of the rules of English grammar, and as their language becomes the standard of correct speaking and writing, we shall introduce examples of writers of reputation to prove that the baptismal formula is elliptical.

SECTION IV.

Testimony to the elliptical character of the baptismal formula. Our first authority will be Butler, the author of the *Analogy*. In his chapter on *The Importance of Christianity*, we have the following: "Christianity is to be considered in a further view, as containing an account of a dispensation of things not at all discoverable by reason, in consequence of which several distinct precepts are enjoined upon us. Christianity is not only an external institution of natural religion, and a new promulgation of God's Providence, carrying on by his Son and Spirit, for the recovery and salvation of mankind, who are represented in Scripture to be in a state of ruin. And in consequence of this revelation being made, we are commanded *to be baptized*, not only *in the name of the Father*, but also, *of the Son, and of the Holy Ghost:* and other obligations of duty, unknown before, to the Son and Holy Ghost, are revealed. Now the importance of these duties may be judged of, by observing that they arise, not from positive command merely, but also from the offices which appear from Scripture, to belong to those divine persons in the Gospel dispensation; or from the relations which we are there informed, they stand in to us. By *reason* is revealed the relation which God the Father stands in to us. Hence arises the obligation of duty which we are under to him. In *Scripture* are revealed the relations which the Son and Holy Spirit stand in to us. Hence arise the obligations of duty, which we are under to them. The truth of the case as one may speak, in each of these three respects being admitted: that God is the governor of the world upon the evidence of reason; that Christ is the Mediator between God and man, and the Holy Ghost our guide and sanctifier, upon the evidence of revelation: the truth of the case, I say, in each of these respects being admitted, it is no more a question, why it should be commanded, that we be baptized in the name of the Son and of the Holy Ghost, than that we be baptized in the name of the Father."—*Butler's Analogy, pages 194, 195.*

When the author in the above extract says, "we are commanded *to be baptized*, not only *in the name of the Father*, but also, *of the Son, and of the Holy Ghost*," it is evident that he understood the *name* that occurs before Father in the baptismal formula, as belonging only to the Father. It is also evident that he understood that name was to be supplied before Son and Holy Ghost. This is proved from the close of the extract: "It is no more a question, why it should be commanded that we be baptized into the name of the Son and of the Holy Ghost, than that we be baptized in the name of the Father." Here he puts name before Son, showing that he understood it to belong there according to the implied sense of the phraseology. He did not put it before Holy Ghost because it was plainly to be understood that it was implied there after he had supplied it before Son.

We give another extract from the same author: "That we be baptized in the name of the Father is as much a positive duty, as that we be baptized in the name of the Son, because both arise equally from revealed command: though the relation which we stand in to God the Father is made known to us by reason, and the relation we stand in to Christ, by revelation only. On the other hand, the dispensation of the Gospel being admitted, gratitude as immediately becomes due to Christ, from his being the voluntary minister of this dispensation, as it is due to God the Father, from his being the fountain of all good; though the first is made known to us by revelation only, the second by reason. Hence also we may see, and for distinctness' sake, it may be worth mentioning, that positive institutions come under a two-fold consideration. They are either institutions founded on natural religion, as baptism in the name of the Father; (though this has also a particular reference to the Gospel dispensation,) for it is in the name of God, as the Father of our Lord Jesus Christ; as baptism in the name of the Son, and of the Holy Ghost."—*Ibid, page 198.* The reader will notice the recognition again of *name* before Son, and it is also evidently to be understood before Holy Ghost. We would also remind him that our author in the last extract alludes to God and the Father as being the same. He says, "it is in the name of God, as the Father of our Lord Jesus Christ."

From Butler's reference to the baptismal formula, it is clear that he understood that in its full and complete construction, name properly belongs to "the Son," and to "the Holy Spirit," as well as to "the Father," and hence in the form in which it occurs in the commission of our Lord, it is elliptical.

Our next authority will be a writer in *The Christian Baptist*, a periodical established by Alexander

Campbell, and through which he first promulgated and defended the reformation for which he contended and which he introduced. The writer of the article from which we make our extract was a contributor to that periodical. He says: "The first instituted act of Christian worship is baptism into the name of the Father, and of the Son, and of the Holy Spirit. Why is it translated '*in* the name,' etc., contrary to the literal and almost universal translation of the particle *eis?* In the name of any dignified character, universally imports, by the authority of such a person. Whereas this is not the proper and obvious meaning of the baptismal institution. For although it is done by virtue of the divine authority enjoining it, that is, by the authority of Christ; yet its proper and primary import is not a mere exhibition of authority on the part of the institutor, and of submission on the part of the baptized, though this is certainly implied in every act of worship; but it is of a much more consolatory and blissful import, being an expression of faith and obedience on the part of the baptized; nay the very first instituted act of the obedience of faith, in and by which the believing worshipper is openly dedicated to be of the household of faith, and of the family of God, being baptized into 'the name of the Father,' of whom the whole redeemed family in heaven and earth is named; and into the name of the Redeemer, the Son, and heir of all things, who makes his people free; and into the name of the Holy Spirit, the sanctifier, the comforter, and perfecter of the saints; that by virtue of his indwelling and sanctifying presence, he, the baptized believer, may be separated to God with all the redeemed, for a habitation of God, through the Spirit."—*Christian Baptist, page 99.* The writer of the above evidently understood *name* to be implied before Son, and before Holy Spirit, in the baptismal formula, and he so used it, and wrote "into the name of the Father," "into the .name of the Redeemer, the Son," and "into the name of the Holy Spirit."

Mr. Alexander Campbell in writing upon the ministry of John, has the following: "Again he did not immerse into the name of the Holy Spirit, because the Spirit was not yet glorified; and these who were immersed by John had not heard anything of the Holy Spirit. [See Acts 19: 1-8] The Son and the Holy Spirit not being yet revealed, he could not immerse into either the name of the Son or of the Holy Spirit."—*Christian Baptist, page 647.* The foregoing language plainly shows that Mr. Campbell looked at the baptismal formula as elliptical, when there was nothing to prejudice his mind against that view of it. He says John "did not immerse into the name of the Holy Spirit." Again he says, "he could not immerse into either the *name* of the Son or of the Holy Spirit." He evidently had the baptismal formula in his mind, and accepted the idea that the apostles were to baptize into the *name* of the Son, and into the name of the Holy Spirit, as well as into the name of the Father. But as the formula had not been given according to Mr. Campbell's view when John baptized, he argues that John could not have immersed "into either the name of the Son, or of the Holy Spirit," as the apostles did. And in the phrase "he could not immerse into either name of the Son or of the Holy Spirit," he did not put name before Holy Spirit, because that would be clearly understood, following as it does, the phrase "in the name of the Son." But when Holy Spirit did not follow the phrase "in the name of the Son," as was the case when he first used the term, Holy Spirit, then he put *name* before Holy Spirit. He pursued the same course in writing the baptismal formula, that writers pursue in writing phrases similarly constructed, which shows that he looked at the formula as elliptical, and as reading when the ellipses are supplied, "*baptizing them into the name of the Father, and into the name of the Son, and into the name of the Holy Ghost."*

We next quote from Dr. Shedd's *History of Christian Doctrine, Vol. I, page 330.* The author is treating upon the Deity of the Second Person in the Godhead, and says, "Again, baptism was to be administered in the name of the 'Son'; but this would have been impious, had filiation in the Godhead denoted only a finite and created relationship. The candidate would in this case, have been baptized into a name that designed nothing eternal or divine; and, furthermore, a merely finite and temporal hypostasis would therefore have been associated, in a solemn sacramental act, in the eternal Trinity. In the controversy respecting the validity of heretical baptism, the church came to the decision that baptism in the name of Christ is not valid. It must be administered according to the Scriptural formula, in the name of the Eternal Three. But if baptism in the name of the God-man, solely, is not justifiable; still less would it be proper to baptize in the name of 'Son,' if that term denoted a merely temporal and transitory distinction and relationship."

Dr. Shedd by putting *name* before "Son," had without doubt the baptismal formula in his mind, and believed that name justly belonged to Son.

And if he put name before Son in the formula of baptizing, he would, no doubt, have put *name* also before Holy Spirit had he had occasion to do so, and thus clearly sanctioned the grammatical construction of the Christian form for administering baptism to be, *baptizing them into the name of the Father, and into the name of the Son, and into the name of the Holy Spirit.*

The following is from Bishop Tomline: "Are we to be baptized in the name of the Father, of the Son, and of the Holy Ghost, and is it possible that the Father should be self-existent, eternal, the Lord God Omnipotent; and that the Son, in whose name we are equally baptized, should be a mere man, born of a woman, and subject to all the frailties and imperfections of human nature? or, is it possible that the Holy Ghost, in whose name also we are equally baptized, should be a bare energy or operation, a quality or power without even personal existence? Our feelings as well as our reason, revolt from such disparity."—*Tomline's Theology, Vol. II, page 85.*

James Purvis, of Edinburgh, a scholar, apparently of considerable literary attainments, and a writer who seems to have been in search of the truth, in a work called *An Humble Attempt to Investigate and Defend the Scripture Doctrine Concerning the Father, the Son, and the Holy Spirit,* having occasion to refer to the *baptismal formula,* has the following in reference to the structure of the language containing it on page 44 of his work: "It is very evident that the word *name* is to be understood as if it were repeated with the Son and the Holy Spirit. For when it is said, 'Baptizing them in the name ef the Father, and of the Son, and of the Holy Spirit'; it is the same or of the same import as to say, 'Bapsizing them in the name of the Father, and in the name of the Son, and in the name of the Holy Spirit.' If this is not the sense, what does name refer to? or what is meant by it? If it does not refer to or mean the name of the Father, the name of the Son, and the name of the Holy Spirit, it would seem that the text should in part have read the very reverse of what it doth; that is, it should have read, Baptizing them in the *name,* not of the Father, nor of the Son, nor of the Holy Spirit, but in the name that denotes the unity of their essence. I suppose any one may see the absurdity of this, and what difficulties it would present to a serious inquirer, while the text as it stands, is suited to convey instruction to the most ordinary capacity."

We next present a quotation from Dr. Wardlaw, of Glasgow. He preached a series of discourses on

The Principal Points of the Socinian Controversy. He took the Trinitarian side of the controversy. In a discourse on the *Divinity and Personality of the Holy Spirit*, preached on Matt. 28: 19, on the text of Scripture containing the baptismal formula, he has the following on page 267 of the volume of his discourses: "The very form of expression seems to convey the idea, not only of a Trinity of Persons, but of that Trinity as subsisting in the one Godhead:—baptizing them in—or into, for the change of translation does not at all affect the present argument—baptizing them in the *name*—not names—but the *one name* 'of the Father, of the Son, and of the Holy Spirit.' If however, it should be insisted, that '*the name*' is to be supplied before each,—'in the name of the Father, and in the name of the Son, and in the name of the Holy Spirit';—then what are we to make of this last phrase, '*the name of the Spirit*,' if the Holy Spirit means an attribute, or a power, or influence? An attribute of Deity it cannot, indeed, be supposed to mean; for all the attributes of Deity are, of course, included in '*the name of the Father*,' previously mentioned; and to baptize in the name of one of his attributes after having baptized in his own name, while the thing itself is most unnatural, would certainly be a very vain repetition." Dr. Wardlaw does not deny the elliptical character of the baptismal formula, but adapts his argument to it with the ellipsis supplied—'the name of the Holy Spirit.'

We call the reader's attention to another important point in Dr. Wardlaw's discourse. This is the point contained in the following words: "An attribute of Deity it cannot, indeed, be supposed to mean; for all the attributes of Deity are, of course, included in *the name of the Father*,' previously mentioned." The doctor makes Father in the baptismal formula equivalent to Deity or to God. This is correct—a just admission. Hence *name* cannot mean the name of God, or the associated name of all three of the divine persons mentioned, as is frequently declared.

We reviewed two articles that were written by Eld. C. Sine, of the Disciple church, and published in the *Christian Union and Religious Review*. The above articles and our review appeared in the *Gospel Visitor* of 1856. Elder Sine admits the elliptical character of the baptismal formula, in the following words: "The ellipsis is supplied simply by a repetition of the word 'name.' The copulative conjunction 'and' is also connective; it is used to join on a word or sentence implying addition. Hence it has the sense of *add*. To the name of the Father, it joins on—or adds the name of the Son," etc.—*Gospel Visitor for 1856, page 95.*

We shall in the next place select some examples from authors to prove that the form of expression used in regard to the names occurring in the baptismal formula, when used in regard to other names, is evidently elliptical. We give the following example from Dr. Dwight. He makes use of the language in an argument to prove *that the Holy Ghost is a Divine Person because he is united with the Father and the Son in the baptismal service and in the blessing pronounced upon Christians by St. Paul.* His language is this: "Nothing but impiety can, so far as I see, be contained in a direction to baptize in the name of God and of a creature. What creature would dare to associate himself with God in such an act of authority, and thus presume to ascend the throne of his Maker."—*Dwight's Theology, Vol. II, page 379.* In the phrase, "in the name of God and of a creature, name is evidently to be understood before creature, for the meaning is, in the name of God and in the name of a creature. Hence the passage as written by Dr. Dwight is elliptical. Since it is a phrase similar to the baptismal formula, it is a confirmation of the elliptical character of the baptismal formula.

Our next example is from Dr. Pierce, of the Georgia Methodist Conference. He uses the language we shall quote in a discussion with John C. Burruss, of the Universalist church. The discussion was on the Doctrine of the Trinity. The discussion was published, and on page 26 of the work, Dr. Pierce says, "How strangely it would have sounded if baptism had been ordered in the name of the Father and of Gabriel and of Michael—one divine and two angelic names." Here we have a form of expression precisely similar to that used in the baptismal formula, but name is only supplied before the first person and is understood before the other two. But in a complete construction of the phrases used by the Dr., name would be supplied before Gabriel, and also before Michael, and with the ellipses supplied, it would read, "How strangely it would have sounded if baptism had been ordered in the name of the Father, and in the name of Gabriel, and in the name of Michael."

"'Thus it appears that the great works of Omnipotence, *creation*, *regeneration* and *resurrection* of the dead, are ascribed equally to the Father, Son, and

Spirit; consequently 'these three' persons 'are one' God. No fourth person is ever associated with the sacred three. No minister of Christ ever baptized in the name of Peter, or even of Mary, the mother of Christ's human nature, nor prayed that the grace of Paul or of Apollos might be with the people of God."—*Tract 221 of the M. E. Church, On the Trinity, page 6.*

There is another way of presenting the baptismal formula to show its elliptical form, and which will confirm what we have already said in regard to the elliptical character of the baptismal formula. And although we have produced ample testimony to prove our position, the following view is worthy of our consideration in treating our subject under the aspect, under which we are treating it.

We have in our language what grammarians call "grammatical equivalents." This means that an idea may be presented in different ways, or embodied in different words. "The preposition *of*, with the objective, is generally equivalent to the possessive case, and is often used in preference to it."—*Bullion's Grammar, page 105.*

According to the above principle as given by Bullion, and recognized by all grammarians, the baptismal formula may be read in the possessive form, instead of the form it has with the preposition of. In the possessive form it will read, *Baptizing them into the Father's name, and the Son's, and the Holy Spirit's.* And this reading is in accordance with the original Greek. This will not be denied. Elder Adamson of the Disciple church, to whom we have already referred, and who wrote a pamphlet against trine immersion, on page 8 of his pamphlet has the following note: "In the phrases, 'of the Father,' 'of the Son,' and 'of the Holy Ghost,' the words *Father, Son,* and *Holy Ghost,* are grammatically in the objective case, but in signification they are in the genitive, denoting possession according to an idiom of the English language, by which the objective with the preposition *of,* is frequently used instead of the possessive. This will be seen by referring to the German translation, and to the Greek, in both of which these words are in the genitive."

We also have the following rules given us by our grammarians to govern us in the use and understanding of the possessive case:

"Nouns denoting a possessive relation to the same object, have the sign annexed to the last only; as, 'Mason and Dixon's line.'

"Nouns denoting a possessive relation to different objects, have the sign annexed to each; as, 'Adams' and Jackson's administration," i. e. 'Adams' administration' and 'Jackson's administration.'"— *Covell's Digest of English Grammar, page 133.*

Applying the foregoing principles to the baptismal formula, we have it in the following form: *Baptizing them into the Father's name, and into the Son's name, and into the Holy Spirit's name.* This is equivalent to the reading, *baptizing them into the name of the Father, and into the name of the Son, and into the name of the Holy Spirit.* And the common form in which we have it, "baptizing them into the name of the Father, and of the Son, and of the Holy Spirit," is equivalent to each of the foregoing forms. The same ideas are expressed but in different forms.

The objection has been made to the supplying of the ellipses, that it is adding to the word of the Lord. But it is not really adding to the word of the Lord. It is only presenting the word of the Lord that we have in the baptismal formula, in another form. In our common reading we have it in an abridged form. With the ellipses supplied we have it in an expanded form,

The translation of the Scripture by the American Bible Union was objected to on the ground that the Baptists were making a Bible to suit their baptism, because the translators translated the word *baptidzo* by the English word immerse. To such an objection it was replied, that their was no changing of the Bible, and no adding anything to it to favor any denominational view of baptism, but simply the translating of the word *baptidzo* in Greek by the English word immerse, which was claimed to be its equivalent. And just so in regard to supplying the ellipses in the baptismal formula. It is only giving some of the ideas contained in it, a little more prominency. The words supplied, "are as much a part of the sentences, as if they were expressed," our grammarians affirm.

A number of our quotations have been taken from writers who were writing upon the subject of the Trinity when they used the language we have quoted to prove that they regarded the baptismal formula to be elliptical. And we wish it understood that it is not with their theology that we are concerned, but it is with their philology or knowledge and use of language with which we have to do. Although they were writing upon the subject of the Trinity, when they added "name" to Son and to Holy Ghost as they so frequently did, this was not generally done, if at all, as will be seen by a careful examination of the connection in which the passages quoted stand, for doctrinal effect. It was done apparently, by the natural prompting of their minds, being educated as they were in the principles of the English language, and the use of the language requiring name to be added in such cases to the person to whom it belongs in a full construction of the sentence, though omitted when the sentence was elliptical, they added it, and thus clearly sanctioned the elliptical character of that form of writing.

We have now developed the subject of this chapter, the elliptical character and the full construction of the baptismal formula, to a considerable extent. The propriety of our doing so will appear in the next chapter. We have produced testimony of different kinds, and from different writers to prove the elliptical character of the baptismal formula. Believing its elliptical character is either not understood, or if understood, not appreciated in its bearing upon the mode of immersion taught in it, we have given it the prominence we have in our work.

1. We have given the authority of several writers for the elliptical form of the baptismal formula, who, when writing upon it, without any special design in view, added name to " the Son," and to "the Holy Spirit," showing that they recognized the principle, that according to our language, *name* was under-

stood in such cases to belong to the person or persons following another to whom it was applied, and though not expressed in the sentence as commonly and correctly written, yet would be expressed, when the construction of the sentence was full or complete. To this class belong Bishop Butler and Dr. Shedd.

2. We introduced another class that did not add *name* to "the Son," and to "the Holy Ghost," but added another person to the baptismal formula, besides the three Divine Persons contained in it, and by the form they gave it, its elliptical character, and the elliptical character of similar sentences clearly appear. Such are the examples from Drs. Dwight and Pierce. Dr. Dwight uses the language, "to baptize in the name of God and of a creature." Here *name*, though not expressed, clearly belongs to "creature," as well as to "God." Dr. Pierce says, "How strangely it would have sounded if baptism had been ordered in the name of the Father, and of Gabriel, and of Michael—one divine and two angelic names." Here name evidently belongs to Gabriel, and to Michael, as well as to "Father," and thus the elliptical character of such sentences in the judgment of those writers is recognized.

3. Then we have seen that other writers directly

affirm the elliptical character of the baptismal formula and add *name* to "the Son," and to "the Holy Spirit," understanding it to belong to them as well as to "the Father."

4. We have also shown that the baptismal formula according to the recognized principles of the English language, may be put into a possessive form, having the sign of the possessive case instead of the preposition *of*, and the objective; that this is not only in harmony with the principles of the Fnglish language, but also according to the original, as the words "Father," "Son," and "Holy Spirit," are in the possessive case in the Greek; that the possessive form is manifestly elliptical.

We have seen that "*Use is the law of language*, whether for single words, grammatical forms, or grammatical construction." And we have also seen that the use of reputable writers proves the elliptical character of the baptismal formula. We are, therefore warranted by acknowledged authority in regarding the baptismal formula as elliptical, and in reading it when the ellipses are supplied, and when there is given to it, its full grammatical construction, "baptizing them into the name of the Father, and into the name of the Son, and into the name of the Holy Spirit."

CHAPTER IX.

AN APPLICATION OF THE PRINCIPLES CONTAINED IN THE BAPTISMAL FORMULA.

IN the treatment of our subject in the previous chapters of our work, various principles have been brought out, being more or less the outgrowth of the baptismal formula. These principles will now be made the basis of a number of arguments to prove that trine immersion is the true Christian baptism. This proposition embodies the truth our present work is designed to develop and maintain. And regarding the baptismal formula as having the materials in it when developed and applied for a successful maintenance of the proposition, our work hitherto has been to prepare those materials, and we shall now make an application of them.

SECTION I.

Argument 1. From the implied admission of single immersionists.

It is plainly implied by single immersionists that a plurality of names in the baptismal formula would show that a trine immersion was intended to be taught by the formula. There is a work called *Notes on the Gospel of Matthew; Explanatory and Practical*, by Rev. George W. Clark. Such is the title of the work, and such is the name of the author. It is published by the *American Baptist Publication Society*, and it is a Baptist work. In commenting upon the baptismal formula, and in referring especially to *name* in the formula, the author says, "The plural would have implied three distinct beings. The singular implies that the three though in a sense distinct are yet one. The fact of the trinity is revealed, but the precise mode of its existence is one of the secret and mysterious things of God. Compare 2 Cor. 13:14. The singular also points clearly to only *one* immersion. If a *threefold* immersion had been intended, the form would have been either *in the names of*, or *in the name of the Father, and in the name of the Son, etc.* The old custom of immersing at the utterance of each name, still practiced by the Greek church, is first mentioned by Tertullian, and appears to have arisen from the superstitions and corruptions which gave birth to infant baptism." We are evidently to infer from the language above quoted, that in the judgment of the author, a plurality of names would have indicated that a plurality of actions or immersions was intended. He says, "The singular also points clearly to only *one* immersion." We infer from this that had *name* been *names*, then a plurality of immersions would have been intended according to his judgment. He also says if a three-fold immersion had been intended, the form would have been either *in the names of*, or *in the name of the Father, and in the name of the Son, etc.* So his language plainly implies that if a plurality of names was in the baptismal formula, it would indicate that a plurality of immersions was intended to be taught. Dr. Conant's view given in Chapter VII, is very similar to Mr. Clarke's idea, and implies the same. The remarks from the *Baptist Advanced Quarterly*, "Trine immersion wrong; 'name' not 'names,'" also quoted by us in Chapter VII, implies the same. Then if a plurality of names indicates a plurality of immersions, and it is implied in the quotations made, that it does, then we surely have a plurality of immersions; for we have showed plainly and conclusively that we have such a plurality of names. This has not only been done by showing that the baptismal formula is elliptical and that when its construction is complete, it will evidently contain three names, but it has been also done by the testimony we have adduced from writers quoted whose testimony will be found in Chapter IV, Section III.

SECTION II.

Argument 2. From a plurality of Persons in the baptismal formula. We shall deduce our second argument for trine immersion from the baptismal formula, from the plurality of Persons recognized in it. We have seen in presenting our first argument, that it is plainly implied in remarks and criticisms upon the baptismal formula by single immersionists, that a plurality of names, would indicate that a plurality of immersions was intended. This, no doubt, is a correct view of the case. For as one name would require one action or immersion, it would seem to follow as a necessary consequence, that if there were three names it would require three actions or three immersions. This is the view we presume that those have taken of the baptismal formula, who say It should read, baptizing them "*into the names of,*" or "*in the name of the Father, and in the name of the Son, and in the name of the Holy Ghost,*" if a trine immersion had been intended to be taught in it.

But it is not simply into the *name* of ihe Father, and into the *name* of the Son, and into the *name* of the Holy Spirit that believers are to be baptized.

They are to be baptized into those Divine Persons themselves. This has been clearly proved in Chapter V. It is there shown that the names representing the Persons in the baptismal formula really represent and stand for the Persons themselves.

Again: it will be seen by a careful reading of the preceding chapters of our work, especially Chapter IV, Section I, that there is a plurality of Persons plainly presented to us in the form of words given for administering baptism. This we have proved by Scriptural testimony and by the testimony of many writers. Indeed, we presume that it will be universally admitted, that there are three Divine agents, or three Personal agents, in the form of baptism presented to our faith, and to our affections, into which we are to be baptized. Upon the character or nature of the three objects in which those who would be saved must believe, and which they must receive, and into which they must be baptized, there may be a difference in sentiment among believers, but upon their tri-plurality we presume there can be but little difference of sentiment. It should also be remembered that these three objects are distinct. See Chapter IV, Section II.

If then a plurality of names in the baptismal formula requires a plurality of actions or immersions, as we have seen it does, for the same reason a plurality of Persons will require a plurality of immersions, for it is into the Persons themselves that we are to be baptized as well as into their names. And could it be proved that there is but one name in the baptismal formula, if there are three Persons into whom believers are to be baptized, three immersions will still be required. But there are three *names*, as well as three *Persons*, and hence trine immersion is plainly taught by the phraseology of the baptismal formula.

SECTION III.

Argument 3. From the marked distinction that characterizes the three Divine Persons and their names as they are given in the baptismal formula.

1. We make the distinction that characterizes the Persons and their names, and the manner in which those Persons and names are referred to in the baptismal formula, the ground of our third argument. There are given in the form of words for administering baptism, a plurality of names, as showed in Chapter IV. There is also a distinction in the work and offices of the three sacred Persons presented to us in the baptismal formula, and into which believers are to be baptized. Each one has his own work to do in Creation, Providence, and Redemption.

And while believers are to be baptizrd into each one to show their need of the help and blessing of each, the apostolic benediction shows the same distinction: "The *grace* of the Lord Jesus Christ, and the *love* of God, and the *communion* of the Holy Ghost be with you all." The distinction in the three Divine Persons in the Godhead and in the baptismal formula is very clearly manifested throughout the Christian Scriptures.

The distinction to which we are referring, and which has been so generally recognized, is remarkably preserved in the phraseology in which the baptismal formula is stated.

Father, Son, and Holy Spirit as they occur in the baptismal formula are not joined together by the conjunction "and" though it occurs between Father and Son, and between Son and the Holy Spirit. For the preposition "of" occurs in connection with the conjunction "and," and prepositions as well as conjunctions have a connecting power. There must be, therefore, some other words, phrases, or sentences connected by the two conjunctions "and," and not merely the words Father, Son, and Holy Spirit. The fact that Father, Son, and Holy Spirit are not joined together as they occur in the phraseology in the baptismal formula, and according to the principles of our language, should not be overlooked in studying the import of the baptismal formula. The three words, "Father," "Son," and "Holy Spirit" are generally looked at as being joined together. But this is not the case. And as they are not joined together by the conjunctions "and" that occur in the sentence, neither are the three names that occur in the full construction of the sentence, the *name* of the Father, and the *name* of the Son, and the *name* of the Holy Spirit, joined together.

3. The argument we are drawing from the marked distinction of the three persons in the Godhead, taught in the baptismal formula, and preserved in its peculiar phraseology, for trine immersion, is strengthened by the following testimonies: Dr. Stier, a learned German theologian, and commentator, in his work called, *The words of the Lord Jesus,* in commenting upon the baptismal formula, says, "All who receive baptism in conformity with this anticipatory institution, require to be baptized *into each of the three names.*" The writer of the article on the Holy Spirit, in Kitto's Cyclopædia of Biblical Literature, says, in referring to the baptismal formula, "He is baptized into the *name* of each of the three." Dr. Doddridge when commenting on

the baptismal formula in his *Expositor*, makes the following remark: "That by this solemn initiatory ordinance they may profess their subjection to *each* of these Divine Persons, and maintaining suitable regard to *each*, may receive from *each* correspondent blessings."

For the reader to get the idea that we desire him to get from the above testimonies, and which will add weight to our argument, he should have a clear view of the import of the word *each*. Webster thus explains it: "This word is a distributive adjective pronoun, used either with or without a following noun, and denoting every one of the two or more individuals composing a whole, considered separately from the rest."

Then as *each* means any number of persons taken separately, and not joined together, the above writters considered the three Divine Persons in the baptismal formula as being presented separately. And if each one of the three is to be taken separately, and the believer is to be baptized into each of the three, the necessity of three immersions is evident, and our position is confirmed by their testimony.

3. The argument we are making for trine immersion upon the distinction in the Godhead plainly taught in the baptismal formula, is confirmed and

strengthened from the peculiar form given to the communion service by our Lord for the commemorating of his death. In his wisdom and benevolence he purposed for the edification and profit of his church, and to enable his followers ever to keep in mind what their redemption cost their divine Master, to institute an ordinance that would represent impressively his death. That ordinance comprises two symbols, the bread and the wine; the bread to represent his flesh, the wine to represent his blood. Now if the distinction in his holy flesh and blood was such, either in themselves, or in their effect in the work of redemption, as to require two symbols or two actions to exhibit the completeness of his sacrifice, is it improbable that there should be in the ordinance of baptism three actions to bring prominently before the believer the three Divine Persons who are engaged in his salvation? It is not improbable. For while their distinction is fully recognized and made manifest, each one has also his separate work to do. And a plurality of actions or of immersions to indicate the plurality of persons in the Godhead and the plurality of their offices, would be in perfect harmony with the plurality of actions in the communion service, designed to indicate both the flesh and blood of Christ.

The ancient Christians regarded baptism in its three-fold action as symbolizing the three Persons in the Godhead, and also the three days' and three nights our Lord was "in the heart of the earth." The three immersions they regarded as symbolizing the three nights and the three emersions, the three days. Whatever may be the symbolic expressiveness of the baptism intended by the phraseology of the baptismal formula, it is very evident that that phraseology was intended to present to the church and to the world, the plurality and distinction of the persons in the Godhead. The words of the baptismal formula in their connection and teaching seem to convey this idea to the mind of the observing reader.

Should it be said that while there are three persons and three names in the baptismal formula, these three persons are also one, and that name refers to the unity and not to the plurality, of the persons in the Godhead, we reply, that we readily admit that there is a sense in which the three are one, and that there is a unity as well as a plurality in the Godhead, but it is the plurality of both names and persons that is presented to us in the baptismal formula. This should be kept in mind. "Is it possible," says Dr. Clark in the quotation from him we have already made, "for words to convey a plainer sense than these do? And do they not direct every reader to consider the Father, the Son, and the Holy Spirit, as three distinct persons?"

In Chapter IV the plurality and distinction of persons, and the plurality of names in the baptismal formula, have been clearly presented and proved. And as the Divine Persons into whom we are to be baptized, are presented to us in the baptismal formula, we should consider them, receive them, and submit to them. We should by no means go to some other passage of Scripture, or to some other representation of those Divine Persons, to get our idea of the manner in which they are to be regarded in baptism. We have already said that it is to the primary and literal meaning of *baptidzo* that we are to go, and not to some secondary or metaphorical meaning to get its true import as a command in the law of Christ. And so it is from the baptismal formula, and the manner in which the Divine Persons into whose names and into whom we are to be baptized are presented to us, and the phraseology that is used, that we are to obtain the true mode of Christian immersion. We are not to leave the form given by Christ to meet the wants of his somewhat inexperienced disciples, "baptizing them into the name of the Father, and of the Son, and of the Holy Spirit," and accept of such forms of expression as "the Triune God" and "the essence of God," as containing what is taught about the Godhead in the baptismal formula. We have the Godhead presented to us in the baptismal formula in three manifestations bearing the impressive and suggestive names, Father, Son, and Holy Spirit. And their distinction is clear and marked. If then there are three distinct persons and three distinct names in the baptismal formula, and if those three distinct persons have three distinct works to perform in creation, in providence, and in redemption, and if they are also kept distinct and not joined together in the peculiar phraseology of the form of baptism, and if it is into those three Divine Persons, that each believer is to be baptized, the necessity of trine immersion will be apparent, for three actions are necessary to put one object into three other separate and distinct objects.

SECTION IV.

Argument 4. From Analogy. We call our fourth argument from the baptismal formula, an argument from analogy. There is another passage of Scripture that bears considerable analogy in its construction in some important respect, to the form of expression used in the baptismal formula. And the explanation that has been put upon the passage alluded to, will afford important help in obtaining a correct understanding of the baptismal formula. The points in the analogous passage that give it some analogy to the baptismal formula are such as are not used to sustain any special doctrine in theology, and therefore the application that we shall find has been made of them, cannot be attributed to any partiality to a favorite theory.

The passage bearing some analogy in its phraseology to the phraseology of the baptismal formula, is the following: "All our fathers were under the cloud, and all passed through the sea: and were all baptized unto Moses in the cloud and in the sea." 1 Cor. 10: 1, 2. "In the cloud and in the sea," is a form of expression bearing a resemblance in its structure to the following parts of the baptismal formula: "into the name of the Father, and of the Son, and of the Holy Spirit." We give the language in its elliptical form. In its full or complete form, it is no less analogous. *"In the cloud and in the sea,"* is a phrase that brings together the conjunction "and" and the preposition "in." "Into the name of the Father, and of the Son," etc., is a phrase that also brings together the conjunction "and" and the preposition "of," "and of the

Son." And herein consists a resemblance between the two passages.

When a conjunction and preposition come together like they do in the phrase, "in the cloud and in the sea," the phrase is not equivalent to "in the cloud and sea" but the occurrence of the preposition enlarges the sentence or adds another. So the phrase, "baptizing them into the name of the Father, and of the Son, and of the Holy Spirit," in the baptismal formula, is not equivalent to the form, "baptizing them into the name of the Father, and Son, and Holy Spirit." This latter form is often used as the baptismal formula. But it does not express the baptismal formula, and should not be so intended. It is not giving the word of God its full expression of power.

We made an allusion in our last chapter to the occurrence of a preposition with a conjunction, and intimated that in such cases the preposition implies the addition of something more to the sentence than the conjunction would imply without the preposition. We shall now develop that principle with a plain illustration, and a strong testimony.

Let us first take the phrase, "in the cloud and in the sea." The occurrence of the preposition "in" with the conjunction implies here that something more is intended than if the conjunction alone occurred. The conjunction implies an addition, and the preposition occurring with it in such connections, implies still more of an addition. In the phrase, "in the cloud and in the sea," under some circumstances, if the preposition did not occur, "cloud" and "sea" might be joined together. "In the cloud and in the sea," is not equivalent to "in the cloud and sea," as already intimated. The occurrence of the preposition "in" implies something more. "In the cloud" and add "in the sea." That which occurred in the cloud also occurred in the sea. Now to ascertain what is to be added, we go back and ascertain what had been done in the cloud. We find that all the Israelites that were journeying at that time, were "baptized unto Moses in the cloud." And it is added, "and in the sea." That which was done in the cloud, was also done in the sea. And as they were baptized unto Moses "in the cloud," so they were baptized unto Moses "in the sea." And so there were two baptisms, one in the cloud, and the other in the sea.

Before we apply the principles that we have applied to Paul's baptisms of the Israelites, to the baptismal formula, we shall confirm our view above stated, by an intelligent and impartial witness. Dr. W. C. Wilkinson, of the Baptist denomination, is the author of a work published by the American Baptist Publication Society, the title of which is, *The Baptist Principle in its Application to Baptism and the Lord's Supper.* The 13th chapter is headed, *Baptism in Symbols.* Among the symbols of baptism that the author introduces, is the baptism of the Israelites "in the cloud, and in the sea," as given by Paul, and which we have quoted.

Dr. Wilkinson takes the position that the Israelites experienced two baptisms, one in the cloud, and one in the sea. This position he attempts to prove, and in our judgment he is altogether successsul in his attempt. We have entertained the same view of the apostle's language. In the *Gospel Visitor* of May, 1861, we have an article on the baptism of the Israelites "in the cloud, and in the sea," and in that article we take the position that there were two baptisms, one in the cloud, and one in the sea, the position that Dr. Wilkinson takes. In his reasoning to prove that there were two baptisms he says, "We conclude, therefore, with much confidence, that Paul introduces in the verses here being considered, not one symbol of baptism made up of two parts, but two different symbols instead. There was a symbolic baptism in the cloud, and there was a symbolic baptism in the sea."—page 103.

But the following remarks of the doctor's are especially relevant to our subject: "The experiences were two: first, that of being under the cloud; secondly, that of passing through the sea. With this understanding of the first verse agrees the phraseology of the second. For it is not said, 'And were all baptized unto Moses in the cloud and sea,' as if sea and cloud united to give them one baptism; it is said, 'And were all baptized unto Moses *in* the cloud and *in* the sea,' the preposition *in* being repeated, as if to indicate two separate experiences on their part, each experience capable of being likened to baptism."—page 102. Now we compare the phraseology of the baptismal formula with the above phraseology used by Paul to describe the baptisms of the Israelites. "Baptizing them into the name of the Father, and of the Son, and of the Holy Spirit;" "Were all baptized unto Moses in the cloud and in the sea." After carefully comparing the phraseology of the two passages together, then let the doctor's explanation be carefully noticed. He remarks, "It is not said, 'And were all baptized unto Moses in the cloud and sea,' as if cloud and sea united to give them one baptism." Precisely so. And we would say in regard to the baptismal formula, it is not said, baptizing them into the name of the Father, and Son, and Holy Spirit, as if Father, Son, and Spirit were united to receive them by one immersion. It is said, "baptizing them into the name of the Father, and of the Son, and of the Holy Spirit," the preposition "of" being repeated, as if to indicate three separate experiences on the part of the baptized, each experience being an immersion. And the three experiences of baptized believers, are glorious experiences, for they realize a blessed fellowship with the three manifestations of the Godhead, the Father, Son, and Holy Spirit, into all of whom they are baptized.

Dr. Wilkinson is a Professor in the Rochester Theological Seminary, and is said by the writer who wrote a memoir of him for The Baptist Encyclopædia, that he is one of the ablest writers in America. When the Doctor looked at Paul's language concerning the baptism of the Israelites, "baptized unto Moses in the cloud, and in the sea," he concluded from the structure of the language, when giving the words their common meaning and power from the form they possessed, that they evidently implied two baptisms. We fully concur with him, and believe that a candid and diligent investigation of the case will lead to such a conclusion.

And then, entertaining such a view of Paul's language, "baptized unto Moses in the cloud, and in the sea," and comparing it with the baptismal formula, "baptizing them into the name of the Father, and of the Son, and of the Holy Spirit," and remembering the Doctor's just criticisms upon the force of the preposition, or the word "in" as it occurs in Paul's language, and applying the Doctor's explanation of the language of Paul, to the language of the baptismal formula as far as there is an analogy between the two passages, the three immersions of the baptismal formula will be made as apparent, as the two baptisms or experiences of the Israelites in the cloud and in the sea.

Thus this argument from analogy, carefully studied with the suggestive points we have stated, and with Dr. Wilkinson's just criticisms and explanation of the baptism of the Israelites, "in the cloud, and in the sea," light will be thrown upon the baptismal formula, and the number of immersions it indicates. And if the Israelites experienced two baptisms, the believer, according to the terms of the baptismal formula, is to experience three immersions.

SECTION V.

Argument 5. From the Positive Admissions of Single Immersionists.

In the baptismal controversy in regard to the action of baptism, it is very common for immersionists to avail themselves of whatever admissions pedobaptists have made, and whatever knowledge they have contributed, that will help them to sustain immersion as the act of baptism.

So in our humble endeavors to sustain trine immersion, we would endeavor to make a judicious use of the admissions that single immersionists have made, to prove our position. We have made the implied admissions of single immersionists a basis of an argument. There is an implied admission by them, and that admission obtains in the passages we shall quote. But there is a positive admission, and it is upon that positive admission that our present argument is based. We shall now give the admissions that several single immersionists have made.

We had occasion to refer to Dr. Conant in Chapter VII of our work. We shall now make a further use of his admission. When he wrote the note that we shall again insert, he was doing the work of a translator, and was translating the Gospel according to Matthew. When he came to the commission of

Christ to his apostles in Matt. 28: 19, in which the baptismal formula occurs, he assumed the character of a commentator and critic, and gave a criticism on the baptismal formula adverse to trine immersion. Whether it was necessary or justifiable for him as a translator to assume the character of a critic and to endeavor to turn the baptismal formula against trine immersion, we shall not take it upon us to decide. He did so and we have his critical note, and though it was designed to disparage trine immersion, we shall use it as a factor in our argument to justify and maintain it. His note is as follows:

"The practice was adopted at an early period of immersing at the utterance of each name. But this is clearly contrary to the terms of the command. To justify such a practice, the form should have been either '*in the names* of,' or '*in the name of the Father, and in the name of the Son, and in the name of the Holy Spirit.*'"

In connection with Dr. Conant's note on the baptismal formula, we give again the explanatory note of a Baptist Commentator, the Rev. George W. Clark. His commentary is published by the American Baptist Publication Society. In referring to the baptismal formula, Mr. Clark says:

"The singular is used; *name* not *names*, pointing to the unity of Father, Son, and Holy Spirit. There is thus a reference to the different parts which the Father, the Son, and the Holy Spirit take in the work of salvation, and to the unity of the Godhead, the fountain of all blessings. The plural would have implied three distinct beings. The singular implies that the three though in a sense distinct, are yet one. The fact of the trinity is revealed, but the precise mode of its existence is one of the secret and mysterious things of God. Compare 2 Cor. 13:14. The singular also points clearly to only *one* immersion. If a three-fold immersion had been intended, the form would have been either *in the names of*, or *in the name of the Father, and in the name of the Son*, etc. The old custom of immersing at the utterance of each name, still practiced by the Greek chnrch, is first mentioned by Tertullian, and appears to have arisen from the superstitions and corruptions which gave birth to infant baptism."

It will be observed that Mr. Clark's view of the baptismal formula, in regard to what would have been its reading, had trine trine immersion been intended to be taught by it, is precisely like unto Dr.

Conant's. His language is very much like Dr. Conant's, though he does not give it as a quotation from Dr. Conant.

There is one point in Mr. Clark's explanation that seems somewhat singular to us. It is that expressed in the following words: "The plural would have implied three distinct beings." The plurality of persons or beings and the distinction of persons, we presume will be readily admitted by all trinitarians, even those of the most moderate views. In Chapter IV of our work we have given a few testimonies in favor of such a plurality and distinction of persons. And the number of such testimonies could have been greatly multiplied. Surely Mr. Clark will not deny, with the views of the Trinity which we presume he holds, that there are three distinct persons or beings recognized in the baptismal formula. Mr. W. R. Williams, a Baptist minister and author, thus speaks of the personality and distinction of the Holy Spirit, and he, of course, would give to the Father and Son the same distinction: "He is as really a person as Abraham or David, or any of the patriarchs, or as Paul, John, or either of the apostles. Is the Son distinguishable from the Father, so is the Spirit also. When you were baptized, it was into his dread and distinct name, invoked upon you, as you sank beneath the entombing waters, and rose again to the upper air."—*The Baptist Pulpit of the United States:* by Dr. Belcher, pages 40, 41. With such a plurality and distinction of persons as Mr. Williams recognizes in the baptismal formula, we shall have a plurality of names and also of persons.

The following is from a work called *The Act of Baptism in the History of the Christian Church:* by H. S. Burrage, a minister of the Baptist church.

"But the great commission is a witness against, not for trine immersion. As Dr. Conant has shown, 'To justify such a practice, the form should have been either 'in the names of,' or 'in the name of the Father, and in the name of the Son, and in the name of the Holy Spirit.'"—page 48.

Dr. Conant declares trine immersion to be "clearly contrary to the terms of the command." Mr. Clark attributes it to "the superstitions and corruptions which gave rise to infant baptism." Mr. Burrage declares "the great commission is a witness against, not for trine immersion." The language of these authors shows that they had but little sympathy for trine immersion.

We are sorry for their sakes and for the truth's sake that they have treated so coolly what Professor Schaaf calls a "venerable usage." We shall show hereafter that trine immersion deserves much more respect from single immersionists than these gentlemen show it. But we proceed to make use of their admissions.

They all admit that the following reading of the baptismal formula would require a trine immersion: "*In the name of the Father, and in the name of the Son, and in the name of the Holy Spirit.*"

The following is the form in which we have the formula given to us: "*In the name of the Father, and of the Son, and of the Holy Spirit.*"

We maintain that we have the first form and what the above writers require as a reading authorizing trine immersion, in the second form, as far as we can have it according to the general principles of composition, and that there is beyond doubt all expressed in the second or common form, that we have in the first. Or, we maintain, as we have done in Chapter VIII of our work, that the common form of the baptismal formula is elliptical, and that when the ellipses are supplied, it will read, "In the name of the Father, and in the name of the Son, and in the name of the Holy Spirit." We have produced arguments and testimonies from various sources, and of various kinds, which will, we believe, if candidly and intelligently examined, and if judiciously applied, satisfy the inquirer after truth, that the baptismal formula is elliptical, and that in its complete and full form, it will read, "Into the name of the Father, and into the name of the Son, and into the name of the Holy Spirit," the very form in which those gentlemen quoted, say it should read to teach trine immersion, and, therefore, we have trine immersion taught in it.

Although we have given considerable attention to the elliptical and full construction of the baptismal formula, and produced testimony of various kinds and from various sources to prove its elliptical character, but standing in the important relation it does to our subject, we shall introduce another witness in connection with the application that we are about making of the materials that we have collected, in developing our present argument upon the positive admissions of single immersionists.

The additional testimony that we shall offer is that of Dr. Meyer. In a note in his Commentary on the New Testament, when explaining the baptismal formula, he says:

"Had Jesus used the words *the names* instead of *the name*, then however much he may have intended the names of the three distinct persons to be understood, he would still have been liable to be misapprehended, for it might have been supposed that the plural was meant to refer to the various names of each separate person. The *singular* points to the *specific name* assigned in the text to each of the three respectively, so that *into the name* is, of course, to be *understood* both before *the Son* and before *the Holy Spirit;* compare Rev. 14:1: '*His name and the name of his Father.*' We must beware of making any such *dogmatic* use of the singular as to employ it as an argument either *for* or *against* the orthodox doctrine of the Trinity."

Such is the judgment of Dr. Meyer on the literal or grammatical structure of the baptismal formula. He admits the elliptical form and adds name to "*Son*" and "*Holy Spirit*" in filling the ellipses, and in giving to it its full form and grammatical construction. He says, "'into the name' is of course to be understood before 'the Son' and 'Holy Spirit.'" Notice, he says *of course*. He considered the elliptical form of the baptismal formula so manifest that there was no argument necessary to prove it. He considered the necessity of supplying name before "Son" and before "Holy Spirit," to be so plain and self-evident as to commend itself to the mind of the reader without any proof.

And who was Dr. Meyer? Let the following recommendations answer:

"Meyer has been long and well known to scholars as one of the very ablest of the German expositors on the New Testament. We are not sure whether we ought not to say that he is unrivalled as an interpreter of the grammatical and historical character of the sacred writers."—*Guardian.*

"The ablest grammatical exegete of the age."—*Philip Schaff, D. D.*

"No exegetical work is on the whole more valuable, or stands in higher public esteem. As a critic he is candid and cautious; exact to minuteness in philology; a master of the grammatical and historical method of interpretation."—*Princeton Review.*

From the above recommendation it will be seen that Dr. Meyer possessed a high reputation for his ability as an expounder of the grammatical and philological import of the Scriptural language. And it is in consideration of his reputation for grammatical and philological knowledge of the language of Scripture that we quote him, and give his judgment upon the full reading of the baptismal formula, the prominence that we do. He was a Lutheran and also a Trinitarian we presume. But neither his Lutheranism nor his Trinitarianism had apparently any influence upon his mind when giving his judgment upon the full and grammatical reading of the baptismal formula. He writes as an independent thinker. And, therefore, when he writes upon the philological aspect of Scriptural exposition, his judgment should be respected by all.

We intimated above that his Trinitarianism had nothing to do with his judgment upon the grammatical meaning of the baptismal formula. We infer this from what he says in regard to the use of the singular number of name in the baptismal formula. He says, "We must beware of making any such *dogmatic* use of the singular as to employ it as an argument either *for* or *against* the orthodox doctrine of the Trinity." The meaning of this is, name was designed to have its common import as when thus connected with the person to whom it belongs, and it should not be turned away to favor either side in the Trinitarian controversy. He was a Trinitarian, but his views of the Trinity did not prevent him from understanding the grammatical import of the baptismal formula. Had all writers and commentators been as free from prejudice as Dr. Meyer, in ascertaining the grammatical meaning of the baptismal formula, the reading he gave it others would give it, and trine immersion would prevail in the west as it does in the east among the immersionists. But its reading and meaning have been more or less darkened and confused by the relation it has been made to sustain to the Trinitarian coniroversy, and its true teaching in regard to Christian immersion is not acknowledged as it would be if its grammatical or full construction was recognized.

Then the reading of the baptismal formula according to Dr. Meyer is, "baptizing them into the name of the Father, and into the name of the Son, and into the name of the Holy Spirit." The testimony of Dr. Meyer given under the circumstances it was, is sufficient of itself to sustain the form of reading of the baptismal formula, that the prominent men of the body of single immersionists, that we have quoted, say that it should have to teach trine immersion. We made his testimony a specialty, because it is so clear, and it comes from such a competent and impartial critic. And if his authority alone is sufficient to produce the condition of the baptismal formula that it is admitted it should have to teach trine immersion, what must all the authority that we have produced be?

To ask for the reading of the baptismal formula in the form, "in the name of the Father, and in the name of the Son, and in the name of the Holy Spirit," in any other way than by supplying the ellipses, is to ask what cannot be furnished unless it would be especially prepared; for such a style of writing is not in accordance with the general principles of composition.

We have given the baptismal formula in the possessive form, instead of the objective form with the preposition of. In that form it reads, "Into the Father's name, and into the Son's, and into the Holy Spirit's." Would this satisfy those who give the baptismal formula the form they think it ought to have to make it require trine immersion, or would they say that if trine immersion was intended it should read, "Into the Father's name, and into the Son's name, and into the Holy Spirit's name?" They surely would not, for they know that the possessive form with name following Father only, and the possessive sign or apostrophe affixed to Son and Holy Spirit would be the same as if name followed Son and Holy Spirit, and it read, "In the Father's name, and into the Son's name, and into the Holy Spirit's name."

It is just the same with the objective form. Into the name of the Father, and of the Son, and of the Holy Spirit, is just the same in meaning as if name was repeated before Son, and before Holy Spirit, and it read, "into the name of the Father, and into the name of the Son, and into the name of the Holy Spirit."

The case is this: All words not necessary to express the ideas of the writer clearly, are to be left out of the composition, and supplied in the mind of the reader. This principle is recognized by grammarians and rhetoricians. Dr. Fowler in referring to the ellipsis says, "This figure is very common in the language, and often serves to avoid disagreeable repetition."—Grammar, page 622. In Chap. VIII of our work will be found authorities for condensing written composition. In this connection we shall quote a few ideas that we have given there. Dr. Blair says, "The first rules which I give for promoting the strength of a sentence, is to divest it of all redundant words." Hart says, "Every redundant word is so much dead matter." We here insert a few of the remarks contained in our quotation from Dr. Conant, on page 125. "The vigorous conciseness and compression of a writer's manner should always be retained, even at the risk of requiring more attention and thought on the part of the reader." With such correct views in regard to the compression of a sentence, it is strange that Dr. Conant would require the baptismal formula to be written in the form he does to show that trine immersion was intended. It could not be written in that way, to be written correctly, or in the style most approved of, according to his own principle. For illustration we take the following sentence: "The Jews revere the name of Abraham, and of Isaac, and of Jacob." This sentence will be understood to mean that the Jews revere the name of Abraham, and the name of Isaac, and the name of Jacob, from its elliptical form as written above, without "name" being repeated before Isaac, and before Jacob, as would be done in its full grammatical construction. And the form in which it is first written above, is the form in which it would be written according to the common custom of writers. And it would be a violation of the principles of composition—the principles that require the omission of all words that are not needed to convey the writer's idea to repeat name. And the repetition of name before Isaac, and before Jacob, is unnecessary, since the meaning is apparent in its elliptical form. Should any person deny the fact stated in the sentence, that the Jews revere all three of the patriarchs mentioned, because *name* is not repeated before Isaac, and before Jacob, such a denial would be considered unreasonable and unsustained.

And so in regard to the baptismal formula. We have it in its common form, "Into the name of the Father, and of the Son, and of the Holy Spirit," and, in this form name is understood before Son, and before Holy Spirit, and with the ellipses supplied we have it, "into the name of the Father, and into the name of the Son, and into the name of the Holy Spirit." And in this way it may be written, as "the words omitted by this figure (ellipsis) as truly belong to the sentence grammatically considered, as those which are expressed."—*Greene.*

And so we have the reading of the baptismal formula that those writers and authors that occupy literary distinction, and denominational influence among single immersionists, say we ought to have to make it teach trine immersion. And that reading is sustained by the principles of our language, and by literary authority of such a character, that allow of no appeal from their decision. We therefore have trine immersion taught in the baptismal formula with a clearness that admits of no doubt, and by an authority that is divine—the authority of Christ.

CHAPTER X.

A COMMON ERROR REFUTED.

WE deem it advisable in the discussion of our subject, to give somewhere in our work, and we shall do it here, refuting testimony to refute the error that seems to be surprisingly common; namely, that the ancient Christians did not claim Scriptural authority for trine immersion. It is admitted that trine immersion was the common manner in which baptism was performed in ancient times by Christians, but with the great amount of evidence to the contrary, it is asserted that they offered no Gospel ground for it, but practiced it only on the ground of tradition. That the people not read in church history or not acquainted with the Antiquities of the Christian Church should fall into such an error, need not, perhaps, surprise us very much. But that men who seem to be somewhat versed in the affairs of the ancient church, should fall into such an error, and circulate it as a fact, does seem strange. It is another evidence that there has been much prejudice against trine immersion, and that the prejudice has interfered at times with men's judgments, and with the correctness of their information.

Mr. Burrage, in his work called *The Acts of Baptism in the History of the Christian Church*, a work from which we quoted in the last chapter, on page 48, has the following: "Certainly the trinity of Persons in the Godhead is the reason assigned for trine immersion by Tertullian, and later by Jerome, Basil, and the *Apostolic Canons*. Scriptural authority was not claimed for it." There are several errors in the above statement, some of which, if not all, will be corrected in the discussion of our subject in the present chapter.

We quote an assertion from Alexander Campbell, showing that strange ideas are attributed to the ancients in regard to trine immersion. The assertion we refer to, occurred in the debate Mr. Campbell had with Mr. Rice. The latter had said, "The first writer of any standing, who speaks of immersion is Tertullian, in the beginning of the third century, and he says, the practice then was trine immersion," etc. To this Mr. Campbell makes the following reply: "The gentleman will have Tertullian to be a sort of a cotemporary with the origin of immersion.

Trine immersion he ought to have said. . . . . Tertullian denies that *three* immersions (not one immersion) had an ancient origin,"

We have read the assertion of Mr. Campbell with surprise and pain. We know that his position in the world was one of great influence. He was well acquainted with the history of the ancient Church. Such assertions as the foregoing from Mr. Campbell would be accepted as true, and of course add to the prejudice already existing against trine immersion. Standing as the assertion does, without anything to qualify it in the least, we cannot but think that it does injustice to Tertullian and to trine immersion.

What did Mr. Campbell mean? Had he any direct declaration from Tertullian in which he positively and plainly denied that trine immersion had an ancient origin? If so, should he not have referred to the place in Tertullian's works in which it could have been found? Or, did he refer to the stereotyped error which makes Tertullian say that trine immersion had only tradition for its authority? Mr. Campbell does not refer to Tertullian's oft-quoted passage about tradition in connection with the assertion he makes, that "Tertullian denies that *three* immersions had an ancient origin," but he quotes that passage in his debate with Mr. Walker, and also in that with Bishop Purcell, but not to disparage trine immersion. Indeed the translation that Mr. Campbell makes of the celebrated passage in Tertullian, does not at all favor the idea that he declares trine immersion to be more than the gospel requires.

But if it is the passage in Tertullian that is wrested to make him say that trine immersion is more than the Gospel requires, that Mr. Campbell alludes to for his authority that Tertullian denies the ancient authority for trine immersion, does that passage warrant Mr. Compbell in making such an assertion? We do not believe that it does. Had Tertullian held the idea that tradition was the only authority that they had for trine immersion, which was not the case, as we shall hereafter prove, still that was not by any means saying it had not an ancient origin. Those who wrote and spoke of it as having the authority of tradition, meant apostolic tradition. So it still might have had even in their judgment, an ancient origin. Did Tertullian declare that he originated trine immersion or that it originated with somebody else of his time? He declared no such absurdity. But Tertullian lived in the latter part of the second century, and not long after the time of the apostles. And for him to say that the trine immersion which he practiced, and which was the common practice of the Christians of his time, had not an ancient origin, is too unreasonable to believe. And as Mr. Campbell does not refer to the place in Tertullian's works where it may be found, and as a number of passages in his works contradict it, we can not believe that Tertullian ever said so.

As we design in this chapter to refute the prevailing error that the ancient Christians recognized no authority but that of tradition for trine immersion, we have thus dwelt upon Mr. Campbell's injudicious assertion. We regard it as injudicious, because he gives no proof of its correctness. And considering what Tertullian wrote of trine immersion, it is of doubtful authority. And yet coming from a man of Mr. Campbell's intelligence and reputation, many may believe it.

We shall proceed to hear some of the ancient Christians. And from their testimony, we shall learn their authority for trine immersion. And we should associate with the authority they claim for trine immersion their competency to judge. Whether Matthew wrote his Gospel of our Lord in the Hebrew or in the Greek language is a question upon which there has been some controversy among the learned. The preponderance however, of the weight of testimony is in favor of the Hebrew origin. But the existence of a Greek copy can be traced so far back as to lead some to think that Matthew himself made the translation.

Then the ancient Greeks had a copy of the Gospel according to Matthew, which contained the baptismal formula in their native language. And when such ancient Greek scholars as Chrysostom and Theodoret, and Pelagius read the baptismal formula in their own native tongue, and understood it to mean trine immersion, their understanding of it in that way is certainly important and strong testimony in favor of the idea that trine immersion was the mode of immersion taught by Christ.

Chrysostom says, "Christ delivered to his disciples one baptism in three immersions of the body, when he said to them, 'Go, teach all nations, baptizing them in the name of the Father, and of the Son, and of the Holy Ghost.'"—*Bingham's Antiquities of the Christian Church, Book XI, Chapter XI.*

Theodoret says, "He (Eunomius) subverted the law of holy baptism which had been handed down from the beginning from the Lord and the apostles, and made a contrary law, asserting that it is not necessary to immerse the candidate for baptism thrice, nor to mention the names of the Trinity, but to immerse once only into the death of Christ."—

Chrystal's History of the Modes of Christian Baptism, page 78.

Pelagius says, "There are many who say that they are baptized in the name of Christ alone, and by a single immersion. But the Gospel command, which was given by God himself and our Lord and Saviour Jesus Christ, reminds us that we should administer holy baptism to every one, in the name of the Trinity and by trine immersion, for our Lord said to his disciples, 'Go, baptize all nations in the name of the Father, and of the Son, and of the Holy Ghost."—*Ibid, page 80.*

The 50th Canon of *The Constitutions of the Holy Apostles,* thus expresses the judgment of those who formed the Constitutions: The Lord did not say, Baptize into my death; but, *Go ye and make disciples of all nations, baptizing them into the name of the Father, and of the Son, and of the Holy Ghost.* Do ye, therefore, O Bishops, baptize them into one Father, and Son, and Holy Ghost, according to the will of Christ and our constitutions by the Spirit.—*Chase's Edition, page 252.*

In the Apostolic Canons it will be noticed that the authority for trine immersion is attributed directly to the command of Christ. And after the command is given, then it is said, "Do ye, therefore," that is in consideration of the command of Christ, "O Bishop, baptize thrice into one Father," etc. These Canons contain the combined wisdom and judgment of the ancients. We are not examining the origin of these Canons, or the age in which they were formed. They are acknowledged to be very ancient. We are examining to see to what authority those who formed them, attribute trine immersion, the only form of immersion which they accept. And we find they acknowledge the gospel to be their authority for trine immersion. This does not agree with the statement of Mr. Burrage, on page 48 of his *Act of Baptism*, "Certainly the trinity of Persons in the Godhead is the reason assigned for trine immersion by Tertullian, and later by Jerome, Basil, and the *Apostolic Canons*. Scriptural authority was not claimed for it."

Now let us hear Tertullian. Reference has already been made to him, and further reference will be made hereafter. But he very justly comes in for a place in this chapter. We give Tertullian's testimony as we find it in a note on page 129 of Prof. Duncan's *History of Baptists*. We give the note as it occurs with its references to Tertullian's works.

"Tertullian, in his treatise 'Against Praxeas' (*Contra Praxeam*) assigns to trine immersion an apostolic origin. 'Christ,' he says, (c. 26) 'appointed baptism to be administered not in the name of one, but three, Father, Son, and Holy Ghost. Therefore, we are dipped (*tinguimur*) not once, but thrice, into every person (of the Trinity) at the mention of each name."

Prof. Duncan was a Baptist minister, and a Prof. of the Greek and Latin languages in the University of Louisiana. Consequently, his scholarship was sufficient to qualify him to read Tertullian in his own native Latin language comprehensively, and to translate him correctly. And while it seems to be altogether probable that he did not feel the opposition to trine immersion that many of his brethren have felt, it is not likely that he was at all partial to it. And therefore he was competent to make a correct translation. And the translation in his note seems to be his own.

Dr. Duncan's translation of the passage from Tertullian's writings that we have given, and his remarks upon it, make the following facts so clear, that there can remain no doubt. 1. Dr. Duncan declares that Tertullian "assigns to trine immersion an apostolic origin." Mr. Campbell declares that "Tertullian denies that three immersien had an ancient origin." So the statements of Dr. Duncan and Mr. Campbell are in direct conflict with each other. And which is correct? This will appear when the second fact alluded to above is considered. That fact is this: 2. Tertullian believed that trine immersion was commanded by Christ. Dr. Duncan represents Tertullian as saying, "Christ appointed baptism to be administered not in the name of one, but three, Father, Son, and Holy Ghost, therefore, we are dipped not once, but thrice, unto every person (of the Trinity) at the mention of each name." Then if Tertullian was dipped "thrice" because Christ appointed that mode of immersion, and so he was according to Dr. Duncan's translation, then it is clear that he (Tertullian) "assigns to trine immersion an apostolic origin." And Mr. Campbell is wrong and Dr. Duncan right in regard to Tertullian's view of the origin of trine immersion.

This should settle the question in regard to Tertullian's view of the authority for trine immersion. It is proved very clearly, that he regarded it as a command of Christ.

In these testimonies of ancient scholars we have their understanding of what the baptismal formula teaches in regard to the mode of immersion contained in the ordinance of baptism. Many of these men were Greeks, and they read the baptismal formula in their own language. It has been often said by single immersionists when arguing for immersion upon the meaning of *baptidzo* that the Greeks understood their own language, and as they understood *baptidzo* to mean immersion, this fact carries with it great weight in favor of immersion. And this is certainly true. And this weight of testimony may justly be claimed for trine immersion as well as for immersion. If the Greeks understood the meaning of the words in their language, they understood the sentences formed by words, especially sentences formed by words used in their ordinary meaning, as it is presumed the words in the baptismal formula were used by our Lord when instituting an ordinance having such an important bearing upon character, and human destiny that the ordinance of Christian baptism has.

And those of the ancient writers from whom we have quoted, who were not Greeks, were scholars and would understand the import of the language of the baptismal formula, and they underetood it to mean trine immersion.

CHAPTER XI.

TRINE IMMERSION IN ITS HISTORICAL ASPECT.

THE following concession is made to trine immersion: "Trine immersion was the general practice of Christians from the end of the second till the close of the twelfth century. The proof of the above statement is overwhelming." The above language occurs in the opening of Dr. Cathcart's work, *The Baptism of the Ages and of the Nations*. The foregoing concession is concurred in by single immersionists generally, if not universally. But beyond the beginning of the third century, trine immersion is denied an existence in the Church by single immersionists. Dr. Cathcart, who makes the above concession, also makes the following declaration, immediately following his concession: "Beyond Tertullian no record in the literature of men, in the book of God, or in any symbol known to mortals utters a single word about three immersions in baptism.." This language is emphasized.

Single immersionists believe that immersion was the action of baptism that prevailed between the beginning of the third century, and the apostolic age, but they believe it was single immersion, while we trine immersionists believe it was trine immersion. And we shall give the ground or evidence of our belief.

The testimony in the first centuries for the action of baptism is very limited. We mean the information we have in the literature of the first two centuries besides the Scriptures, to prove the manner in which baptism was performed, is limited. And this should not surprise us. The general practices and doctrine of the apostolic church were maintained in their general integrity for some time after the apostles, perhaps till about the third century. It is altogether probable that the ordinance of baptism continued during that time to be practiced as it had been in the apostolic age. And as there was no special or general attempt made to change it, there was little or no controversy, and hence we have so little testimony in regard to baptism. There are, however, a few allusions to it, and the circumstances plainly indicate that the action was immersion, as the word itself imports. And whether it was single or trine, will hereafter appear.

There are other witnesses in the first two centuries, besides the divine witnesses, whose testimony is used by immersionists to prove immersion. These are Barnabas, Hermas, and Justin Martyr.

BARNABAS: "Blessed are they who, placing their trust in the cross, have gone down into the water." And again: "We indeed descend into the water full of sins and defilement, but come up, bearing the fruit in our heart, having the fear and trust in Jesus in our spirit."—*Anti-Nicene Christian Library, Vol. I, page 121.*

HERMAS: "The seal, then, is the water: they descend into the water dead, and they arise alive. And to them accordingly, was this seal preached, and they made use of it that they might enter into the kingdom of God."—*Ibid, page 420.*

JUSTIN MARTYR: "I will also relate the manner in which we dedicated ourselves to God when we had been made new through Christ; lest, if we omit this, we seem to be unfair in the explanation we are making. As many as are persuaded and believe that what we teach and say is true, and undertake to be able to live accordingly, are instructed to pray and to entreat God with fasting, for the remission of their sins, that are past, we praying and fasting with them.

"Then they are brought by us where there is water, and are regenerated in the same manner in which we were ourselves regenerated. For, in the name of God, the Father and Lord of the universe, and of our Saviour Jesus Christ, and of the Holy Spirit, they then receive the washing with water.

"And for this (rite) we have learned from the apostles this reason. Since at our birth we were born without our own knowledge and choice, by our parents coming together, and were brought up in bad habits and wicked training; in order that we may not remain the children of necessity and of ignorance, but may become the children of choice and knowledge, and may obtain in the water the remission of sins formerly committed, there is pronounced over him who chooses to be born again, and has repented of his sins, the name of God the Father, and Lord of the universe; he who leads to *the Laver* the person that is to be washed, calling him by this name alone. For no one can utter the name of the ineffable God; and if any one dare to say that there is a name, he raves with hopeless madness. And this washing is called illumination, because they who learn these things are illuminated in their understandings. And in the name of Jesus

Christ, who was crucified under Pontius Pilate, and in the name of the Holy Ghost, who through the prophets foretold all things about Jesus, he who is illuminated is washed."

The foregoing passages contain about all the testimony to immersion that we have between Tertullian and the apostolic age. From what Barnabas and Hermas say, we learn that believers when they were baptized went into the water. There is more allusion to the result of baptism than to the manner in which it was performed. And what they say is as favorable to trine immersion as it is to single.

Justin's testimony is very different from that of the other two. It is a very valuable testimony. Dr. Wall says of this passage in Justin's writings, "it is the most ancient account of the way of baptizing next the Scripture; and shows the plain and simple manner of administering it. The Christians of these times had lived, many of them at least, in the the apostles' days."—*History of Infant Baptism, Vol. I, page 69.*

There is something very impressive in the description Justin gives of the way in which the Christians of his time, just after the apostolic age, baptized. It is very evident that he had reference to the baptismal formula given by Christ to his apostles, and that he and the Christians of his time baptized according to it.

It is also evident that he had the baptismal formula before his mind under a two-fold aspect,—in its elliptical form, and in its full construction. "Then they are brought by us where there is water, and are regenerated in the same manner in which we were ourselves regenerated. For, in the name of God, the Father and Lord of the universe, and of our Saviour Jesus Christ, and of the Holy Spirit, they then receive the washing with water." Here it will be noticed that "name" is only added to God the Father, as we have it expressed in the baptismal formula. Then he proceeds to describe it more fully, and says there is pronounced over him who chooses to be born again, and has repented of his sins, the name of God the Father, and Lord of the universe. . . . . . And in the name of Jesus Christ, who was crucified under Pontius Pilate, and in the name of the Holy Ghost. Then according to Justin, believers were baptized in his time, *in the name of God the Father and Lord, and in the name of Jesus Christ, and in the name of the Holy Ghost.*

Now let us look at the way the baptismal formula should read according to Dr. Conant and others to require a trine immersion: *"baptizing them into the name of the Father, and into the name of the Son, and into the name of the Holy Ghost.* See Chapter IX, Section V. Then Justin's form of baptizing in its structure, being similar to the form that Dr. Conant and others say requires trine immersion, the conclusion is plain and legitimate that Justin's form of baptizing was by trine immersion. We, therefore, arrive at the conclusion, by a fair course of reasoning, from facts stated by Justin, and from principles admitted by single immersionists, that trine immersion prevailed in the church in the second century, and as early as the time of Justin Martyr. Of this there can be no reasonable doubt.

Let it be kept in mind that it is admitted to be a fact, and admitted too, by the opponents of trine immersion, and a fact admitted by them to be sustained by "overwhelming proof," that trine immersion was general at the close of the second century. We want this fact distinctly remembered, as we shall now make it the basis of another historical argument.

Mr. Orchard is the author of *A History of Foreign Baptists*. Mr. J. R. Graves has published an edition of the work in the United States. It was originally published in England, and is highly spoken of by the American publisher. In giving the testimony of historians upon baptism in the third century, Mr. Orchard says: "The most respectable historians affirm, that no evidence exists as to any alteration in the subject or mode of baptism during the third century." After Mr. Orchard makes the above affirmation, he quotes two authors to sustain his position. The first declares, "We have no testimony as to any alteration as to the rites of baptism." The other says in reference to the Christians of the third century baptizing, "They baptize with some ceremonies those that were well instructed in their religion, and who had given satisfactory signs of their sincere conversion; they generally dipped them thrice in water, invoking the name of the Holy Trinity."—*Orchard's History of Foreign Baptists, Vol. I, page 35.* The authorities quoted above as given by Mr. Orchard, are named, and reference is made to their works in his history.

Having previously given the authority of the advocates of single immersion to prove the fact that trine immersion was the prevailing form of immersion at the close of the second century, and in the third, and then proving from Mr. Orchard, the Baptist historian, that baptism was not altered in the third century, but remained as it had been in the second, what then is the legitimate conclusion to be drawn from such premises or data? The logical conclusion is that trine immersion was the prevailing mode of immersion in the second century, and not at the close of it only. The prevalence of trine immersion in the second century as well as in the third, is a fact well sustained by ecclesiastical writers. As we have seen above, Mr. Orchard, the Baptist historian, presents us with proof to sustain the fact. Dr. Cathcart quotes Dr. Coleman, an author of Christian antiquities, as saying, "In the second century it had become *customary* to *immerse three times*, at the mention of the several names of the Godhead."—*The Baptism of the Ages and of the Nations, page 75.*

In Gregory and Rutter's *Church History*, a work originally published in England, and republished in the United States with improvements by Dr. Rutter, president of Augusta College, we find the following in the account given *Of Government, Doctrines, Rites and Ceremonies* of the second century: "Baptism was publicly performed twice a year. The catechumens (or probationers for baptism) assembled in the church on the great festivals of Easter and Whitsuntide; and after a public declaration of their faith, and a solemn assurance from their sponsors that it was their intention to live conformably to the Gospel, they received the sacrament of baptism. This rite was performed by three immersions."—page 53. Notice, it is not said that trine immersion was the manner in which baptism was occasionally performed, nor the manner in which it was frequently performed, "*This rite was performed by three immersions.*" This language plainly indicates, that according to the authors, trine immersion was the accepted, the established, and the authorized way of performing baptism. And this plainly declared fact in church history, agrees with, and confirms the way that Justin Martyr describes as that in which the Christians of his time baptized.

The position at which we have now arrived by different arguments that trine immersion was the prevailing manner of baptizing in the second century as well as in the third, is greatly confirmed and strengthened by another consideration that naturally grows out of the admission of single immersionists in regard to the prevalence of trine immersion in the third century. It is admitted by single immersionists, (let it be remembered) that "trine immersion was the general practice of Christians from the end of the second till the close of the twelfth century." But it is maintained by the opponents of trine immersion, that, that mode of immersion had its origin about that time and that it does not extend beyond that.

If then trine immersion was the general practice of Christians about the end of the second century, it must have had its origin long anterior to that period, or to the period in which it generally prevailed. It would be unreasonable to suppose that it would attain unto a general prevalence immediately upon its beginning. There were in the second century, according to Dr. Haven, as given by Mr. Bate in his *Cyclopædia of Illustrations*, under the head of the *Progress of Christianity*, two millions of Christians.

Now it will not only be admitted, but it will be maintained by all immersionists, single and trine, that the two millions of Christians in the second century were all immersed; or if there were any exceptions the number was so small, that it will not affect our argument. Then, according to the admission of single immersionists, the generality or large majority of those two million Christians, were trine immersionists. And if at the close of the second century, there were any thing near two millions of Christians, and if a majority of them were trine immersionists, then trine immersion had its origin a considerable while before the beginning of the second century. This is so evident that it admits of no doubt.

Then the train of thought that we have been pursuing, leads to the conclusion, that all our other arguments in this connection have led to, namely, this, that trine immersion did not originate in the time of Tertullian, or in the end of the second century, but at a time considerably before that, or it could not have attained to such a general prevalence as is conceded to it at that time.

We have then established by arguments of different kinds, and among them the positive declaration of the fact, that trine immersion was the prevailing mode of immersion in the church in the second century. We shall now proceed to show that it was the mode of immersion that prevailed in the church in the first century.

We quote again from Mr. Orchard. And as he is a Baptist historian, and single immersionist, he will have no partiality to trine immersion. In closing his history of the second century in his *History of Foreign Baptists*, he says: "Although unwarrantable customs and ceremonies began to prevail at the conclusion of this century in some churches, yet the ordinances of religion were not diverted or altered from their scriptural subject, which is supported by the best historians, as, 'It does not appear by any approved authors, that there was any mutation or variation in baptism from the former century.'"

Now as we had proved by disinterested witnesses, and "by the mouth of two or three witnesses," that trine immersion prevailed in the second century, and now prove by Mr. Orchard, the Baptist historian, that no mutation or variation in baptism from the former century (first century) had been made, it follows as a just and legitimate inference, that trine immersion prevailed in the first century, and in the apostolic age, and therefore is the mode of immersion practiced by the apostles. Such a conclusion cannot be justly avoided. It has been reached by a fair and logical course of reasoning upon historical ground, and that ground admitted, and even furnished by single immersionists.

1. The concession of Dr. Cathcart, that "Trine immersion was the general practice of Christians from the end of the second till the close of the twelfth century," makes trine immersion the general practice of Christians in the third century. Mr. Orchard's testimony in reference to the third century that we have already quoted, contains the following two points to be noticed: (1) He quotes

Bingham as saying in reference to the mode of immersion practiced in the third century, "they generally dipped them thrice in water." (2) He quotes the *Magdeburgh Centuriators* as his authority, and an authority that is said to be very reliable, as saying, "We have no testimony as to any alteration as to the rite of baptism." Then as it is proved from the above testimonies and Dr. Cathcart's admission, that trine immersion prevailed in the third century, and as it is stated as a historic fact by Mr. Orchard, that there was no change in the rite of baptism from what had been in the second century, the prevalence of trine immersion in the second century follows as a necessary consequence. Then having well established the prevalence of trine immersion, in the second century by the testimony above alluded to, and by the testimony of Gregory and Rutter's *Church History*, positively declaring that baptism in the second century "was performed by three immersions," and by the description of the manner of baptizing as given by Justin Martyr, which so plainly indicates trine immersion, we have only to apply the principle laid down by Mr. Orchard, upon reliable historic authority, namely, that, "It does not appear by any approved authors, that there was any mutation or variation in baptism from the former century," meaning that there was no change in baptism from the first to the second century, and we have trine immersion in the first century and in the apostolic age. For if trine immersion prevailed in the second century, as we have seen it did, and if there was no variation in baptism from the first century, and it is declared there was not, then as trine immersion prevailed in the second century, it must also have prevailed in the first, and so we plainly have trine immersion in the first century and in the apostolic age.

Before we dismiss our historic argument, we have a few thoughts to offer in regard to the silence that obtains upon the subject of trine immersion beyond the time of Tertullian. This silence is turned against trine immersion. And Dr. Cathcart's strong language alludes to this silence. "Beyond Tertullian no record in the literature of men, in the book of God, or in any symbol known to mortals utters a single word about three immersions in baptism." We examined the records of history upon the subject of immersion, and found there are three writers beyond Tertullian who allude to immersion. But we have seen that two of them in their testimony favor trine immersion as much as single, as they only speak of going into the water. While if we accept the reading of the baptismal formula as Dr. Conant,

Mr. Clark, and Mr. Barrage say it should read to require a trine immersion, Justin Martyr was a trine immersionist. So the silence of the time beyond Tertullian, upon single immersion, is more profound than it is upon trine immersion.

CHAPTER XII.

THE TESTIMONY OF REFORMERS, THEOLOGIANS, AND LITERARY MEN IN FAVOR OF TRINE IMMERSION.

WE present the judgments of several men, eminent and honored in their day, and among their people, upon the subject of trine immersion. They are important witnesses. They were not biased in their judgments by any special preference to trine immersion. We do not know that any of those who have borne such faithful testimony to trine immersion, practiced it. Many of them would have preferred it to any other action of baptism. But there were difficulties in their way, and not regarding the action of baptism as of very great importance, they did not make any very great sacrifices to overcome the difficulties that were in their way. But it is interesting to have an expression of their minds, and such an expression we have in their testimonies that we give.

LUTHER: In the year 1530 Luther was written to

by a preacher inquiring about the manner in which he should baptize a converted Jewess. The following is Luther's reply: "As to the public act of baptism, let her be dressed in the garments usually worn by females in baths, and be placed in a bathing tub, up to the neck in water; then let the baptist dip her head three times in the water, with the usual words: 'I baptize you in the name of the Father,' etc."— *Luther's Works, ed. Walch, Part X, page 2637. Translated by C. L. Loos, for the* DISCIPLE.

JOHN WESLEY: "When Mr. Wesley baptized adults professing faith in Christ, he chose to do it by trine immersion if the person would submit to it, judging this to be the apostolic method of baptizing."—*Moore's Life of Wesley, Vol. I, page 425.*

ROBERT ADAMS: "They baptized by immersion, and they used the trine immersion, or form of dipping the child thrice in the water; which is no doubt the most ancient manner."—*Religious World Displayed, Vol. I, page 303.*

Mr. Adams was a minister of the Church of England. In writing his work, The Religious World Displayed, he had occasion to make himself extensively acquainted with the various religious systems in the world. And after all his researches, he declares that trine immersion, without doubt is the most ancient manner of baptizing.

CHAMBER'S CYCLOPÆDIA: BAPTISM, in Theology; formed from the Greek baptidzo of bapto, I dip or plunge; a rite or ceremony by which persons were initiated into the profession of the Christian religion. The practice of the Western Church is, to sprinkle the water on the head or face of the person to be baptized, except in the church of Milan, in whose ritual it is ordered that the head of the infant be plunged three times into the water, the minister at the same time pronouncing the words, 'I baptize thee in the name of the Father, the Son, and the Holy Ghost'—importing that by this ceremony the person baptized is received among the professors of that religion, which God the Father of all revealed to mankind by the ministry of his Son, and confirmed by the miracles of his Spirit. 'A triple immersion was first used and continued for a long time.''

A triple immersion was first used, and continued a long time, affirms the learned work. If it was first used—used by divine authority, should it not have been continued? The wisdom that originated it was perfect, and it knew what was best.

Vossius: "What son of the church will not willingly hold to that custom which the ancient church practiced all over the world except Spain? etc. Besides at present the trine immersion is used in all countries; so that the custom cannot be changed without an affectation of novelty, and scandal given to the weak."—*Wall's History of Infant Baptism, Vol. 2, page 424.* Vossius wrote in the latter part of the sixteenth and beginning of the seventeenth century. His language shows how extensively trine immersion prevailed in his time.

Strabo: "Which single immersion, although at that time pleasing to the Spaniards who asserted that the trine immersion should be disused because certain heretics, for the purpose of denying the consubstantiality of the Son, had dared to propound the dogma that there are dissimilar substances in the Trinity: notwithstanding the more ancient use and the reason above stated prevaled. For if we are to desert everything which heretics perverted, nothing will be left us, since they have erred concerning even God himself, and they have twisted everything which seems to pertain to his worship, and have applied it as though it were peculiarly designed for the support of their errors. But why should I speak farther. Suffice it to say, that the trine immersion prevails everywhere in the world this day, and that it can by no means be changed unless in accordance with a rash desire of novelty and to the scandal of the weak." Strabo lived in the eighth century. He in referring to his time, says *trine immersion prevails everywhere in the world this day.*

The PANTALOGIA, under the article "Greek Church," thus explains:—That part of the Christian church which was first established in Greece, and is now spread over a larger extent of country than any other established church. It comprehends in its bosom a considerable part of Greece, the Grecian Isles, Wallachia, Moldavia, Egypt, Abyssinia, Nubia, Lybia, Arabia, Mesopotamia, Syria, Cilicia, Palestine. . . . . It may be observed that among all their trifling rites, they practice trine immersion, which is unquestionably the primitive manner."—*Pengilly's Scripture Guide to Baptism, page 73.*

The author or authors of the above express themselves very strongly in regard to trine immersion—*which is unquestionably the primitive manner.*

WILLIAM WHISTON, M. A., Translator of Josephus: (1) "That the practice in baptism seems not to have been as now, *I baptize thee in the name of the Father, and of the Son, and of the Holy Ghost:*

But while the Person to be baptized, (or his surety if an infant,) repeated the Creed and Renunciation after the Bishop, or Presbyter, at least their Abridgement the second time, the Bishop or Presbyter dipped him, *once* at his naming of the Father, a *second* time of the Son, and a *third* of the Holy Ghost. Which manner of baptizing agrees exactly with the rule in the Constitutions, and the practice in *Cyril of Jerusalem;* and seems the proper meaning of the original command of baptizing or dipping *eis to honoma at the* respective *names* of the Father, Son, and Holy Ghost, and not according to the common exposition *in their name* by their authority, or to their worship. Since baptism is only designed originally *into the death of Christ;* though so ordered as to put us in mind of the Father, who *sent* him; and of the Holy Ghost who *witnessed* to him, at the same time as the Constitutions particularly inform us. (2) That therefore the *Trine Immersion* is directly of our Saviour's own appointment, and the very meaning of the original command for baptism, both in Matthew and the Constitutions; and is not to be altered by any Christian."—*Primitive Christianity Revived, Vol. 3, pages 399, 400.*

Mr. Whiston most enthusiasticrlly pursued the study of Christian antiquity to obtain all the knowledge he could in regard to the origin or date of the Apostolic Canons. He had great regard for those Canons. But Mr. Whiston was a student and a scholar, and in his reading and study, he was strongly impressed with the divine authority of trine immersion. He affirms it to be "directly of our Saviour's own appointment, and the very meaning of the original command for baptism."

Dr. J. G. King: "The Greek Church practices the trine immersion, undoubtedly the most primitive manner."

Dr. King wrote upon the ceremonies of the Greek church. He thoroughly investigated those ceremonies. He was brought into connection with various sources of knowledge in regard to the faith and practice of this large and ancient body of professing Christians. And the result of his reading and observation was, that trine immersion was *undoubtedly the most primitive manner*. The proof must have been very clear and abundant to his mind.

Archbishop Tillotson: "To be baptized into the death and resurrection of Christ, is to be baptized into the similitude and likeness of them; and the resemblance is this: that as Christ being dead was buried in the grave, and after some stay in it, that is, for some days, he was raised again out of it, by the glorious power of God, to a new and heavenly life, being not long after taken up into heaven to live at the right hand of God; so Christians, when they were baptized were immersed into the water three times; their bodies being covered all over with it, which is therefore called our being buried with him by baptism unto death; and after some short stay under water, were *raised* or taken up again out of it, as if they had been recovered to a new life; by all which was spiritually signified our dying to sin, and being raised to a divine and heavenly life, through the faith of the operation of God, that is by that divine and supernatural power, which raised up Christ from the dead."—*Tillotson's Works, Vol. 3, page 255.*

BISHOP BEVERIDGE: "Neither did the Church ever esteem that baptism valid, which was not administered exactly according to the institution, in the Name of all the three Persons; which the primitive Christians were so strict in the observance of, that it was enjoined, that all persons to be baptized should be plunged three times into the water, first at the 'Name of the Father,' and then at the 'Name of the Son,' and lastly, at the 'Name of the Holy Ghost'; that so every person might be distinctly nominated, and so our Saviour's institution exactly observed in the administration of this sacrament."—*Beveridge's Works, Vol. 8, page 336.* And Mr. Chrystal, in his *History of the Modes of Baptism*, and on page 194, quotes from Bishop Beveridge, the following: "That this (trine immersion) was in some way handed down from the Apostles we dare not deny."

We have given the foregoing testimonies from the authors to whom they are attributed, not with any expectation that they will amount to much as a direct argument for trine immersion. But if they are carefully read as the sentiments of their distinguished authors, they may constitute a presumption that there is some ground for trine immersion, as the mode of immersion taught in the baptismal formula. And thus remove préjudice, and prepare the way for a candid examination of the claims of trine immersion upon Christian belief. With a desire that they may have this effect, we have introduced them.

CHAPTER XIII.

THE CHURCHES THAT HAVE PRACTICED TRINE IMMERSION.

AS we shall take some little notice, in the discussion of our subject, of the different Christian churches that have practiced trine immersion, it may be of some interest to notice the trine action in aspersion and effusion as well as in immersion. If the baptismal formula requires a trine immersion when immersion is accepted as the action of baptism, when pouring or sprinkling is accepted as the action, it should be done by a trine affusion or a trine aspersion. And so it was done in former times.

There seems to be something associated with the trine action in the performance of what is done as Christian baptism, whether it is a trine immersion, a trine affusion, or a trine aspersion, that makes a trine action preferable to a single one, as the church for a long time in all its branches, whether those branches were distinguished for their hetrodoxy or orthodoxy, showed a decided preference to a trine, er than to a single action. For it is known to student of church history, that the single action, whether it is the single immersion, or the single affusion or aspersion, is comparatively of modern origin. Before the Reformation it was only a very small minority of all in all countries that received what they called baptism, in any form, that received it in a single act. And after the Reformation, the trine action continued a considerable time in all countries.

We have said there seems to be a preference to a trine rather than to a single action. The idea of having the Godhead presented in the three-fold manifestations of Father, Son, and Holy Spirit, with that marked distinction of name and person, in which we have them presented in the baptismal formula, seems to be more acceptable than to have it presented in one undefined name. The three persons named, the Father, Son, and Holy Spirit, are so familiar in the gospel, that when there is a foundation laid for Christian culture in the new birth, such a Christian culture will be experienced that those names will be readily apprehended, though they may not be fully comprehended.

Again: The number three is one of the sacred numbers of Scripture, and the number symbolical of the Godhead. And this perhaps may go to account in some measure for the preference that is shown for the number three. Such a preference is shown both by Jews and Christians. In their sacred ablutions, the Jews used a trine washing. "Another person," says Wall, "very learned in Jewish customs, assures me, that their way of washing any person, or thing, that was by their law to have *tevillah*, or solemn washing, was to do it three times over: so that a vessel that was to be washed, was drawn three times through water. And Mr. Selden says, 'it must be the same quantity of water as that wherein a proselyte was baptized.' Whence it is probable that they gave the proselyte a trine immersion."— *Wall's History of Infant Baptism, Vol. I, page 38, 39.*

The idea prevailed among the ancients that our Lord received a trine immersion from John the Baptist. Wall says, "In England there seems to have been some priests so early as the year 816, that attempted to bring in the use of baptism by affusion in the public administration; for Spelman recites a canon of a council in that year, 'Let the priests know, that when they administer holy baptism, they must not pour the water on the head of the infants: but they must always be dipped in the font. As the

Son of God gave his own example to all believers, when he was thrice dipped in the waters of Jordan; so it is necessary by order to be kept and used.'"—*Ibid, Vol. II, pages 395, 396.*

1. The Roman Catholic Church. This church has always held baptism in high esteem. And it practiced trine immersion until about the time of the Reformation. But by an exercise of power which it claims to have to change the rites of the church, it discontinued trine immersion and adopted affusion. But it is charged with insincerity by protestant writers, and not without reason, as it boasts of its conformity to the practices of the church in ancient times, but cannot deny that the practice of the church in ancient times was to baptize by trine immersion, but it has abandoned the practice of antiquity, and adopted the modern custom of affusion.

But while the Roman Catholic church has discontinued trine immersion, it continues the three actions in affusion.

The following directions for baptizing are given in the ritual of the church:

"Q. Ought baptism to be administered by dipping or by pouring of the water, or by the sprinkling of the water?

"A. It may be administered validly any of these

ways; but the custom of the church is to administer this sacrament either by dipping in water, which is used in the East; or by pouring of the water upon the person baptized, which is more customary in these parts of Christendom. Moreover it is the custom in all parts of the Catholic church, and has been so from the Apostles' days to dip or pour three times at the names of the three divine persons.

2. *The Greek Church.* The Greek Church through all the changes that it has come in its long and eventful history has closely adhered to the trine immersion, the ancient form of baptism. And all the organizations that have separated from the great body of the Greek church, have done the same. This is not a little remarkable, but nevertheless, it seems to be true.

Dr. Stanley in his history of the *Eastern Church,* has the following just remarks in regard to the Greeks and their language:

"The early Roman Church was but a colony of Greek Christians or Grecized Jews. The earliest Fathers of the Western Church, Clemens, Irenaeus, Hermas, Hippolytus, wrote in Greek. The early Popes were not Italians but Greeks. The name of Pope is not Latin but Greek—the common and now despised name of every pastor in the Eastern church.

It is true that this Grecian color was in part an accidental consequence of the wide diffusion of the Greek language by Alexander's conquests through the East, and was thus a sign not so much of the Hellenic as of the Hebrew and Oriental character of the early Christian communities. But the advantage thus given to the Byzantine Church has never been lost or forgotten. It is a perpetual witness that she is the mother and Rome the daughter. It is her privilege to claim a direct continuity of speech with the earliest times, to boast of reading the whole code of Scripture, old as well as new in the language in which it was read and spoken by the Apostles. The humblest peasant who reads his Septuagint or Greek Testament in his own mother tongue, on the hills of Boetia, may proudly feel that he has an access to the original oracles of divine truth, which Pope and Cardinal reach by a barbarous and imperfect translation; that he has a key of knowledge, which in the West is only to be found in the hands of the learned classes."—*Stanley's History of the Greek Church, pages 101, 102.*

In looking at the great body of the Greek church in the strong light in which Dr. Stanley pictures it, and remembering that the Greeks occupy the same country that the apostles did, and that they speak the same language that those faithful servants of God spake, the circumstance that they read the baptismal formula in their own language, and have always understood it to mean a trine immersion, and have adhered to it for nearly two thousand years, we must feel that in the experience and practice of the Greek Church we have not only a strong argument for immersion, as immersionists justly claim, but also a strong argument for trine immersion.

3. The Church of England. The Church of England is a witness of trine immersion. In the first years of its history, and for some time afterwards, it practiced trine immersion. And many of its eminent scholars and theologians have expressed a strong desire to return to this mode of baptism.

There were two Books of Common Prayer authorized by Parliament under the reign of Edward VI, in the sixteenth century. In these we have the form of baptism given as follows:

1. "Then the Priest shall take the child in his hands, and ask the name; and naming the child, shall dip it in the water thrice. First, dipping the right side; second, the left side; the third time dipping the face toward the font: so it be discreetly and warily done, saying, N, I baptize thee in the

name of the Father, and of the Son, and of the Holy Ghost. Amen."

2. In the second book the baptismal service is as follows: "Then the Priest shall take the child in his hands, and ask the name; and naming the child, shall dip it in the water, so it be discreetly and warily done." Then follow the same words as in the first. It will be observed that in the first book, trine immersion was the order. In the second the trine was omitted. And now the immersion is omitted and sprinkling is the order in practice, of the Church of England, although it is said, there has been no change in the written form.

4. *The Lutheran Church.* The Lutheran church practiced the trine pouring according to the following: "*Lutherean Baptism, as it is practiced by established rituals in Saxony, Denmark and Norway.* After the preparation is completed, then the naked head of the child is held over the font, and the priest pours water three times over it, while he is pronouncing the usual words, pouring once in the name of the Father, a second time in the name of the Son, and a third time in the name of the Holy Ghost. Then he covers the head of the child, and before he returns it to the godfather, he pronounces

with his hand upon the head a short benedictory prayer."—*Robinson's History of Baptism, page 483*.

5. *The River Brethren.* There is a small body of Christians in the United States and Canada, known by the name of River Brethren. They practice the trine immersion in baptism. In their practices and principles in several points, they resemble the Brethren or German Baptists.

6. *The Congregation of James Chrystal.* James Chrystal was a minister in the Episcopal Church, and becoming impressed with the necessity of being baptized by a trine immersion, and not being able to obtain it in his own church, he went to Greece, and was baptized by a Greek Bishop. Mr. Chrystal was very anxious to have the Episcopal Church return to the practice of trine immersion—the form of baptism that it had originally held. And to further the purpose that he took much interest in, he wrote a work called, *History of the Modes of Baptism*. In this he sustains trine immersion as the form of baptism instituted by Christ. The work shows learning and diligence, and contains much information. Our acquaintance with Mr. Chrystal impressed us favorably with the sincerity and uprightness of his character.

Mr. Chrystal becoming discouraged in his labors

trine immersion restored to his church, or-
d a congregation in Jersey City, New Jersey,
,rding to his principles, and is now preaching
and laboring successfully in that congregation.

7. *The Brethren or German Baptists.* When
the humble and devoted brethren re-organized the
Church in 1708, with the doctrine and practices as
we now have them in our Christian community, they
became concerned in regard to baptism as well as to
other matters pertaining to Christian faith and practice. They had been sprinkled, but with this they
were not satisfied. And by prayer, fasting, and
reading, they asked and sought for "the old paths,"
and "the good way," and settle down upon trine
immersion, as the form of baptism taught in the
gospel, and practiced by the first Christians. And
it has been retained in our Fraternity.

8. *The Seventh Day Baptists.* There are a few
congregations of Seventh Day Baptists in the United
States, and they practice trine immersion.

Trine immersion prevailed extensively in the christian world for fourteen hundred years. There was
comparatively but little immersion of any kind during that time but trine immersion. And what was
done as baptism, that was not immersion, was done
by pouring. Sprinkling was scarcely known. And

whether it was pouring or immersion, it was but little exception by a trine action. It was immersion or trine affusion. And the prevalence of a trine action in baptism, no doubt mainly grew out of a deep and general conviction that the baptismal formula teaches a trine action.

And this general conviction that prevailed so long in the Christian world that a trine action is taught in the baptismal formula, constitutes a strong probability that such a trine action is taught in it.

CHAPTER XIV.

OBJECTIONS TO TRINE IMMERSION ANSWERED.

IF the various arguments we have advanced in favor of trine immersion are carefully and candidly examined, and the trains of thought that we have suggested are carried out, we do not think that many objections will present themselves to a candid inquirer, that will have much weight. There have been many objections offered against trine immersion, as there have been against immersion. But these objections are frequently more in appearance than in reality.

We shall notice some of the more common objections that have been urged against trine immersion.

1. It is said that it conflicts with the figures used to represent immersion. Baptism is compared to a burial, and it is said that as there is a plurality of actions in trine immmersion, and as we bury people but once, the figure is destroyed. This is no valid objection whatever, to trine immersion. What is it

to bury? To bury is to cover, to hide, or to conceal. And as this is done by trine immersion as well as by single, the former may be compared to a burial as well as the latter.

There are well defined rules given for the explanation of figures. The following is one given by Mr. Alexander Campbell: "In the interpretation of symbols, types, allegories, and parables, this rule is supreme. Ascertain the point to be illustrated; for comparison is never to be extended beyond that point—to all the attributes, qualities, or circumstances of the symbol, types, allegory, or parable."—*Campbell on Baptism, page 61.* There is usually one prominent point in which the type agrees with the anti-type, and when we have that agreement it is sufficient. There need not be a resemblance found in every particular. The point to be illustrated in comparing baptism to a burial is the covering or concealing. And, as has been already observed, this is done by trine immersion as fully as by single.

The ancient Christians indulged much in comparing baptism to the burial and resurrection of Christ. And instead of there being any thing in their judgment in trine immersion against the comparison, it increased the resemblance. Gregory Nyssen of the fifth century, uses the following language: "We who receive baptism, in imitation of our Lord, and Teacher, and Guide, are not buried in the earth, for this covers the entire lifeless body, and enwraps the weakness and corruption of our nature; . . . . but coming to the water, the element cognate to the earth, we hide ourselves in it, as the Saviour hid himself in the earth; and this we do three times, to represent the grace of his resurrection performed after three days."—*Chrystal's History of the Modes of Baptism, page 76.*

Dr. Cathcart, after speaking in high terms of the splendid abilities of Leo the Great, in the fifth century, quotes from him the following words, "Trine immersion is an imitation of the three days' burial [of Christ], and the elevation from the waters is a figure [of the Saviour] rising from the grave;" and adds, "These words of Leo were used for centuries by the Church teachers of the Old World, as the Nicene Creed was quoted as a general expression of orthodoxy."—*Baptism of the Ages, page 143.*

Among the many passages Dr. Cathcart quotes from the ancients, is the following from one the Doctor calls a cultivatd Englishman. He lived in the twelfth century: "Whilst the candidate for baptism in water *is immersed, the death of Christ is suggested; whilst immersed, and covered with water, the burial of Christ is shown forth; whilst he is raised from the water*, the resurrection of Christ is proclaimed. *The immersion is repeated three times*, out of reverence for the Trinity and on account of the three days' burial of Christ. In the burial of the Lord the day follows the night three times; *in baptism, also trine* emersion accompanies trine immersion." Dr. Cathcart adds to the above, "The most beautiful exposition of Rom. 6: 4 ever penned!"

We then see that there is nothing in the figure of a burial to which baptism is compared, that will conflict in the least with trine immersion according to the ancients, and also according to the moderns. And so it is with all the other figures. Keep in mind that a leading point both in the type and in the anti-type, is sufficient resemblance to justify the comparison.

2. It is objected that the one baptism of Paul, Eph. 4: 5, conflicts with trine immersion. When baptism in the verse is translated, and rendered "*one immersion*," it is urged, this rendering conflicts with trine immersion. This, however, is by no means the case. There is one immersion for Jews and Gentiles, and for all believers. This trine immersionists accept as cordially as single immersionists. But that one immersion is the immersion

that is performed according to the baptismal formula, that requires an immersion "into the name of the Father, and into the name of the Son, and into the name of the Holy Spirit."

The administrator in administering trine immersion, immerses the subject into the name of the Father. This is an immersion, but it is not the "one immersion" of Paul, for that is the Christian ordinance of immersion, in which the subject is immersed into the three names. He then immerses him into the name of the Son. This is also an immersion, but it is not the one immersion alluded to by Paul. He then immerses him into the name of the Holy Spirit. And now the subject has the one immersion, comprised of the three immersions, one into each of the Divine names contained in the baptismal formula.

This manner of writing is sanctioned by good usage. A word may express an idea of something in a more limited sense, and the same word may express the same idea of the thing in an enlarged sense. Dr. Carson thus expresses it: "The three immersions used by the ancients in the performance of the rite called *tria baptismata, three baptisms,* that is, *three immersions,* for it could not be *three purifications:* it was only one purification. I am well aware that three immersions may be called also one baptism. *My philosophy* can account for this. When there are said to be three baptisms, the word is used in reference to the act of immersion; when they are called one baptism, the word is used in reference to the rite in its appropriated sense. The three immersions are, in the estimation of those who used them, only one rite, which was designated by the name baptism."—*Carson on Baptism, pages 491, 492.*

Dr. Waterland in writing upon the unity and plurality of the Godhead, says, "Neither is there any difficulty in admitting that three things may be *three* and *one* in different repects; distinct enough to be *three*, and yet united enough to be *one*."—*Waterland's Works, Vol. V, page 350.*

Mr. Alexander Campbell in writing upon the Church, says, "This institution, called *the congregation of God*, is a great community of communities—not a community representative of communities, but a community composed of many particular communities," &c.—*Christian System, page 73.*

"Jerome, in his notes on Ephesians 4: 5, says, 'We are immersed three times to receive the one baptism of Christ.'"—*The Baptist Encyclopædia, Art. Immersion.*

Chrysostom says, "Christ delivered to his disciples one baptism in three immersions of the body, when he said to them, 'Go, teach all nations, baptizing them in the name of the Father, and of the Son, and of the Holy Ghost."—*Bingham's Antiquities of the Christian Church, Book XI, Chapter XI.*

There is nothing then in Paul's "one immersion," that is not easily reconcIled with trine immersion, when intelligently read, and read in the light of the reputable usages of our language. But if Paul speaks, Eph. 4:5, of "one immersion," in Heb. 6:2 he recognizes as distinctly a plurality of immersions: "the doctrine of immersions." And this plurality of immersions has been understood to refer to trine immersion by De Wette, an eminent German Commentator, and others. See Lange and Millegan *in loco*.

3. It is objected to trine immersion that it was introduced to add weight to the doctrine of the Trinity. It is thus stated by Dr. Fairbairns: "It very probably took its rise about the period when the doctrsne of the Trinity came to be impugned by the theories of ancient heretics, toward the middle or latter part of the second century, with the view of obtaining from each subject of baptism a distinct and formal acknowledgment of the doc-

trine."—*Fairbairn's Hermeneutical Manual, page 296*. The substance of this objection we find in different writers. It is mere surmising. There is no ground whatever for it.

Those who attribute the introduction of trine immersion to this cause, are usually single immersionists and trinitarians. Then according to the statement thus made, and according to the views of those who make it, the friends of the trinitarian doctrine, must have felt their cause to be weak to be driven to change the sacred ordinance of baptism given by Christ to strengthen it. This is not at all probable. If the trinitarian doctrine was true, it needed no such support. And if it was not true, it would not have been likely to obtain the general support it did at that early age of the church.

Again: The opponents of trine immersion intimate that it was introduced by Tertullian, or about his time. But he, in his controversy with Praxeus, when he was sustaining the doctrine that there are three persons in the Godhead instead of one, as Praxeus held, appealed to the practice of trine immersion to sustain his position. The following is Tertullian's language as translated by Bingham: "Christ appointed baptism to be administered not in the name of one, but three, Father, Son, and

Holy Ghost. Therefore we are dipped not once, but thrice, unto every person at the mention of each name."—*Bingham's Antiquities of the Christian Church, Book XI, Chapter III.*

If trine immersion had been introduced to strengthen the argument for the trinitarian doctrine, Tertullian would not have had the face to appeal to it to prove the plurality of persons in the Godhead. His opponents would have known of its introduction, and they would have turned it to the defeat of Tertullian and his sympathizers. But as he appealed to it as a divine command to prove the plurality of the persons in the Godhead, it is evident that it was a divine command. For had he appealed to it as such, when it was not, it would have ruined his cause. So there is no ground whatever, for the idea that trine immersion was introduced to strengthen the doctrine of the Trinity, or "to emphasize the three persons in the Godhead," as has been affirmed of it.

We have now answered a few objections that have not come up so distinctly in the discussion of our sueject. Others will be met and answered as we proceed.

CHAPTER XV.

TRINE IMMERSION AN IMPORTANT SUPPORT TO IMMERSION.

IN the baptismal controversy, and in the defence that immersionists make of immersion, trine immersion is often called in to assist them in their defence. Trine immersion having been the common form of baptism from the early ages of Christianity down to the Reformation, examples of immersion in that way occur very often in history, and their testimony has been used frequently and effectually in defence of immersion. Among the witnesses used by immersionists to prove immersion, will be found many trine immersionists. And the cause of immersion is unquestionably greatly indebted to trine immersion. Dr. Cathcart's *Baptism of the Ages and of the Nations*, one of the most recent productions on the side of immersion, is a striking evidence of the truth of our affirmation. The whole work is almost entirely made up of examples of trine immersion. And the Doctor must have thought that the testimony of his witnesses will promote the cause of immersion.

Trine immersion having rendered the support it has to the cause of immersion, we have been surprised and grieved at the great impropriety, and inconsistency, to use no stronger language, of single immersionists, in the manner in which they have spoken of trine immersion, though they have derived the help from it that they have. In a pamphlet bearing the title, *Trine Immersion Weighed in the Balances and Found Wanting*, published it appears originally in England by Mr. R. Robertson, and republished in America by Mr. F. M. Bowman, of Newtonia, Mo., the following language occurs on page 15: "*The foolishness of trine immersion.*" In the *Baptist Encyclopædia*, and in the article on *Trine Immersion*, the following language occurs, "The ordinance had been enlarged by two extra dippings, *and increased in other foolish ways.*" In Mr. Clark's Commentary, a Baptist publication, the author when referring to the baptismal formula, says, "The old custom of immersing at the utterance of each name, still practiced by the Greek church, is first mentioned by Tertullian, and appears to have arisen from the superstitions and corruptions which gave birth to infant baptism."

A SUPPORT TO IMMERSION.

A correspondent of *The Church Advocate* the following from *The Evangelist,* a paper edited by Elder B. W. Johnson, of the Disciple church: "There is little doubt that trine immersion was introduced by the Trinitarians in order to emphasize the three persons in the Godhead." The following is also quoted as part of the article: "No well informed person doubts that trine immersion is a corruption of the ancient practice, just as much as sprinkling." The correspondent of the *Advocate* adds the following remarks: "These are plain sayings; but facts support their truthfulness. If trine immersion has no support from New Testament authority, then it originated since Christ's day, and may be classed among the corruptions of past ages." —*Church Advocate, July 5th, 1882.*

Single immersion being related to trine immersion as it is, and having received the support from it that it has in the conflict between immersion and sprinkling, single immersionists are guilty of great impropriety when they speak so irreverently of trine immersion. But their impropriety and inconsistency become more apparent, and more reprehensible when we consider the fact that prominent and leading single immersionists have recognized ancient trine immersionists to be their brethren, and the churches in ancient times that practiced trine immersion to be the churches of Christ, and Baptist churches.

Mr. Orchard quotes from Robinson's Ecclesiastical Researches the following important testimony in regard to the character of the ancient churches: "During the first three centuries, Christian congregations all over the East subsisted in separate independent bodies, unsupported by government, and consequently without any secular power over one another. ALL THIS TIME THEY WERE BAPTIST CHURCHES."—*Orchard's History of Foreign Baptists, Vol. I, page 36.* The emphasizing was done by Mr. Orchard.

In connection with the above, we will read the concession made to trine immersion, as stated in the language of Dr. Cathcart. "Trine immersion was the general practice of Christians from the end of the second to the close of the twelfth century. The proof of this statement is overwhelming."

"The second century dawns on the world, and in proportion as it recedes from New Testament times, errors in doctrine creep into the church. According to Mosheim, 'about the middle of the second century, Montanus, the first dissenter entitled to notice, undertook a mission to restore Christianity to its native simplicity. He was successful, his doctrines spreading through Asia, Africa, and some portions of Europe.' Numerous converts to his theory were made, and 'amongst several others of no mean rank, two opulent women.' 'This sect continued to flourish down to the fifth century, and the list of its members was ennobled by not a few names distinguished both for learning and genius.'

"That the Montanists were Baptists, is evident from the fact that Tertullian joined them, and became eminent among them. Neander calls him 'the Montanist Tertullian,' and speaks of him as 'assuming a more important place,' in Montanism, than its founder, on account of the superiority of his intellectual character. Mosheim gives Tertullian the same relation to Montanism as does Neander. His writings abound in Baptist sentiments, as we have seen in the chapter on the history of baptism. It is this distinguished writer who says of the mode of baptism in his time: 'They were let down into the water, and dipped between the utterance of a few words.' When the Donatists arose (and we shall shortly see that they were Baptists), they were often called Montanists, from their resemblance to this more ancient sect.

"It should be remarked that in forming the connection between the New Testament Baptists and the Montanists, a period of only fifty years is unprovided for, as the Montanists appear 'about the middle of the second century.' This is the only defect in the chain, if, indeed, this can be called one. The New Testament history leaves the churches in a favorable conditton, and fifty years is not a long period for the innovations to have reached a point requiring dissent."—*The Baptist Denomination, page 41, 42.*

The foregoing extracts are taken from a work called the *Baptist Denomination.* The author D. C. Haynes, declares the Montanists to be Baptists. And to prove that they were Baptists, he states the fact "that Tertullian joined them." And then in speaking of Tertullian, he says, "his writings abound in Baptist sentiments." He also says in speaking further of Tertullian, "It is this distinguished writer who says of the mode of baptism in his time: 'they were let down into the water, and dipped between the utterance of a few words.'"

Another Baptist author, Dr. Ford, in his *Origin of the Baptists,* in speaking of Tertullian, says, "He plead for the purity of the Church, and the rejection of all unregenerate persons. He joined the now numerous sect of the Montanists, and finally proclaimed with them that the one immersion '*can relate only to us who know and call on the true God and Christ. The heretics have not this God and Christ. These words, therefore, can not be applied to them, and as they do not rightly administer the ordinance, their baptism is the same as none.*'

"Such were the principles of the Tertullianists in the second century. *Were they not Baptists?*"—*Origin of the Baptists, page 151, 152.*

Mr. Orchard says of Tertullian, "Tertullian's writings prove that he as a Baptist stood between contending parties; he explained duties to some, enforced them on others, while some of his instructions gave a check to the innovations of the times." —*History of Foreign Baptists, page 33.*

The above quotations are nearly all from Baptist authors, and it is claimed as has been seen, that all the churches for the first three centuries, all over the east were Baptist churches. Then as it has been conceded that trine immersion was the general practice of Christians from the end of the second century, trine immersion must have been the form of baptism practiced in those churches.

The dissenters that constitute the churches of the first three centuries, claimed by Mr. Orchard to be Baptist churches may be comprised under three general names. The Montanists were the first as we have seen in our extract from Mr. Haynes. The Montanists were succeeded by the Novatians. And the latter by the Donatists. We have seen that Mr. Haynes recognizes the Montanists and Donatists as Baptists. The Novatians were also recognized as Baptists. Dr. Ford says, "The people called Novatians were Baptists."—*Origin of the Baptists, page 148.*

The Montanists, Novatians, and Donatists were, without doubt, trine immersionists. As Tertullian was a well known trine immersionist, and as he joined the Montanists, and as the body was called Tertullianists, they were unquestionably trine immersionists. And let it be remembered that Mr. Haynes says (see our quotation) "It should be remarked that in forming the connection between the New Testament Baptists and the Montanists, a period of only fifty years is unprovided for, as the Montanists appear 'about the middle of the second century.' This is the only defect in the chain, if, indeed it can be called one."

The Novatians were likewise trine immersionists. This will probably not be doubted. If it is, it can be clearly proved. The following testimonies constitute one proof: "The Novatians called themselves Kathari or Puritans."—*Baptist Encyclopædia,*

Art. Novatians. Robinson says, "The first council at Nice took notice of two sorts of dissenters. . . . . . . These were Cathari and Paulianists. The first held the doctrine of the Trinity, as the Athanasians in the church did: but, thinking the church a worldly community, they baptized all that joined their assemblies by trine immersion in the name of the Father, Son, and Holy Ghost, on their own personal profession of faith, and if they had been baptized before, they re-baptized them."—*Ecclesiastical Researches, page 72.*

That the Donatists were trine immersionists is proven from the following testimony: "The Donatists were determined to have only godly members in their churches. . . . . They regarded the Church universal as having forfeited her Christian character by her inconsistencies and iniquities, and they refused to recognize her ordinances and her ministry. Hence they gave the *triple immersion* a second time to those who had received it in the great corrupt church."—*Baptist Encyclopædia, Art. Donatists.*

From the foregoing testimonies the following points are fairly proved: 1. The churches of the first three centuries, are claimed by good Baptist authority, to have been Baptist churches. And the bodies of dissenters known as Montanists, Novatians, and Donatists, are claimed by the same authority to have been Baptists. 2. It has also been proved that the churches within the period above named, practiced trine immersion, and that the bodies of dissenters claimed as Baptists, were trine immersionists. It is also claimed that "the Montanist Tertullian" was a Baptist. Hence it follows, that the early churches called by Baptists, Baptist churches, practiced trine immersion, and that those early Christians called by the same authority Baptists, were trine immersionists.

And while it was our intention in this chapter simply to vindicate trine immersion from the injudicious and irreverent remarks made against it by single immersionists, and to show how it has been used to support immersion, which we have done, our testimonies introduced, form a basis for an additional historical argument of great strength to prove that trine immersion can be traced to the apostolic age of the church.

We would only add in concluding our present chapter, if, according to the testimony of single immersionists, the early churches practiced trine immersion as we find they did, where shall we find the churches in those times that practiced single immersion? It seems there were none from the foregoing testimony.

CHAPTER XVI.

THE POSTURE OF THE BODY IN BAPTISM.

WHILE immersionists differ in regard to the number of immersions the baptismal formula requires to constitute Christian baptism, they also differ in regard to the position that the person receiving baptism should assume, when receiving it. Several positions have been assumed, but there are only two that are common, the bowing, and the supine position. 1. In the practice of trine immersion, the person bows in the water, under the hands of the administrator. 2. In the practice of single immersion, the person baptized is put into the water in a supine position.

Mr. Robinson thus describes the manner of performing trine immersion in America. "The administrator with the candidate goes into the river. The candidate kneels down into the water, aad the administrator puts his hand on his head, and bends him forward till he is immersed; he does this three times, pronouncing during the ceremony the usual baptismal words. The baptized continues kneeling till the administrator prays, and lays on hands, then he rises and departs. Trine immersion is very easily performed this way."—*History of Baptism, page 500*.

1. Trine immersionists observe the manner they do in baptism, in regard to the posture of the body from the following considerations: (*a*) As baptism may be regarded as an act of worship, it seems to be proper in paying the Divine homage and worship we do to the three divine objects of worship, to do it in a way that becomes both the worshipper, and the being worshipped. And this is done by presenting ourselves in an humble posture before the Divine beings whom we worship.

"Wherewith shall I come before the Lord, and bow myself before the high God."—Micah 6: 6.

"O come, let us worship, and bow down; let us kneel before the Lord our maker."—Ps. 95: 6.

"At the name of Jesus every knee should bow."—Phil. 2: 10.

"And all the angels stood round about the throne, and about the elders, and the four beasts, and fell before the throne on their faces, and worshipped God."—Rev. 7: 11.

(*b*) How was our Lord baptized? Did he bow forward, or was he put into the water in a supine position? We presume there would be a very general unanimity of sentiment in answering this question where the mind is free to decide, and makes the decision deliberately. If there is nothing to incline the mind to any other decision, the natural deduction would be that he bowed under the hands of his forerunner. And this seems to have been the conclusion that has been arrived at, and it has been embodied in a stanza of a hymn on baptism by Dr. S. F. Smith, a Baptist minister.

> "Meekly in Jordan's holy stream
> The great Redeemer *bow'd;*
> Bright was the glory's sacred beam
> That hush'd the wond'ring crowd."

This is a familiar baptismal hymn. The author was a poet of some reputation. As stated above he was a Baptist. And though he probably was baptized in the ordinary way that Baptists perform the ordinance, he accepted the idea that would be likely to be suggested to the reflecting and unbiased mind, that our Lord, in his baptism, "meekly bowed in Jordan."

And if John the Baptist baptized our Lord by bowing him forward, he no doubt baptized all that he baptized in the same way. And if the apostles of our Lord were baptized by bowing forward, they no doubt baptized those that they baptized in the same way.

And if the apostles before our Lord's death, baptized by bowing the candidate for baptism forward, they would continue to do the same after his death, unless they had received instruction to do otherwise. And as we know of no such instruction being given, the strong probability is, that after the apostles received their great commission to preach and baptize, they baptized by bowing the candidate forward.

With the manner of bowing the candidate forward till he is covered in the water, agree the references made to baptism in the writings of the ancients when the head is named especially as the part baptized. The following is Chrysostom's reference to baptism: "For when we immerse our heads in the water, the old man is buried as in a tomb below, and wholly sunk for ever; then as we raise them again, the new man rises in its stead. As it is easy to dip and lift our heads again, so it is easy for God to bury the old man, and to show forth the new. And this is done thrice, that you may learn that the power of the Father, the Son, and the Holy Ghost fulfilleth all things."—*Homilies on St. John, Part 1, page 211, 212.*

Mr. Robinson, in giving the manner in which the

Christians of the middle ages baptized, represents the candidate as standing, and the administrator as bowing him gently forward till he is under the water.—*History of Baptism, page 497.*

The forward action seems to commend itself as the more proper and consistent way of performing immersion even to some of those who practice the mode of putting the candidate into the water in a supine manner. Dr. Judson was a Baptist, but he considered the forward action the apostolic method of performing immersion, as the following from his pen will show:

"Immersion, however, maintained its ground, until the middle of the seventeenth century, when the Westminster Assembly of Divines voted, by a majority of one, that immersion and sprinkling were indifferent. Previously to that period, the Baptists had formed churches in different parts of the country; and having always seen infants, when baptized, taken in the hands of the administrator, and laid under water in the baptismal font, and not having much, if any, communication with the Baptists on the continent, they thought, of course, that a candidate for baptism, though a grown person, should be treated in the same manner, and laid backward under the water. They were probably confirmed in this idea, by the phrase, 'buried in baptism.' The consequence has been, that all the Baptists in the world, who have sprung from the English Baptists, have practiced the backward posture.

"But from the beginning, it was not so. In the apostolic times, the administrator placed his right hand on the head of the candidate, who then, under the pressure of the administrator's hand, bowed forward, aided by that genuflection, which instinctively comes to one's aid, when attempting to bow in the practice, until his head was submerged, and rose by his own effort."—*Judson on Baptism, page 112.*

Mr. Isaac Errett, of Cincinnati, one of the most able and influential ministers and writers among the Disciples, and editor of the *Christian Standard*, a leading paper in that church, in replying to a correspondent's query involving the manner of putting a person into the water when he is baptized, gives the following candid answer upon that subject: "As to the *mode* of the immersion, whether forward or backward, we have no certain knowledge. But we incline to the opinion that the backward motion in immersion is *modern and western—that in the east the candidates knelt in the water, and were immersed face foremost.*"—*Christian Standard.*

2. The following from Mr. Robinson will explain

the origin of the backward action of immersion among the modern single immersionists: "The first English Baptists, when they read the phrase *buried* in baptism, instantly thought of an *English* burial, and therefore baptized by laying the body in the form of burying in their own country; but they might have observed that Paul wrote to Romans, and that the Romans did not bury, but burned their dead, and buried nothing of the dead but their ashes in urns: so that no fair reasoning on the form of baptizing can be drawn from the mode of burying the dead in England."—*History of Baptism, page 500, 501.*

To take the apostle's figure of a burial to which he compares baptism, Rom. 6:4; Col. 2:12, to govern us in regard to the posture we assume when we are immersed, does not seem to be advisable, as such a course must necessarily lead to a variety of postures, as the customs of burying the dead in different nations are so very different, as will appear from the following account of burial customs given by Burder in his *Religious Ceremonies:*

Pagan Nations. The coffin was laid in the tomb on its back; in what direction among the Romans is uncertain; but among the Athenians, looking to the west.—Page 572.

Funeral Ceremonies of the Russian Greek Church. "To conclude, the coffin is nailed up and let down into the grave, the face of the deceased being turned towards the east."—Page 189.

Persian Ceremonies. The graves are smaller in Persia than in other countries, only two feet broad, six in length, and four in depth. On that side of them which is toward Mecca, they dig a slanting vault, which is as long and broad as the first grave; they thrust the corpse into it without a coffin, the face towards Mecca, and place two tiles to cover the head from the earth, when the grave is filled up.—Page 134.

Polynesians. "When about to be interred, the corpse was placed in a sitting posture, with the knees elevated, the face pressed down between the knees, the hands fastened under the legs, and the whole body tied with a cord."—Page 695.

Now as there is no uniformity among the nations in regard to burial customs, it is not at all probable that the posture of the body in baptism would be left to be governed by those customs. And as Mr. Robinson justly remarks in the quotation we have made from him, "No fair reasoning on the form of baptizing can be drawn from the mode of burying the dead in England." And we may add, nor from the mode of burying the dead in any other nation.

And as the idea that our Lord bowed in his baptism, and was baptized by a forward motion, is so generally accepted as we have seen it seems to be; and as his disciples baptized by John were in all probability baptized in the same way; and as it is also probable that they baptized what they did in the same manner in which they themselves were baptized, and as there was no change apparently made, the bowing posture and the forward motion have much to recommend them.

CHAPTER XVII.

REVIEW OF DR. FORNEY.

DR. Forney is a minister of "the Church of God," the organization that Mr. John Winebrenner commenced. He is also the editor of the *Church Advocate*, the church organ of his denomination.

Dr. Forney is the author of a work having the following title: *The Christian Ordinances; Being a Historical Inquiry into the Practice of Trine Immersion, the Washing of the Saints' Feet and Love-feast.*

The Doctor kindly sent us a copy of his work, but as we were preparing our book for publication, and expecting at the time to have it ready for the press before very long, and regarding some of his positions to be of such a character as to make a notice of them a proper subject for our book, we deferred a notice of the work until we should publish our own. We have thus delayed noticing his book a longer time than we desired, but we could not well do otherwise. With due respect to the

Doctor and his book, we shall notice the principal points in his work bearing on trine immersion. He has referred to us, and to some of our writing in a way that makes it proper for us to notice his work. And fidelity to the mode of immersion which is as dear to us, as the Doctor's favorite mode can possibly be to him, imposes upon us the duty of noticing some of his positions. The headings of his chapters will furnish us with points that will enable us to present what we may think should be presented, and what our limited space yet remaining, will allow us to present.

1. The testimony for Trine Immersion. This is the heading of one of the chapters of the Doctor's work. The Doctor endeavors to destroy the historic testimonies both of a direct, and indirect character, cited to prove trine immersion, intimating that as the historians lived after the time in which the events recorded occurred, their testimony is not reliable. He says, "It is a recognized principle in all rules of evidence, that *in testifyieg to a question of fact, no man is a competent witness who lived after the fact, except in so far as he cites authorities or witnesses who lived at the time.*" The italicizing is the Doctor's. The above principle is only partially applicable to historians. What historians state as facts should be facts. But historians do not always cite the authorities for the facts they state. We have before us in our library, *Gibbon's Rome*. He wrote of things that occurred long before his time, and he does not always cite his authorities. The case is this in regard to all kinds of history. The historian should be a man of truth as well as of talents. And if he has the confidence of his readers, what he states as facts will be believed, though he does not give his authority. They will take it for granted that he had authority for what he stated, and it will be believed. A historian may be criticised and if it is found that he has not stated the truth, his statements should be rejected. But if his statements cannot be disproved, we are bound to receive them.

The Doctor, entertaining such principles as above stated, says, "they" meaning trine immersionists, "frequently cite Dr. Wall, Doctor Hinton, and other modern authors. But these we dismiss at once, for their testimony is wholly second handed." And does the Doctor reject all testimony that is second-handed? Then he does not believe much history.

But let us examine the cases the Doctor intended his principle to apply to. Now let us hear Dr. Wall. This well known and popular author read all the authors of antiquity that he had access to, and searched most diligently the records of antiquity to find infant baptism. But he did not find it in the times immediately after the apostles, though he thought he did. But he found trine immersion. This is what he says: "The way of trine immersion or plunging the head of the person three times in the water, was the general practice of all antiquity." —*History of Infant Baptism, Vol. II, page 419.* Now, however Dr. Wall obtained his testtmony, it must have been strong and satisfactory. He spoke with positiveness.

And so in regard to the statement of Theodoret and Sozomon. These two writers of ecclesiastical history both allude to what is stated by many writers to be a fact, namely, that Eunomius corrupted the ordinance of baptism by substituting the single for the trine immersion. We have said, both these writers allude to Eunomius as making the change. But let us see how they allude to it. Theodoret thus alludes to it: "He (Eunomius) subverted the law of holy baptism, which had been handed down from the beginning from the Lord and the apostles, and made a contrary law, asserting that it is not necessary to immerse the candidate for baptism thrice, nor to mention the names of the Trinity, but to immerse once only into the death of Christ."—*Chrystal's History of the Modes of Baptism, page 78.* Theodoret speaks positively. And, no doubt, he felt he was declaring the truth. He lived in the century following that in which Eunomius lived. We may reasonably suppose he knew whereof he affirmed. Sozomen says, "Some say that this Eunomius was the first who dared to bring forward the notion, that the divine baptism ought to be administered by a single immersion," &c.—*Ibid, page 78.* Sozomen was not sure that it was Eunomius who changed baptism from the trine to the single action. And hence he speaks with caution. His language shows that he knew a change had been made. And, further, it shows that it was not Theodoret alone who believed that Eunomius changed the form of baptism.

We cannot regard these writers as the Doctor seems to have done. He makes some insinuations that we think he should not have made. He says, in speaking of Theodoret, "As to baptism by a three-fold immersion, he testifies that it was abandoned by Eunomius, though it had been handed down from the beginning from the Lord by *tradition*. Whether it was a true or false tradition he did not inquire."—page 21. There are two points in this language of the Doctor to which we must take exception. In the Doctor's language, tradition is italicized by him. Now the reader will find by referring to our quotation from James Chrystal's work, of Theodoret's language, that he, Theodoret, does not say that trine immersion had been handed down from the beginning from the Lord and the apostles, by *tradition*. He simply says, "He subverted the law of holy baptism, which had been handed down from the beginning from the Lord and the apostles." What would Dr. Forney think if he should preach that immersion was handed down from Christ and the apostles, and somebody would report that he preached that it was handed down by *tradition*. Would he not think that he had been misrepresented? Theodoret had the Scriptures. And he believed it had been handed down through them. So affirms Bingham. After declaring that Chrysostom made trine immersion a part of the first institution, and quotes him as referring trine immersion to the formula of baptism given by Christ, he says, "And Theodoret was of the same opinion: for he charges Eunomius as making an innovation upon the original institution of baptism, delivered by Christ and his apostles."—*Bingham's Antiquities of the Christian Church, Book XI, Chapter XI.*

The Doctor makes another insinuation that reflects upon the character of Theodoret. It is in the quotation we made. After representing Theodoret as saying the three-fold immersion had been handed down by tradition, the Doctor says, in referring to Theodoret, "Whether it was a true or false tradition he did not inquire." See our quotation from Dr. Forney. This is a pretty hard charge. It is representing Theodoret as being a very careless writer. We have seen that he did not use the word *tradition*. And if he had used it, how did the Doctor know that Theodoret had not inquired to ascertain whether the tradition was true or false. Surely Theodoret never said that he had not so inquired.

The Doctor, in the chapter we are noticing, has showed a very strong desire to invalidate the testimony of historians favoring trine immersion. We presume he has felt the force of their testimony. And if he can weaken that testimony by proper means, he has a lawful right to do so. But we must regard some of his remarks in regard to the witnesses referred to, as injudicious. And as we have quoted Theodoret, we feel that it is proper for us to vindicate his character, as far as it can be fairly vindicated. Any historian that is careless in his examination of facts, and reckless in his statements, is not worthy of confidence. But we have no reason to believe that such was the case with Theodoret.

Then when writers, whether historians, reformers, or theologians, bear testimony to the primitive or apostolic character of trine immersion, we receive their testimony as the result of their judgments with the information they possessed, whether that information was obtained from their personal knowledge, or through other sources, and the weight of authority to which their testimony is entitled, will depend upon various circumstances.

Our eleventh and twelfth chapters contain testimony more or less of the character above alluded to, and when that testimony is candidly examined, though much of it has been given long since the apostolic age, still, when we consider the character of the witnesses, and the circumstances under which the testimony has been given, and find as we shall do, that they were intelligent men, and disinterested witnesses, their testimony should have considerable influence.

2. *Testimony of the Early Fathers.* Such is the heading of one of the Doctor's chapters. He examines several of the early Fathers, but does not, according to his judgment, find anything of importance in them for trine immersion. We shall find

something more. He first notices Chrysostom. The words of Chrysostom alluded to, are these: "Christ delivered to his disciples one baptism in three immersions of the body, when he said to them, 'Go, teach all nations.'" The Doctor says, in quoting this passage, "It would be a justifiable act to reject this testimony entirely, if it may be dignified as testimony. The reason is, that it does not state a matter of fact at all, but simply gives an opinion. He does not say that trine immersion was *practiced* in his day, though we are ready to concede that it was. But his testimony is worthless to establish that fact."—Page 26, 27. The foregoing words of Chrysostom do not contain his only testimony to trine immersion. He says also, "For when we immerse our heads in the water, the old man is buried as in a tomb below, and wholly sunk forever; then as we raise them again, the new man rises in its stead. As it is easy for us to dip and lift our heads again, so it is easy for God to bury the old man, and to shew forth the new. And this is done thrice, that you may learn that the power of the Father, the Son, and the Holy Ghost fulfilleth all this."—*Homilies on John, Homil XXV.* This is clear testimony, and shows not only that Chrysostom carried out his own views of baptism, but it shows it was the practice of the Church in his day, "For when *we* immerse our heads in the water," &c. This indicates it was the common practice. Then what have we in the case of Chrysostom? He was a learned Greek. He retired awhile from the world, and shut himself up in a cave, and studied most diligently and prayerfully the Scriptures. And after all his study, and his acquaintance with the Greek language, and his knowledge of the Scriptures, when he read the baptismal formula, "baptizing them into the name of the Father, and of the Son," &c., he believed the language conveyed the idea of a trine immersion. And this surely, is a considerable testimony for trine immersion. Then he was a witness to the practice of trine immersion in his day.

We are sorry the Doctor did not understand more fully the case of James Chrystal. He says, "that we are not putting it too strongly when we say that the words quoted from Chrysostom do not prove that trine immersion was practiced in his day can be readily illustrated. Mark, he does not say it was *practiced*. Mr. Chrystal, in his *History of the Modes of Baptism*, declares just as unequivocally as Chrysostom, that 'Christ delivered one baptism in three immersions.' Yet Mr. Chrystal was an Episcopalian, and practiced as his church does—sprinkling, and not trine immersion." James Chrystal received trine immersion from a Greek Bishop, and has organized a church with trine immersion as the form of baptism. He is consistent in regard to trine immersion, as Chrysostom also was.

We next notice Ambrose among the Early Fathers the Doctor mentions. The Doctor quotes Ambrose, but quotes him as testifying not to trine immersion, but to only two immersions. We give the Doctor's language: "We do not say that three actions were not common under Ambrose; but he certainly does not so testify. An advocate of trine immersion has acknowledged this. He says, 'He only speaks of the two first actions in baptism; the other, in the name of the Holy Ghost, must be inferred.' In that way it is easy to derive trine immersion by tradition from the Apostles. It is unscientific and misleading. It is known to all readers of church history that the distinct personality of the Son was first defined, and not until a later Council was the equally distinct personality of the Spirit accepted. Hence in the testimony of Ambrose we may have a hint as to the origin of trine immersion. We do not affirm this, for it is not in evidence as yet; but we have ample reason to believe that such was the origin of the three-fold immersion or baptism."—Page 29.

It will be seen from the above, that the Doctor found the familiar passage in Ambrose, for it is familiar to those who are acquainted with the writings of the ancient Fathers, in somewhat of an abridged or imperfect form, and conceived the idea from it, that it was a step from single to trine immersion. But we wonder that the Doctor entertained such a thought, as according to his concession, trine immersion was quite general before the close of the third century, see page 10 of his book, and Ambrose was not born until about A. D. 340, according to Dr. Lardner. If we were inclined to draw upon our imagination for ideas, rather than to reason them out logically, or to obtain them from historic facts, we would say, if we received Ambrose's two immersions, as correct, that this was the beginning of a departure from the trine to the single immersion. But we do not say so. And the Doctor's theory is spoiled when we pronounce his reading an incorrect reading of Ambrose. And such no doubt it is. The Doctor, we presume, read it in an abridged form, and thought it was designed as the whole. And so the "advocate of trine immersion" to whom the doctor refers, must have read it. We are much surprised that such a mistake was made. And the more so, as the Doctor refers to James Chrystal's *History of the Modes of Baptism*, which would indicate that he read that work. The passage from Ambrose is in James Chrystal's book in full, the three questions and the three immersions. Bingham also has the three immersions, with the three questions.

We shall briefly refer to Monulus, one of the Early Fathers to which the Doctor refers. There was a Council called at Carthage, A. D. 256, comprised of eighty-seven Bishops. Monulus was one, and the following is his language: "The true doctrine of our holy mother, the catholic church, hath always, my brethren, been with us, and especially in the article of baptism, and the trine immersion wherewith it is celebrated; our Lord having said: *Go ye, and baptize the Gentiles, in the name of the Father, and of the Son, and of the Holy Ghost.—Marshall's Translation, Vol. I, page 241*. Such is the testimony of a Bishop in the Council of Carthage, A. D. 256. It is very clear. He declared that trine immersion had been always with them. And he does not refer it to tradition, but to the words of Christ.

And how does Dr. Forney dispose of this? He

seeks to weaken it, as he usually does such testimony. He says, "There are some rather suspicious circumstances connected with it." And what are the suspicious circumstances? "It is said," the Doctor remarks, "that this language was used 'at the famous Council of Carthage.'" But "no Ecumenical Council was ever held at Carthage," the Doctor says. Can no council be famous but an Ecumenical Council? Surely other councils may be famous. And this one was famous, for it was composed of eighty-seven bishops, and it had under consideration subjects of great interest to the Church at that time. The Doctor says he had not been able to verify the quotation, though he had diligently examined the works of Cyprian. This is very strange! We have two copies of Cyprian's Works, and it is in both. It is in the copy of his Works which is in the Ante-Nicene Library. The passage is all right, and it is a strong testimony for trine immersion. The other testimonies, those of Cyril, Augustine, and the Apostolic Constitution, all are on the side of trine immersion, but as there is nothing special connected with them, we shall not notice them further.

3. *The first witnesses for trine immersion.* This is the heading of the 5th chapter of the Doctor's book. He says: "The concurrent testimony of his-

torians and archæologists is that Tertullian is the first author who speaks of trine immersion." P. 35. After quoting the following well-known, but misapplied passage from Tertullian, "Then we are thrice dipped, answering somewhat more than the Lord prescribed in the gospel," he says, "Here we have trine immersion, as conceded in the opening of this discussion; but beyond this it is not possible to carry it." P. 36. To this we reply:

First: The idea has obtained very extensively among learned men of research and judgment, and who had no prejudices in favor of trine immersion, that this mode of immersion was the original manner of performing Christian baptism. We refer the reader to chapters XI and XII, where he will find the testimony of such men as we above referred to, showing that they believed that trine immersion existed before the time of Tertullian, even as early as the Apostolic age. It is therefore very evident that testimony for trine immersion is to be found beyond the time of Tertullian and before A. D. 200, according to the judgment of the authors quoted, or they never could, and they never would have affirmed so positively that trine immersion was the original manner of baptizing.

Secondly: We have shown in chapter XI that Justin

Martyr is a witness to trine immersion. And we recommend the reader to carefully examine what we have said in regard to the passage in Justin, in which he explains the manner in which baptism was performed in his day. A careful reading of the passage in Justin to which reference has been made, and to our remarks upon it, will, we think, convince the candid reader that trine immersion was plainly recognized by Justin in his description of the manner of baptizing in his time.

Inasmuch as Dr. Forney has misunderstood and misapplied the language of Justin, it seems to be necessary that we here should give his language again, and we shall do so. The Doctor justly remarks, "The testimony of Justin Martyr is of great importance in this connection. He was born about A. D. 89. . . . . He is the recognized link between the apostolic Fathers and the more distinct periods of the early church." P. 51. As the testimony of Justin is important, we want it read just as it was given by him. In describing the manner in which Christians of his time baptized, after alluding to the preparation of the candidate for baptism, he says: "Then they are brought by us where there is water, and are regenerated in the same manner in which we were ourselves regenerated. For in the name of God, the Father and Lord of the universe, and of our Saviour Jesus Christ, and of the Holy Spirit, they then receive the washing with water. For Christ also said, 'Except ye be born again, ye shall not enter into the kingdom of heaven.' Now, that it is impossible for those who have once been born to enter into their mother's wombs, is manifest to all. And how those who have sinned and repent shall escape their sins, is declared by Esaias the prophet, as I wrote above; he thus speaks: 'Wash you, make you clean; put away the evil of your doings from your souls; learn to do well; judge the fatherless, and plead for the widow; and come and let us reason together, saith the Lord. And though your sins be as scarlet, I will make them white like wool; and though they be as crimson, I will make them white as snow. But if ye refuse and rebel, the sword shall devour you: for the mouth of the Lord hath spoken it.'

"And for this [rite] we have learned from the apostles this reason. Since at our birth we were born without our own knowledge or choice, by our parents coming together, and were brought up in bad habits and wicked training; in order that we may not remain the children of necessity and of ignorance, but may become the children of choice and knowledge, and may obtain in the water the remission of sins formerly committed, there is pronounced over him who chooses to be born again, and has repented of his sins, the name of God the Father and Lord of the universe; he who leads to the laver the person who is to be washed calling him by this name alone. For no one can utter the name of the ineffable God; and if any one dare to say that there is a name, he raves with hopeless madness. And this washing is called illumination, because they who learn these things are illuminated in their understandings. And in the name of Jesus Christ, who was crucified under Pontius Pilate, and in the name of the Holy Ghost, who through the prophets foretold all things about Jesus, he who is illuminated is washed."—*The Writings of Justin Martyr*, pp. 59, 60.

It will be noticed that in Justin's description of the manner of baptizing, there is a considerable amount of explanation given. He seems to have thought this was necessary. Let it be also observed, that he describes the manner of using the formula for baptizing twice, first in its abridged, or elliptical form, saying it was done "in the name of God, the Father and Lord of the universe, and of our Saviour Jesus Christ, and of the Holy Spirit." This corresponds with the elliptical, or abridged form of the formula as we have it in the written form given by our Lord. Then we have it in a full form with name preceding each of the three divine Persons named in the baptismal formula, and into each of whom the believer is baptized, thus: "There is pronounced over him who chooses to be born again, and has repented of his sins, the name of God the Father and Lord of the universe; he who leads to the laver the person that is to be washed calling him by this name alone. . . . And in the name of Jesus Christ, who was crucified under Pontius Pilate, and in the name of the Holy Ghost." This last form is equivalent to *into the name of the Father, and into the name of the Son, and into the name of the Holy Spirit*. But this form is the form that Dr. Conant and others say the baptismal formula should have to require trine immersion. Dr. Conant says, in referring to the practice of trine immersion, "To justify such a practice, the form should have been, either 'in the names of,' or 'in the name of the Father, and in the name of the Son, and in the name of the Holy Spirit.'" Therefore, as Justin gives the form of baptizing, that Dr. Conant says it should have to justify trine immersion, Justin is manifestly a witness to the practice of trine immersion in his day.

Dr. Forney has misinterpreted Justin's language, and that, too, in a way which seriously affects its meaning, and hence we notice it. The Doctor gives correctly the first part of Justin's description of the manner of baptizing. And after he gives the first part, he continues to quote Justin as follows: "Further on he says: 'The name of God, the Father and Lord of the universe, is pronounced over him who is willing to be born again, and hath repented of his sins; he who leads him to be washed [or bathed] in the laver of baptism saying this only over him.'" Now, according to the above reading of the Doctor's book, he makes Justin say, that the administrator of baptism pronounced only the name of God, the Father and Lord of the Universe, over him that was baptized. Whereas, if the whole of the last part of Justin's description of baptizing is read, it is plain that "the name of Jesus Christ" and "the name of the Holy Ghost" were also pronounced, or repeated in the performance of baptism. It was not the name of God "only" that was pronounced, for we have seen there were two other names into which the believer was baptized, or which were pronounced over him. But the qualifying word "only," or "alone," as "alone" is used in the *Writings of Justin Martyr,* in the Ante-Nicene Library, as will be seen in our quotations, refers to the name of the first person in the Godhead that was used in baptism. It was the name of "God the Father and Lord of the universe," and no other of the several names which are applied to him, that was to be the first name used in baptism.

Webster, in explaining the term JEHOVAH, has the following in the explanation: "the sacred, unpronounceable name of the Eternal." And this probably is the "ineffable" name referred to by Justin, and which was not to be used;—"the name of God the Father and Lord of the universe," was the name of the first person in the Godhead that was to be used in baptism, "he who leads to the laver the person who is to be washed calling him by this name *alone.*" The administrator was to use the name of God alone as the first name he was to call over the person baptized, or it was to be the first name into which the person that desired to be born again, was to be baptized. After this the person baptized was baptized into the name of Jesus Christ, and into the name of the Holy Ghost, according to Justin, and he thus recognizes in his baptism a trine immersion.

In Reeve's translation of Justin, the latter part of the description of the way of baptizing is made somewhat plainer, and we shall here insert it. It is as follows: "The penitent, who now makes his *Second Birth* an act of his *own choice*, has called over him the Name of God the Father and Lord of all things (when we conduct the Person to be baptized to the Place of Baptism, we call God by no other Name because we have not any appellation for the *ineffable Majesty* of God, that can explain his Nature, and if any man pretends to that, We think him *mad* in the highest Degree: this baptism is called *Illumination* because the Minds of the Catechumens who are thus washed are Illuminated) and moreover the Person baptized and Illuminated is baptized in the *Name* of Jesus Christ who was crucified under Pontius Pilate, and in the *Name* of the Holy Ghost." By omitting the parenthetical part of the foregoing, and reading the remainder, it will read very much like the baptismal formula with the ellipses supplied, —baptizing them into the name of the Father, and in the name of the Son, and in the name of the Holy Ghost, which indicates a trine immersion.

Thirdly: In our XIth chapter, that on the Historical aspect of trine immersion, we have traced, logically and plainly, trine immersion to the Apostolic age. There must therefore have been witnesses beyond the time of Tertullian, from which the Church historians obtained their information upon which they affirmed the early practice of trine immersion.

4. Testimony in favor of immersion before A. D. 200. The Dr. has a chapter under the above heading, in which he labors to prove that the Apostolic Fathers ."speak at some length of *immersion*," but "are all totally silent touching trine immersion."— P. 43. The Doctor says in the same connection, "In some instances they could not readily avoid testifying in favor of trine immersion had it been in vogue." See the testimonies of Barnabas and Hermas on page 200 of our work. The Doctor is surely not warranted in excluding trine immersion so positively from the testimonies of those Fathers, and in making them speak at "length of immersion." They do not directly and positively testify of immersion. It was not apparently their design to testify to the action of baptism, but rather of its happy effects. They testify of going down into the water, and of coming up out of the water. They, no doubt, were immersed. But this is to be inferred from the circumstance that they went into the water, and from the meaning of the word that expresses the ordinance which they obeyed. Whether they were immersed once or thrice, cannot be learned from what is said by them of baptism. They say nothing to prove a single immersion, or to disprove a trine immersion. Whatever the baptismal formula given by Christ required, they undoubtedly did when they went down into the water.

We must remark again that for the first two hundred years after its organization, there was no general change in the doctrine and practice of the church; and there being no great change in its ordinances, there was no necessity for a special defence of them. And it was particularly so in regard to baptism. And hence this ordinance was simply referred to, and but little said designed to prove the manner in which it was to be performed, as it was presumed this would be understood. In our chapter XI, in which we have discussed our subject in its historical aspects, we have proved, and that from Baptist testimony, that there was no change in baptism in the third century from what it was in the second, and that there was no change in the second century from what it was in the first. Hence we have so little in the first 200 years of the history of the Church, said in regard to the action of baptism.

In later ages we find more said in regard to it, as there was not the same harmony in the views of Christians concerning it.

The advocates of sprinkling make the same objection to immersion because the history of the church for the first 200 years is so silent on it, that the Doctor makes against trine immersion. See our reference to the *Braden-Hughy Debate,* in the sixth section of the present chapter. Others besides Mr. Hughy have taken the same position. We refer the reader to chapter XI of our work, for proof that Tertullian was not the first witness for trine immersion.

Dr. Schaff has published an edition of *The Teaching of the Twelve Apostles,* an ancient document that has excited considerable interest in the Christian world. He considers it an important document, and has given it considerable attention. In considering various things bearing upon its date, he comes to the following conclusion concerning the time it was written: "We may therefore assign the *Didache* with some confidence to the closing years of the first century, say between A. D. 90 and 100." P. 122. He speaks of its character in the following honorable manner: "It takes its place among the genuine documents of the Apostolic Fathers, so called—Clement of Rome, Polycarp, Ignatius, Barnabas, Hermas."—P. 14. In remarking upon the article on baptism, Dr. Schaff says: "Baptism must be administered into the triune name (*eis to honoma*) of the Father, and the Son, and the Holy Spirit. This is the prescribed form of Christ (Matt. 28:19). The shorter form 'into the name of Jesus,' is not mentioned. The normal and favorite mode of baptism is threefold immersion 'in living water,' *i. e.* fresh, running water, either in a stream or fountain, as distinct from standiug water in a pool or cistern." In a note the Doctor adds, "'Three times' is only mentioned in connection with pouring, but must, of course, be supplied in the normal form of immersion."—Page 32. Then, according to Dr. Schaff, this witness for trine immersion is as old as are the Apostolic Fathers.

In giving the early date to the *Didache* that Dr. Schaff gives it, he dates its origin in the Apostolic age, as the Apostle John, at least, was living when he believes it was written. And by giving the document the early date that he has given it, and by declaring that trine immersion is the "normal mode" of baptism taught in it, Dr. Schaff has virtually revoked what he said in regard to trine im mersion when he said, "The old practice of a *three-*

fold immersion, which is first mentioned by Tertullian, is a venerable usage, but cannot be traced to the Apostolic age (see Dr. Schaff's note on Matt. 28: 19, in Lange's Commentary), for he admits that trine immersion can be traced to the Apostolic age, according to what he has written concerning the *Teaching of the Twelve Apostles.*

But why does Dr. Forney dwell so much upon the silence concerning trine immersion among the ancient Fathers, when the same silence obtains to a very great degree concerning feet-washing? As the title of the Doctor's book shows, as we have given it, he wrote upon the ordinance of feet-washing in its historical aspect, as well as upon the historical aspect of trine immersion. And in treating of feet-washing, he has a chapter under the heading, "*The Post-Apostolic Practice of Feet-Washing.*" The first authority for feet-washing after the age of the apostles that the Doctor cites, is Justin. He does not cite one of the Apostolic Fathers. And why does he not cite some of them? We presume it was because he found them "all totally silent touching" feet-washing, as he declares they were touching trine immersion. And if their silence is so much against trine immersion, is it any the less against feet-washing? It certainly is not. And as the Doctor does not, we presume, consider the silence of the Apostolic Fathers upon the subject of feet-washing as an evidence that it was not practiced in their time, he should not urge their silence upon trine immersion as an evidence that *it* was not practiced in their age.

The Doctor says in referring to Justin as a witness to feet-washing, "He is the first author after the Apostles, so far as we know, in whose writings this subject is mentioned. We have not his words at our command, and so can only state upon the authority of others that he speaks of the washing of feet as a religious rite."—P. 106. We are somewhat surprised that the Doctor did not himself examine Justin so that he could upon his own authority declare him to be a witness to the washing of feet as a religious rite. We presume he could have had access to Justin's works. But the Doctor has quoted a considerable amount of testimony second-handed to prove that the ancient Christians washed feet as a religious rite, though he depreciated so much, such testimony in defence of trine immersion. And in this he is not very consistent.

We doubt whether any testimony for feet-washing as a religious rite is to be found in the writings of Justin Martyr. We do not affirm there is no such testimony, for this we would not do without carefully reading Justin's works. And this we cannot now do. We have examined his writings to some extent, but find no testimony to feet-washing as a religious rite. And from the circumstance that Dr. Forney does not refer to such testimony, and from other circumstances, we entertain some doubts whether there is such testimony in Justin's writings.

If Justin is a witness to feet-washing, the Doctor has but one witness in his historical argument for feet-washing in about 225 years, as he claims none after Justin until the time of Origin. And he claims none before Justin—none among the Apostolic Fathers. Such being the fact in regard to testimony among the ancient Fathers concerning feet-washing, according to the Doctor's own claims, he cannot with any propriety whatever, urge with so much persistency as he has done, the silence of the ancient Fathers upon trine immersion as an argument against its divine authority, as the same argument may be used against feet-washing.

5. *Trine Immersion based on Tradition.* In the chapter of his work having the above heading, the Doctor says: "We hence propose to show further that the weight of testimony, even in the times when trine immersion was so widely practiced, is in favor of its traditionary origin." P. 57. This is the

common opinion of single immersionists. We did something to refute this error in the tenth chapter of our work, but as Dr. Forney has said so much upon the subject of tradition, we shall say something more to set the Ancient Fathers right upon the subject of trine immersion.

Tertullian, Jerome, Basil, and other ancient Fathers practiced trine immersion, as is universally admitted. But Dr. Forney and single immersionists say, that they practiced it upon the authority of tradition alone. Now single immersionists hold that those ancient Fathers believed immersion to be the action of baptism taught in the Scriptures. And if single immersionists were asked what mode of immersion they thought those ancient Fathers believed was taught in the Scriptures, the answer undoubtedly would be, single immersion. Then those ancient Fathers found, according to the views of single immersionists, single immersion in the Scriptures, and trine immersion in the traditionary teaching in the times in which they lived. And by practicing trine immersion and not single, they plainly exalted tradition above the Scriptures, and also made tradition and the Scriptures contradict each other. This is the unavoidable conclusion that we must come to in accepting the theory of single immersionists that the ancient Fathers believed in single immersion as taught in the Scriptures, and yet practiced trine immersion. And such a conclusion fastens a stigma upon their Christian characters which renders them utterly unworthy of the least respect as Christian teachers. We quote a passage in the Doctor's book in reference to Basil. It is on page 60.

"Basil (died A. D. 379) furnishes strong testimony for our position. With others of the Fathers of the Church, he speaks of immersion as having been established as an ordinance by the Lord, but that *trine* immersion was derived through tradition. Thus he says: 'There is but one death for the world and one resurrection from the dead, of both which baptism [or immersion, as Chrystal renders it, an advocate of trine immersion] is a type. Therefore has the Lord, the dispenser of life, *established* the rite of baptism [immersion—Chrystal] for us, that it might afford a figure of death and life.' But when he refers to the three-fold baptism, or triple immersion, he states that it was derived through tradition (De Spirit. Sanct., CXXVII)." Would Dr. Forney have us to understand that Basil referred to single immersion when he speaks of baptism in the above language attributed to him? It would seem so. But surely we cannot accept of such an idea.

Whenever he refers to Christian baptism, he refers to trine immersion. In connection with the above ideas, Basil has the following: "In three immersions, therefore, and in the same number of invocations, the great mystery of baptism is finished, so that both the figure of death is exhibited and the souls of the baptized are illuminated by the transmission (or gift) of the knowledge of God."—*History of the Modes of Baptism*, p. 71. In the language above quoted, Basil expressly names trine immersion, showing plainly that it is trine immersion that he means when he speaks of immersion in the passage quoted by Dr. Forney. We cannot then avoid the conclusion, that if those ancient Fathers believed immersion was taught in the Scriptures, they believed it was trine immersion.

Though we have said something in the tenth chapter of our work to correct the error which has been circulated through a wrong interpretation of a passage in the writings of Tertullian, as Dr. Forney has repeated the error, and tried to justify the misconstruction of Tertullian's language, we shall offer further testimony to correct the error to which an allusion is above made. The error is that which makes Tertullian say, that trine immersion is more than the Lord commanded. Such was his scholarship, his zeal, and his piety, and living so near the Apostolic age that he did, he possessed considerable influence in the church at the time in which he lived, and his writings still possess considerable influence, as is shown by the frequent use that is made of them. And very frequent use has been made of the passage we have referred to, against trine immersion. And we have no doubt that it has had much influence in producing the strong prejudice that exists against trine immersion. We therefore feel that a full exposition of the error is demanded in our discussion of trine immersion.

We shall quote the passage in Tertullian, in which his words occur, that have been so erroneously construed. He says: "To deal with this matter briefly, I shall begin with baptism. When we are going to enter the water but a little before, in the presence of the congregation and under the hand of the president, we solemnly profess that we disown the devil, and his pomp, and his angels. Hereupon we are thrice immersed, making a somewhat ampler pledge than the Lord has appointed in the Gospel. Then, when we are taken up [as new-born children], we taste first of all a mixture of milk and honey, and from that day we refrain from the daily bath for a whole week. We take also, in meetings before daybreak, and from the hand of none but the presidents, the sacrament of the Eucharist, which the Lord both commanded to be eaten at meal-times, and enjoined to be taken by all [alike]. As often as the anniversary comes round, we make offerings for the dead as birthday honors. We count fasting or kneeling on the Lord's day to be unlawful. We rejoice in the same privilege also from Easter to Whitsunday. We feel pained should any wine or bread, even though our own, be cast upon the ground. At every forward step and movement, and every going in and out, when we put on our clothes and shoes, when we bathe, when we sit at table, when we light the lamps, on couch or seat, in all the ordinary actions of daily life, we trace upon the forehead the sign [of the cross]. If for these and other such rules, you insist upon having positive Scripture injunction, you will find none. Tradition will be held forth to you as the originator of them, custom as their strengthener, and faith as their observer."—*Ante-Nicene Christian Library, Vol. XI, pp. 336, 337.*

Now the question is, how much ampler was the pledge they made than the Lord in the gospel commanded? Dr. Forney and many of the single immersionists say it was two dips in baptism. Some of the advocates of sprinkling say it was the three dips.

In a lengthy debate between Mr. Braden, of the Disciple church, and Mr. Hughy, of the M. E. church, the latter says, "The gentleman asserted that I misrepresented Tertullian. Tertullian says: 'We are immersed three times, fulfilling somewhat more than our Lord in the gospel commands.' Mr. Braden says that Tertullian meant that the two extra dips were more than 'our Lord in the gospel commands;' but what authority has he for that statement? I say Tertullian meant 'the three extra dips,' that he meant immersion was 'fulfilling somewhat more than our Lord in the gospel commands.' I challenge the gentleman to show a single case of immersion before the time of Tertullian, A. D. 200, and with the first mention of immersion we have the acknowledgment, it is 'more than our Lord requires!' Tertullian never heard of the single dip in baptism."—*Braden-Hughy Debate, p. 152.* What do Dr. Forney and the single immersionists think of this? They, no doubt, think that Mr. Hughy's construction of Tertullian's language is a manifest misrepresentation of his meaning. And so we must regard the construction of Tertullian's language that makes him say, that the three immersions which were practiced in his time were "fulfilling somewhat more than our Lord in the gospel commands." With the same propriety that Dr. Forney and Mr. Hughy say that Tertullian meant that three immersions in baptism are more than the Lord commands, the Quaker Friends may say that he meant water baptism altogether.

It was evidently in regard to what is called the renunciation, that Tertullian says they made a somewhat ampler pledge than the Lord commands. This renunciation had been enlarged in Tertullian's time. "We disown the devil, and his pomp, and his angels." We have not this full form of renunciation given by our Lord in the gospel. And hence Tertullian could say as he did. And what they did on the authority of tradition was not trine immersion, but those ceremonies that he enumerates, as following baptism.

There are two reasons for believing that Tertullian did not design to say in the passage quoted, that trine immersion is more than the Lord required. *First.* His language fairly and intelligently construed, will plainly show his meaning is not what single immersionists put upon it. We have seen in the quotation that we have given above from his writings what he says according to his translator. We now give Dr. Duncan's rendering of the passage: "Being about to approach the water, both there, and also in the church a short time before, we testify, under the hand of the president, that we renounce the devil, his pomp, and his angels. Then we are immersed three times; having responded somewhat more at length than the Lord has determined in the Gospel."—*History of the Baptists*, pp. 128, 129. Alexander Campbell renders the passage thus: "To begin with baptism, when we are ready to enter into the water, and even before we make our protestations before the bishop, and in the church, that we renounce the devil, all his pomp and ministers: afterward, we are plunged in the water three times, and they make us answer to some things which are not precisely set down in the gospel."—*Campbell and Purcell Debate, p. 124.*

Dr. Forney says, in referring to Dr. Wall, on page 61 of his book, "And as quoted by Dr. Wall, Tertullian distinctly admits that the practice of trine immersion is without Scriptural authority." Now we shall give Dr. Wall's translation of the passage in Tertullian under consideration. It is as follows: "We do renounce the Devil, and his pomp, and his angels. Then we are three times plunged into the water: and we answer some few words more than those which our Saviour in the gospel has enjoined." *Wall's History of Infant Baptism, Vol. II, p. 420.*

It surely is not in the passage in Tertullian under consideration that Dr. Wall finds an admission by him that the practice of "trine immersion is without Scriptural authority." For Dr. Wall's rendering of the passage shows very plainly that what was more than the Lord requires, was not additional immersions in baptism, but the answering "*some few words more.*" Let this be carefully noticed. Dr. Wall's translation settles the matter, for it shows that it was not baptism that Tertullian alluded to when he speaks of doing something more than the Lord commanded.

We shall next give Dr. Conant's translation of the passage: "Then we are three times immersed, answering somewhat more than the Lord prescribed in the Gospel."—*Baptezein*, p. 77. Dr. Conant's translation is correct, but we think it was not judicious in him to detach the words he gives from the context, as they are likely to convey a wrong idea in being so detached.

Dr. Forney thus refers to Dr. Conant: "'Then we are three times immersed, answering [or fulfilling] somewhat more than the Lord prescribed in the Gospel.' This is Dr. Conant's translation, who is fully able to determine the meaning of Tertullian's words." If Dr. Conant was "fully able to determine the meaning of Tertullian's words," and translated *respondentes* "answering," why did Dr. Forney add "fulfilling" to answering in Dr. Conant's translation, as it will be seen he did, by comparing Dr. Conant's translation as we have given it, with his translation as given by Dr. Forney?

Let the reader carefully notice that in all the translations of Tertullian which we have given, from Dr. Duncan, Mr. Campbell, Dr. Wall, Dr. Conant, and the translator of Tertullian in the *Ante-Nicene Library*, not one translates *respondentes* by "fulfilling," as Dr. Forney would do. Three translate it by *answering*, one by *responding*, and one by *pledging*, clearly showing that it was the renunciation, and not the three immersions in baptism to which Tertullian alluded when he says, "Hereupon we are thrice immersed, making a somewhat ampler pledge than the Lord has appointed in the Gospel."

The second reason which we have for believing that Tertullian does not affirm in the passage we have been considering, that trine immersion is more than the Lord has commanded in the gospel, is contained in the fact, that he plainly declares that trine immersion is commanded in the gospel.

Dr. Forney introduces the passage at length from Tertullian which we have examined, and after using it as best he could, against trine immersion, he proceeds to say, "Trine immersion is introduced only in this connection, where Tertullian is speaking of practices for which 'you will find no Scripture injunction.' He also wrote a treatise (*De Baptismo*) on baptism, but he nowhere therein refers to the triple immersion. We have here a definite and positive reason for holding that Tertullian, the first to mention trine immersion, classes it among those practices for which, if 'you insist upon having positive Scripture injunction, you will find none.'" P. 63. The Doctor is mistaken in asserting that "trine immersion is introduced *only* in this connection," that is, he is mistaken, and greatly mistaken, in asserting that the passage in Tertullian, in his work on the Soldier's Crown, which we have had under consideration, is the only place in his writings in which trine immersion is introduced. The several mistakes that the Doctor has fallen into concerning the writings of the Fathers, would seem to indicate that he had not read those writings with the care that he should have done before he made the use of them he did in his work against trine immersion.

In referring to Tertullian Dr. Forney says, "He also wrote a treatise (*De Baptismo*) on baptism, but he nowhere therein refers to the triple immersion."

And were his treatises on the *Soldier's Crown* and on *Baptism* the only ones he wrote? By no means. His works comprise four volumes in the *Ante-Nicene Christian Library*. He wrote a treatise (*Adversus Praxeas*), Against Praxeas. And in that treatise he refers to trine immersion, and gives not tradition as his authority for it, but the command of Christ. The object of his writing against Praxeas was to show that the views of Praxeas concerning the Trinity were not according to the Scriptures, and that his own views were. It was not in an argument to prove trine immersion that the reference to trine immersion was made by Tertullian in his treatise against Praxeas, but in an argument to prove the distinct personality of the Father and the Son in the Godhead.

The passage reads as follows: "Christ appointed baptism to be administered not in the name of one, but three, Father, Son, and Holy Ghost. Therefore we are dipped not once, but thrice, unto every person at the mention of each name."—*Antiquities of the Christian Church, B. XI, ch. III.* We have given Bingham's translation of the passage. On pages 194 and 195 of our work we have given Dr. Duncan's rendering of the passage. And by comparing the two translations it will be seen that they are very similar. And this passage proves to a moral demonstration that Tertullian considered the direct authority of Christ in the baptismal formula as the origin of trine immersion. He declares that "Christ appointed baptism to be administered not in the name of one, but three, Father, Son, and Holy Ghost. Therefore we are dipped thrice, unto every person at the mention of each name." Trine immersion is directly attributed to the appointment of Christ. "Therefore we are thrice dipped." Why were they thrice dipped? Because "Christ appointed baptism to be adminis'ered not in the name of one, but three, Father, Son, and Holy Ghost." And while this passage in his controversy with Praxeas, proves that Tertullian understood trine immersion to be authorized directly by Christ, it follows that the interpretation of the passage in the Soldier's Crown, which makes him say that trine immersion is somewhat more than the Lord appointed, is an erroneous interpretation of the passage.

We have with care, and considerable thoroughness, examined the testimonies of Tertullian, and find that he has been greatly misrepresented to the prejudice of trine immersion. And instead of saying the least to disparage it, he has given positive testimony to its divine origin. And why men, who should have known better, have so misrepresented him, and that to the prejudice of a fair examination of the correct action of a Christian ordinance, we know not, and we judge not, but regret that it has been done.

Dr. Forney apparently has relied on others for an interpretation of Tertullian on trine immersion, and he has been greatly misled. He says: "Tertullian died A. D. 220, and wrote his principal works within the last twenty years of his life. How long before that date trine immersion was practiced he does not in any wise intimate; although, according to the opinion of many learned authors, he does testify that it was not instituted by Christ and practiced by the Apostles." P. 36. Had Dr. Forney and his "learned authors" read more thoroughly and more carefully, the writings of Tertullian, they would have known more in regard to Tertullian's real sentiments concerning trine immersion, and those "learned men" would never have entertained the opinion that Tertullian "does testify that it [trine immersion] was not instituted by Christ and practiced by the apostles," for he did not so testify. But he testifies just the reverse of what they say. He testifies that Christ appointed trine immersion, as we have proved by his own language translated by competent and impartial men.

6. Origin of Trine Immersion. The above is the heading of the last chapter of the Doctor's work against trine immersion. We would give the entire chapter if our space permitted. But it does not. We shall, however, give several paragraphs of the chapter, that his views and arguments may be properly stated, and our reply understood.

The Doctor states several circumstances that he thinks had a tendency to introduce errors and innovations into the church; and names infant baptism as an illustration and confirmation of his position. He had previously devoted a chapter of his book to "The innovations based on Tradition." But we do not think it necessary to refer especially to his remarks upon innovation, for, though they were designed to bear against trine immersion, they do not properly apply to it, for it was not, as we have shown, an innovation, but the form of immersion appointed by Christ. Whether trine immersion or single was an innovation is the point we are discussing. If trine immersion is the form of baptism instituted by Christ, as we have proved it is, then single immersion is an innovation. Then after his general remarks upon innovations and errors in the doctrine and practice of the early church, the Doctor proceeds as follows:

"If such results have followed the development of these doctrines, is not the possibility clearly evident that a modification or a more positive formation of trinitariah ideas might lead to a triplication of the baptism instituted by Christ? History records the fact that the doctrine concernidg the Father, the Son, and the Holy Spirit, and their interrelations, was gradually evolved. Into the details of this evolution we cannot now enter, but our readers can readily verify our statement by consulting any standard work on the history of Christian doctrines. Suffice it here to say, that the term *trinity* did not take its place in the language of Christian theology until the time of Tertullian. Through his teachings the term *Son* was first quite distinctly applied to the *personality* of the Logos; and by him also, or by Theophylus, A. D. 183, the word *trinitas* was first employed to designate the Divine mystery of three persons in the unity of one Godhead (Hodge). Before this date it could, with little truth, be said that the doctrine of the essential Trinity was adequately understood. Some confounded the Logos with the Spirit, and others denied him a co-ordinate relation to the Father and the Son; while still others held to that peculiar system of subordination in which the

Son was made inferior to the Father, and the Holy Spirit to both the Father and Son.

"That these views might have some influence on the mode of baptism, changing it from a single to a threefold immersion, is quite possible. And the more so if it should be made apparent that either the whole of Matthew's Gospel, which alone contains what is designated as "the longer *baptismal formula*" (Matt. 28 : 19), or that paragraph embracing the said *baptismal formula*, was unknown in Africa before the doctrine of the Trinity had been so fully developed. Eusebius tells us (Eccl. Hist.) that the Hebrew Gospel of Matthew was found among the Christians in India in the latter part of the second century, by Pantænus, the missionary and philosopher; who afterwards with so much celebrity presided over the catechetic school at Alexandria in Egypt (Hist. Books of the Bible, p. 166). What more natural than that the concurrence of these two facts, viz.: The more complete and perfect development of the *trinus*, threefold or three-in-one God, and the discovery of the Gospel by Matthew with its baptismal formula, 'into the name of the Father, and of the Son, and of the Holy Ghost,' should have had sufficient influence to change the single into a threefold baptism—the 'one baptism in three immersions' to correspond with the one Godhead in three persons? And how natural, too, that it should at once and with assurance, be asserted that this mode of baptism is authorized by the formula, and so is of *Apostolic* origin. Such a change would be of no .moment compared with ihe introduction of infant baptism.

"And now let it be remembered that about this time trine immersion was probably first practiced, according to the testimony which we have reviewed, and that it is first mentioned in the very place to which for the first time Pantænus brought the Hebrew Gospel by Matthew. Before this time we have also no record of the use of the baptismal formula in Matthew in the administration of the ordinance. Baptism had been generally administered only in the name of Jesus. Neander, the prince of modern ecclesiastical historians, says that the formula of baptism which is regarded as the older is the shorter one which refers only to Christ, io which there is allusion in the New Testament. Dr. Hare also says in his Church History: 'Baptism as an initiatory rite was performed simply in the name of Jesus.' This sentence occurs in his chapter on the 'Apostolic Church,' in his 'History of the Christian Church.' Robinson, in his History of Baptism, says: 'There is no mention of baptizing in the name of the Father, and of the Son, and of the Holy Ghost, in immediately post-Apostolic times.' This testimony, of a negative character, certainly becomes very strong and significant in view of the fact that Peter enjoined baptism 'in the name of Jesus Christ' (Acts 2:38); that when Philip preached in Samaria, to which place Peter and John were sent upon hearing 'that Samaria had received the Word of God,' those who believed 'were baptized in the name of the Lord Jesus' (Acts 8:5; 12:16); and that under the instructions of Paul those who had been baptized 'unto John's baptism' were 'baptized in the name of the Lord Jesus' (Acts 19:3, 5).

"But as soon as the doctrine of the Trinity was developed, and the Gospel of Matthew brought from India to Egypt, trine immersion, with individual exceptions, became gradually the rule. To the use of the formula furnished by Matthew in the administration of trine immersion, we have the testimony of Augustine (de Bapt., lib. vi., cap. 25), Cyprian (Epist. lxxiii.), Tertullian (de Bapt., c. 13), and others. Basil speaks of baptism as invalid if not administered with the words of the formula in Matthew (De Sp. Scto., cap. 12). But Ambrose favored the use of the shorter formula. But the formula found in Matthew had, probably, as much, if not more, to do with the introduction of trine immersion as a correct and dogmatic view of the doctrine of the Trinity, though Marcion and his followers continued at least for some time to use the shorter formula. The Marcionites, the Valentinians, the Praxeans, and the Monarchians were distinct schools or sects which originated about the middle of the second century and before its close. At least the former two were Gnostic sects. Some of these Gnostic sects wholly rejected baptism; but the Marcionites and Valentinus and his followers held baptism in high esteem (Hagenbach). They did not belong to the church—the Catholic church—of that time, and Hagenbach testifies that their 'mode of baptism *differed from that of the Catholic* church.' What was their mode of baptizing? Hagenbach says it was *trine* immersion—'The threefold baptism of the Marcionites.' Thurman also states that Marcion, the leader of the Marcionites, *commenced* 'to baptize the Gentiles by dipping them three times.' Marcion pretended to bring about the restoration of primitive doctrine and polity; but is set down here by these two authorities as deviating from the practice of the Catholic, or general church as it was then, in the matter of baptism. We do not know upon what authority these statements are made, as no ancient writer mentions trine immersion before Tertullian, who was born A. D. 160. But we know that Hagenbach is an almost undisputed authority on matters of church doctrine, and that Thurman is not likely to state so important a point without some adequate testimony to sustain it. It is also in perfect harmony with other ascertained facts. Thus it will account for the silence of all the Fathers down to the time of Tertullian on the subject of trine immersion. And it fully agrees with the inference naturally to be drawn from the testimony of Tertullian and the instance of baptism with sand already noticed, that trine immersion must have been introduced before A. D. 200."

Then according to the Doctor's explanation of the origin of trine immersion, there are two causes that originated it in Africa, in which country he thinks it originated. The first of these is the more full development of the Trinity. And the second is the introduction of the Gospel of Matthew into Africa by Pantænus from India. "What more natural," says the Doctor, "than that the concurrence of these two facts, viz.: The more complete and perfect development of the *trinus*, threefold or three-in-one

God, and the discovery of the Gospel by Matthew with its baptismal formula, 'into the name of the Father, and of the Son, and of the Holy Ghost,' should have had sufficient influence to change the single into a threefold baptism—the 'one baptism in three immersions' to correspond with the one Godhead in three persons?" The Doctor continues: "But as soon as the doctrine of the Trinity was developed, and the Gospel of Mattbew brought from India to Egypt, trine immersion, with individual exceptions, became gradually the rule. . . . But the formula in Matthew had, probably, as much, if not more, to do with the introduction of trine immersion as correct and dogmatic views of the doctrine of the Trinity."

It would appear from the Doctor's language, that he would have his readers to understand that the views of the Trinity developed at the time to which he refers, that is, at the time he thinks trine immersion was introduced, were correct views. And it is reasonable that the Doctor should consider those views as generally sound, as we presume he is in harmony with his church, and it is represented as holding trinitarian views in regard to the Godhead. That the prevailing sentiments of the Christians at the time to which the Doctor refers were tolerably sound, may be inferred from the fact that Tertullian's views which seem to have generally prevailed then, are considered orthodox by trinitarians.

Mr. Jones, the Baptist Church historian, says of Tertullian's views and treatise on the Trinity: "It is, however, due to him to say, that he defended, with great clearness and ability, the doctrine of the revealed distinction in the Godhead, against Praxeas, who had propagated sentiments subversive of the Christian faith. In that work he treats of the Trinity in unity—Father, Son, and Holy Spirit—yet one God;—of the Lord Jesus Christ as both God and man; as at once the Son of man and the Son of God;—and of the Holy Spirit as the Comforter and Sanctifier of believers; and this he describes as the rule of the faith which had obtained from the beginning of the gospel." *History of the Christian Church*, by William Jones, Vol. I, p. 174.

Now if trine immersion in Africa followed upon the introduction of the Gospel of Matthew, and the complete development of the Godhead, into that country, is not this circumstance a strong, and conclusive argument in favor of its Divine authority, if we accept the baptismal formula in Matthew as of Divine authority? We believe it is. And if we understand the Doctor's statements and reasoning, he seems to concede to trine immersionists what they claim, when they claim that trine immersion is the form of baptism taught in the baptismal formula contained in the gospel of Matthew. That formula is our authority for trine immersion. If Church history, or any other source, will afford us confirming testimony, we accept it, and use it, but our main authority is the baptismal formula as given in the gospel of Matthew. This is seen throughout our discussion of the subject.

But we do not overlook the idea, that, though the Doctor seems to admit that the introduction of the gospel according to Matthew, and the perfect development of the Godhead, led to the practice of trine immersion in Africa, that he regarded this as a change from single immersion. He considered single immersion as the original mode; and trine immersion as an innovation. But Matthew wrote his gospel in the age of the Apostles, and the effects of its teaching were felt in that age. And who will doubt for a moment that the development of the Godhead was as complete in the faith and preaching of the apostles as it was at the time the Doctor dates the origin of trine immersion? If then the Gospel according to Matthew with its baptismal formula as appointed by our Lord, and the knowledge of the complete development of the Godhead, were in existence in the apostolic age, and if these led to the practice of trine immersion in a later age in Africa, they would also lead to the same practice in the Apostolic age in whatever country they existed. This will be readily acknowledged by the reflecting, intelligent, and candid.

Again: The Gospel according to Matthew was translated into the Greek language in the Apostolic age, if it was not written originally in that language. See Introduction to the Gospel of Matthew in Lange's Commentary. And further, it will be admitted that Matthew preached the gospel as he wrote it. Then, as he wrote the baptismal formula, so he preached it. And as he wrote that the Lord commanded his disciples to baptize "into the name of the Father, and of the Son, and of the Holy Spirit," so he no doubt himself baptized. And as he baptized, so did all the apostles. And as we have already remarked, no doubt the apostles, as they were inspired by the Holy Spirit, would have as correct a view of the Godhead as those had at the time the Doctor says trine immersion was introduced into Africa. If then, according to his theory of the origin of trine immersion, as complete a development of the Godhead had prevailed in the Apostolic age as prevailed when trine immersion was introduced, and there certainly had, and if the gospel of Matthew prevailed also in the Apostolic age, as it surely did, then did trine immersion also prevail in the age of the apostles, and in all places in which those influences existed, which, the Doctor thinks, led to the practice of trine immersion.

And according to the above legitimate deductions drawn from the Doctor's theory of the origin of trine immersion, it did not originate in Africa in the latter part of the second century, when Pantænus brought the Gospel by Matthew from India to Alexandria. For the causes to which the Doctor attributes trine immersion had evidently existed before it was introduced into Egypt, in the latter part of the second century.

The idea advanced repeatedly by Dr. Forney that trine immersion originated in Africa, is contradicted by very good authority. The following testimony is positive: "In the Greek church we find the *threefold* immersion earlier and more prevalent than in the Latin; whence the Greeks objected to the Latins."—*Knapp's Christian Theology*, p. 486. Then according to good authority trine immersion was practiced among the Greeks before it was among the Latins. And we have no reason whatever to believe that trine immersion was an innovation, and that it took the place of single immersion in Africa. Our course of reasoning with the Doctor's admissions have conclusively proved, that trine immersion was the mode of immersion practiced in the Apostolic age.

But as the baptismal formula given by Matthew so plainly indicates a trine immersion, and as it was regarded by Dr. Forney as one of the things that led to trine immersion, to counteract its influence and thus prevent it from promoting the cause of trine immersion, the Doctor insinuates it was not practiced by the apostles nor their immediate successors. He says, "Before this time [referring to the latter part of the second century], we have also no record of the use of the baptismal formula in Matthew in the administration of the ordinance. Baptism had been generally administered only in the name of Jesus." See this language in our quotation from the Doctor. In the first chapter of our book, we have discussed at some length *The Baptismal Formula of the Church*, and have proved that the formula in Matthew is the form of baptism to be used by the church. And we do not think it necessary to say much upon this subject here.

We cannot but question the correctness of the

Doctor's statements, with the testimonies that we have in Christian writers in regard to the prevalence in the early church of what he calls the shorter form of baptism, namely, that administered "in the name of Jesus." He says, near the beginning of the third paragraph that we have quoted from his chapter on the origin of trine immersion, as will be seen in referring to the quotation, "Before this time [meaning the latter part of the second century], we have also no record of the use of the baptismal formula in Matthew in the administration of the ordinance. Baptism had been generally administered only in the name of Jesus." He refers to the same authorities, and uses nearly the same languages, in another place of his work, namely, on page 55. He there says, "It is generally conceded that during the time of the Apostles, as well as in the earliest post-Apostolic times, baptism was administered in the name of Jesus." By referring to our authorities in the first chapter of our work, the reader will find that it is not only generally, but almost universally, conceded that baptism was performed in the early church according to the baptismal formula in Matthew.

The Doctor mentions a few authorities to sustain him in his position. He names Dr. Smith's *Diction-*

ary of Christian Antiquities. We have the full and strong testimony of Dr. Smith's *Dictionary of the Bible*, in support of the early and general use of the baptismal formula in Matthew. See on pages 14 and 15 of our work. He quotes Robinson as saying, in his *History of Baptism*, "There is no mention of 'baptizing in the name of the Father, and of the Son, and of the Holy Ghost,' in immediately post-Apostolic time." The fact that Justin Martyr, in explaining the manner in which baptism was performed in his time, represents it as having been done according to the baptismal formula given by our Lord, is evidence that what Robinson says is not correct, as Justin lived but a short time after the Apostolic age. He was born, according to authority produced by Dr. Lardner, A. D. 103. See our quotation from Justin on page 201.

Dr. Knapp has the following in relation to the early use of the baptismal formula: "In the ancient Christian church immediately after the time of the apostles, the words prescribed by Christ at the establishment of this rite were certainly used (Just. M. Ap. 1, 80). It may therefore be rightly inferred that it was the same at the time of the apostles; and that it is right and proper to continue in this use." *Knapp's Christian Theology*, p. 487. We yet add the following: "Baptism was originally performed by immersion in the name of the trinity." *Guericke's Church History*, p. 141.

It will be seen from our authorities quoted, that the testimonies of writers ancient and modern, are strong, and almost unanimous in favor of the early practice and of the binding authority of the baptismal formula in Matthew's gospel.

If the statement the Doctor makes when he says, "It is generally conceded that during the time of the apostles, as well as in the earlier post-Apostolic times, baptism was administered in the name of Jesus," is correct, he indirectly imputes a gross inconsistency to the Christian world, for it is almost, if not altogether, unanimous in the practice of the baptismal formula as given by our Lord in Matthew's gospel. And, indeed, his implied imputation is worse than even an inconsistency. For if the inspired Apostles and their immediate successors performed baptism in the name of Jesus only, then are all those wrong who perform it "in the name of the Father, and of the Son, and of the Holy Spirit," for surely the inspired Apostles knew what form of baptism was right.

If we would accept the idea that the apostles and their successors practiced baptism in the name of Jesus, we would at once adopt that form. And all who hold that idea should do so to be consistent. But the Doctor is wrong, as we have seen, in his statement in declaring "It is generally conceded that during the time of the apostles, as well as in the earlier post-Apostolic times, baptism was administered in the name of Jesus." And though the Christian world is guilty of much inconsistency, it is not guilty of that which the Doctor indirectly imputes to it.

But why should Dr. Forney and other single immersionists, in their ardent zeal in opposing trine immersion, seek to depreciate and invalidate the form of administering baptism contained in the gospel of Matthew, and which the Christian world has so generally practiced, and which they themselves practice? There must be some cause for them to pursue a course so inconsistent, and therefore, so injudicious. And must we not infer that the cause is in the fact that there is in the structure of the baptismal formula, "baptizing them into the name of the Father, and of the Son, and of the Holy Spirit," a power that produces a conviction that they cannot readily relieve themselves of, that the formula indicates a trine immersion? If this were not the case, why attempt to destroy the binding power of the form for administering baptism that is so plainly taught in the gospel, and of which the Christian world has, with so much unanimity of belief, accepted?

In the closing part of the Doctor's chapter on *The Origin of Trine Immersion*, he introduces the ancient heretic, Marcion. Hagenbach, an author quoted by the Doctor, represents the form of baptism practiced by the Marcionites as different from the form used by the general or Catholic church. And the Doctor quotes Hagenbach and Thurman to prove that the Marcionites practiced trine immersion. Then as the Marcionites practiced trine immersion, if their form of baptism differed from that of the general church, the inference the Doctor would have his readers to draw is, that the general church practiced single immersion.

The Doctor, in introducing Marcion as he has done, has made a wide departure from his general course in the preceding part of his book. Our readers have seen from our quotation from the Doctor, and from our replies to him, that he has made the silence of the ancient Christian Fathers upon trine immersion an argument against it. He has dwelt upon this argument at length, and repeatedly urged it. The position that he has taken in his book is, that there is no testimony for trine immersion before the time of Tertullian, or before A. D. 200. And in referring to this time, he says, on page 36 of his book, "But beyond this it is not possible to carry it." According to Dr. Cave and others, Marcion lived early in the second century, and was an avowed heretic as early as A. D. 130. *Lardner's Works, Vol. IV, p. 589.* Then the Doctor, by admitting the existence of trine immersion as early as the time of Marcion, has destroyed the force of his own argument based upon the silence of writers before the time of Tertullian. He has himself broken the silence upon trine immersion before the time of Tertullian, by admitting that Marcion in the first of the second century practiced trine immersion. The admission of the existence of trine immersion in any age, is testimony in proof of its existence in that age. Hence the Doctor's position that Marcion practiced trine immersion, is testimony that trine immersion was practiced in the early part of the second century. And his position that Marcion practiced trine immersion is in direct conflict with the position taken by the Doctor on pages 35 and 36 of his book, where he thus expresses himself: "Tertullian also testifies to the practice of trine immersion in Egypt, as follows: 'Then we are thrice dipped, answering somewhat more than the Lord prescribed in the Gospel.' Here we have trine immersion, as conceded in the opening of this discussion; *but beyond this it is not possible to carry it.*" The italicizing is ours. And the position the Doctor has taken is also in direct conflict with the statement made by all writers who declare that trine immersion cannot be traced beyond the time of Tertullian. If, then, Marcion practiced trine immersion, we have trine immersion early in the second century. But if he practiced single immersion, then, according to the Doctor's theory, the general church practiced trine immersion at that time, for he takes the position that the practice of the general church was different to that of Marcion. So his theory founded upon the case of Marcion, proves the existence of trine immersion early in the second century, and destroys the force of his repeated arguments against trine immersion founded on the want of testimony for it before the time of Tertullian.

We shall now dismiss the Doctor's "*Historical Inquiry into the Practice of Trine Immersion.*" And we feel greatly surprised that he should write so disparagingly against trine immersion, when he has so clearly failed to furnish satisfactory historical testimony against it as we have shown. We have proved that a chain of historical arguments can be furnished from the testimony of impartial witnesses, showing that trine immersion can be traced to the Apostolic age of the Christian Church.

CHAPTER XVIII.

REVIEW OF DR. CATHCART.

DR. Cathcart is an eminent minister in the Baptist church. He is now pastor of a church in Philadelphia. He is the author of several works. He has written one of the most recent works on Baptism that has been written on the immersionist side of the subject. He is also the author of the Baptist Encyclopædia, a work that has appeared within the last few years. In both the works named, the Doctor has used very hard language in writing against trine immersion. And as he has done so, we feel that justice to our subject requires of us some notice of his attempt to repudiate trine immersion.

The title of his first work we shall notice is, *The Baptism of the Ages and of the Nations.* This work is principally made up of records of immersions that have occurred in the different ages of the church, and in different countries. The work is somewhat peculiar. A large proportion of the baptismal occurrences cited by the Doctor, are baptisms performed by trine immersion. And yet, in the opening of his subject, the Doctor has, in strong language, repudiated trine immersion, the very mode of immersion that the most of his witnesses testify to. The Doctor's course is very much like that of an attorney who was about calling up the witnesses for his client, and before he has them to testify, he criminates them, or charges them with being guilty of some crime.

The following is almost the entire preface to the book: "The primary object which claimed the attention of the writer of this little work when he began its preparation was to secure and record reliable information about the *mode of baptism* used by the great missionaries who planted Christianity among the pagan communities now constituting the chief nations of the earth. How did St. Remigius baptize Clovis and his three thousand soldiers? How did St. Patrick baptize the Irish? How did St. Augustine baptize King Ethelbert and ten thousand of his subjects? How did Paulinus baptize the thronging thousands of Englishmen whom he was the means of converting in Northumberland? How did Boniface baptize his hundred thousand Germans? How did St. Anschar baptize the Scandinavians? How were the whole people of Kieff baptized when their Russian master, Vladimir the Great, just rescued from heathenism, ordered them to become Christians?" Now we may affirm, without any fears of a successful contradiction, that the answer, *by a trine immersion*, is the true answer to be given to each one of the questions given by the Doctor in his preface; for it is certain that all the baptisms to which he has referred were performed by trine immersion. This we presume Dr. Cathcart himself would not deny.

Is it not then very strange, that after a preface containing questions which, if properly answered, bear such strong testimony to trine immersion, and before he proceeds to supply the contents of the book, the greater part of which, like the preface, testifies to trine immersion, we should find in the opening of the book, the following passage repudiating trine immersion, the mode of immersion sanctioned so generally by the authorities quoted. "TRINE IMMERSION was the general practice of Christians from the end of the second till the close of the twelfth century. The proof of this statement is overwhelming. But the proof that triple immersion was the usual mode of baptism prevailing for a thousand years among Christians *begins* with Tertullian at the end of the second century, not with Christ.

Beyond Tertullian no record in the literature of men, in the book of God, or in any symbol known to mortals utters a single word about three immersions in baptism. There is not the *faintest shadow* of evidence, before the close of the second century, that ever has been brought forward, or that can be secured, to prove the existence of trine immersion." The great difference between Dr. Cathcart's position as expressed above, and the great body of his authorities quoted, will be readily perceived by the intelligent readers of his book. And as we presume his work was intended to promote the cause of immersion, the difference to which we have above referred, cannot but operate unfavorably upon a class of persons for whom the book was intended. We mean those who advocate sprinkling and pouring as the action of baptism. They will see the want of agreement between the Doctor and his authorities, and the testimony of the latter will not have much influence upon them, for they will see that the author of the work has repudiated the practice of his own witnesses.

When the Doctor says, "There is not the *faintest shadow* of evidence, before the close of the second century, that ever has been brought forward, or that can be secured, to prove the existence of trine immersion," his language is entirely too strong, and his position untenable, and in direct conflict with one of his authorities, and an authority, too, which he highly recommends for honesty and intelligence. We refer to Dr. Coleman. Dr. Cathcart quotes him as follows: "*In the second century* it had become *customary to immerse three times*, at the mention of the several names in the Godhead."—*Baptism of the Ages, p. 75.* The italics in the above are not ours. Dr. Cathcart, in referring to his quotations from Dr. Coleman, among which occurs the one we cited above, says: "Professor Coleman in these declarations speaks as an honest man who had read the writings of the first twelve hundred years of the Christian era, which were penned by the followers of the Saviour. He who speaks otherwise has not surveyed the rich and large harvest-field of testimony, or he misrepresents it."—*Ibid*, pp. 76, 77. Prof. Coleman says, "*In the second century* it had become *customary to immerse three times.*" Dr. Cathcart affirms, "There is not the *faintest shadow* of evidence, before the close of the second century, that ever has been brought forward, or that can be secured, to prove the existence of trine immersion." There was not only the *shadow of evidence*, before the close of the second century, to prove the existence of trine immersion, but there was also the body of evidence, for Prof. Coleman affirms that "*in the second century* it had become *customary to immerse three times.*" And Dr. Cathcart endorsed Prof. Coleman as an "honest man," and as one well read in "the writings of the first twelve hundred years of the Christian era." Therefore Dr. Cathcart's assertion that "there is not the *faintest shadow* of evidence, before the close of the second century, that ever has been brought forward, or that can be secured, to prove the existence of trine immersion," is shown to be incorrect, by one of his own witnesses, and by one, too, whose honesty and competency to decide upon such a question, he has endorsed. We shall now pass from the *Baptism of the Ages* to *The Baptist Encyclopædia*.

Dr. Cathcart is the editor of *The Baptist Encyclopædia*. In this work there is an article on *Trine Immersion*, and it bears strong marks as having been written by the author of the *Baptism of the Ages*. And if it was not written by Dr. Cathcart, it no doubt had his sanction, and from the relation he bears to the work in which it appears, we presume he accepts the responsibility of the article. And in our notice of the article we shall consider it as written by him.

After an introduction of a historical character containing similar facts to those contained in the *Baptism of the Ages,* he proceeds to say:

"If the Scriptures had been read after the third century as they were before it, and if baptism had been translated as it had been previously instead of being transferred, trine immersion could not have been perpetuated. It is one thing for an error to creep into the churches, but with a faithful Bible, widely read and reverenced, errors must perish. Jerome, in his Vulgate, transfers baptism, in Eph. 4 : 5, 'One Lord, one faith, and one *baptism.*' If Jerome had been a faithful reviser, and had rendered baptism *immersion,* how difficult it would have been all over Western Europe, where his Bible was read, to see the words, 'One Lord, one faith, *and one immersion,*' and at the same time to practice *trine* immersion! Jerome saw the difficulty even with the Greek word baptisma in Roman letters in his Latin text; and in the Commentary which he added to his revised New Testament he gives explanations about the reason why, as he says, 'We are immersed three times' (ter mergimur).

"It would appear as if 'baptize' was transferred into the Latin Vulgate to hide the meaning of the word. The ordinance had been enlarged by two extra dippings, and increased in other foolish ways, but the Greek word baptism covers everything to the masses of readers of the Vulgate. If Jerome had not transferred the baptismal words, and the Christians had continued Bible-reading, trine immersion could not have been permanently sustained among Bible-loving Christians. There is absolutely nothing in the Scriptures to support it, and its historical chain of evidence has no links uniting it to the apostles or their times.

"Tertullian quotes from a Latin New Testament, two hundred years older than Jerome's, and his quotations from it, in his treatise 'De Baptismo,' always translate the verb 'baptize.' In the commission, Matt. 28, it reads, 'Go teach all nations, *immersing* them,' etc. (tinguentes). Here Jerome has 'baptizing them.' In Matt. 3:6, Tertullian quotes, 'They were immersed (tinguebantur), confessing their sins,' cap. 13, 20; Jerome again transfers 'baptized.' The New Testament quoted by Tertullian translates the word, and in all probability it was one of the versions the revision of which we have in the Vulgate edition. Jerome's translation of the Old Testament is more faithful than his translation of the New."

We have quoted the Doctor in full, except the

first paragraph, which contains allusions to the torical bearing of the subject, in order that no advantage in any way may be taken of it, and that our review of it may be the better understood.

It will be observed that Dr. Cathcart blames Jerome's translation of the New Testament for the prevalence of trine immersion in Western Europe. For Jerome, like the translators of our common English version, transferred the word baptize, instead of translating it. And so he is blamed by the Doctor for covering over the true meaning of baptism in Eph. 4:5. The Doctor says: "If Jerome had been a faithful reviser, and had rendered baptism *immersion*, how difficult it would have been all over Western Europe, where his Bible was read, to see the words, 'One Lord, one faith, *and one immersion*,' and at the same time to practice *trine immersion*." The Doctor further says: "It would appear as if 'baptize' was transferred into the Latin Vulgate to hide the meaning of the word. The ordinance had been enlarged by two extra dippings, and increased in other foolish ways, but the Greek word baptism covers everything to the masses of the readers of the Vulgate."

Now do the facts bearing on the Doctor's references to Jerome's translation, sustain his position in attributing the prevalence of trine immersion in Western Europe to that translation in which the word baptism in Eph. 4:5 is transferred, and not translated? By no means. And the facts in the case do not only fail to sustain him, but those facts are fatal to his position or theory. We call the attention of our readers to some well-known facts. It is known to all persons acquainted with church history, that the Greek church with its many millions of members, and its numerous branches extending over the countries in which Christianity was first planted, and through which Christ and the apostles traveled and baptized, have always baptized, and they still baptize by trine immersion. These all read the Bible in the Greek language, which is their native tongue. Then, as all those Greeks baptize by trine immersion, it is very evident that there is nothing in the words *one baptism* in Eph. 4:5, when properly understood, that is against trine immersion. If the words *one baptism*, when translated, would settle the question in regard to the gospel mode of immersion, as Dr. Cathcart declares it would, why have they not in the native language of the Greeks settled it with them that one immersion is the true mode of Christian immersion? Whatever meaning words or phrases have in a good translation, they must also have in the original. And, consequently, if a proper translation of the words *one baptism* in Eph. 4:5, would prove one immersion to be the true Christian baptism, those words in the original Greek would be sufficient to prove the same. But they do not, as is seen in the fact that the Greeks, who read the words *one baptism* in their native language, baptize by trine immersion. Hence Dr. Cathcart's theory for accounting for the prevalence of trine immersion in Western Europe, on the ground of Jerome's imperfect translation of the New Testament, is not correct.

Again: Take the ancient Greek Fathers, Clement of Alexandria, Chrysostom, Basil, Augustine, and Cyril of Jerusalem, with many others. These all were Greeks, and Greek scholars, and they read the Scriptures in their native tongue, and yet they all advocated, and practiced trine immersion. If they read *one immersion* in Paul's reference to baptism in Eph. 4:5, they read three immersions in the baptismal formula in Matt. 28:20. Chrysostom, who was a Greek, and a Greek scholar, and who studied very diligently, and prayerfully, the Scriptures, says, "Christ delivered to his disciples one baptism in three immersions of the body, when he said to them, 'Go, teach all nations, baptizing them in the name of the Father, and of the Son, and of the Holy Ghost.'"—*Bingham's Antiquities of the Christian Church, B. XI, Ch. XI, Sec. 7.*

These Greek scholars and theologians did not interpret a positive law of Christ by an incidental allusion to that law by an apostle, but they went directly to that law, and interpreted it according to its plain and literal meaning. Hence they practiced the one ordinance, or the one baptism of Paul in Eph. 4:5, by a trine immersion, according to the meaning of the prescribed law, in Matt. 28:20. We add here as appropriate to our purpose in showing the illogical reasoning of Dr. Cathcart to account for trine immersion in Western Europe, some remarks of Dr. Stanley in his work on *The Eastern Church.* In referring to that church, he says: "It is her privilege to claim a direct continuity of speech with the earliest times, to boast of reading the whole code of Scripture, old as well as new, in the language in which it was read and spoken by the Apostles. The humblest peasant who reads his Septuagint or Greek Testament in his own mother tongue, on the hills of Bœotia, may proudly feel that he has an access to the original oracles of divine truth, which Pope and Cardinal reach by a barbarous and imperfect translation; that he has a key of knowledge, which in the West is only to be found in the hands of the learned classes."—*History of the Eastern Church, pp. 101, 102.*

And, further: While Dr. Cathcart censures Jerome for not being a faithful translator, he says that "Tertullian quotes from a Latin New Testament, two hundred years older than Jerome's, and his quotations from it, in his treatise 'De Baptismo,' always translate the verb 'baptize.'" Let the reader refer to our quotation from the Doctor's article given above. It appears, then, according to the Doctor's statement, that in the time of Tertullian there was a translation of the New Testament used by the Latin Fathers, in which *baptize* was translated *immerse*. As will be noticed in our quotation, the Doctor gives several examples in which this was done. He does not give Eph. 4: 5, as one of the examples in which baptize is translated immerse, but perhaps it might have been given. If not, we do not see the propriety of the Doctor's reference to the translation to which reference is made. But let that be as it may. It is to be understood from the Doctor's statement, that in the time of Tertullian, there was a translation of the New Testament, in which the word baptize was not transferred, as it is done in Jerome's Version, and in various others, but it was translated, and translated *immerse*. It is also claimed by the Doctor that the prevalence of trine immersion is owing to unfaithful translations of the Scriptures, and that if there is a faithful translation, it will be against trine immersion. Now what do the facts in this case prove? What does the fact that there was a faithful translation in the time of Tertullian prove? Does that fact sustain the Doctor's position? Were Tertullian and the Latin Fathers of his time single immersionists? Not at all. Behold, they were all trine immersionists! We cannot but express our surprise. We are not at all surprised that Tertullian should be a trine immersionist. But we are surprised that the Doctor should attempt to disprove trine immersion, for this seems to have been his object, in a way that is so destitute of logical points and arguments. Trine immersion, then, does not depend upon unfaithful translations, even according to the Doctor's own showing. But it depends upon a proper understanding of the Scriptures where read in the original language, or in faithful translations. The Greeks who read the Scriptures in the original language, are trine immersionists. The Latin Fathers were trine immersionists, and they read a faithful translation, according to Dr. Cathcart.

We take leave of the Doctor, feeling a sincere regret that while he would use so many facts and testimonies presented in the practice of trine immersionists, to prove immersion to be the action of Christian baptism, to find him speaking so disparagingly of trine immersion as he does when he uses the following language which occurs in our quotation from *The Baptist Encyclopædia:* "The ordinance had been enlarged by two extra dippings, and increased in other foolish ways." And with the feeling of regret above expressed, we also feel no little surprise that the Doctor should reason so illogically as he has done in regard to the translations of Jerome and Tertullian. The fact that the Greeks had the Scriptures in their native language, and the Latin Fathers a correct version in the translation of Tertullian, according to the Doctor's statement, and that they were trine immersionists, is fatal to his theory to account for the spread of trine immersion in Western Europe. Trine immersion having prevailed so generally as it has done among the Greeks, who read the Scripture in the Greek language, the inference that the Greek language is in favor of, rather than adverse to trine immersion, is lawful and just. And if the Scriptures in the original Greek teach trine immersion, a faithful translation will do the same.

CHAPTER XIX.

REVIEW OF F. M. BOWMAN.

THERE is a pamphlet published with the title, *Trine Immersion Weighed in the Balances and Found Wanting*. The first part of it was published in England by Robert Robertson. Mr. F. M. Bowman, of Missouri, published Mr. Robertson's work and added a chapter of his own to it. The whole work greatly lacks close and logical reasoning. It abounds in vague charges against trine immersion. The first chapter, that written by Mr. Robertson, is mainly devoted to W. Thurman. We shall only notice one point in this chapter. To the chapter written by Mr. Bowman, we shall give a little more attention, and notice what we consider the substance of his objections to trine immersion.

1. We shall notice that point in Mr. Robertson's part of the work which represents trine immersion to be the form of baptism practiced by the general or Catholic church, and single immersion to be that form which was practiced by the Dissenters from the

main body of the Church, or by the Reformers. The following paragraph from his work states Mr. Robertson's idea in his own words:

"The practicers and upholders of trine immersion were men of learning in the worldly sense, and popular with the world; and claiming power as successors of the apostles to settle all questions of faith and discipline. This establishes a three-fold presumption against the Scripturalness of their doctrine; for (1) human learning (which Paul styles 'Philosophy and vain deceit') incapacitates men for retaining or receiving the truth of CHRIST in its purity and simplicity; (2) popularity is evidence of their being uninspired; and (3) their claim to possess spiritual legislative power makes it morally certain that any changes that took place in the institutions of CHRIST would originate, without scruple, in their hands as the 'mystery of iniquity' already working in the days of Paul, which was to develop, and did finally develop, the power exalting itself above every authority, and arrogating to itself the right to 'change times and laws,' viz., the Roman Papacy. The practicers of single immersion, 'the heretics' whom the trine immersionists strove to suppress, and of whom we have but scanty and incredible accounts in the writings of their enemies, were poor men who made no such pretensions, and who having nothing to gain by it, were little likely to 'change the ordinances.'" P. 15.

Dr. Forney, in his work which we have reviewed, also intimates that it was in the Catholic church that trine immersion prevailed so generally. His first concession, on page 10 of his work, intimates this. His language is as follows: "That trine immersion was practiced in the early part of the third century, and that it had become the quite general practice of *the main body of the Catholic church, so known then*, before the close of the third century." But Dr. Cathcart makes no such restriction. His language is this: "Trine immersion was the general practice of Christians from the end of the second till the close of the twelfth century."

But the prevalence of trine immersion among the early Christians, was not only in the general body, but it was also the form of baptism that prevailed among the Dissenters. In the fifteenth chapter of our work, clear and abundant testimony will be found to prove this. We have proved by Baptist authority, that the Montanists, Novatians, and Donatists were all trine immersionists, and they were all Dissenters from the general or Catholic church. And Robinson says, the first council of Nice took notice of two sorts of dissenters. . . "These were the Cathari and Paulianists. The first held the doctrine of the Trinity, as the Athanasians in the church did: but, thinking the church a worldly community, they baptized all that joined their assemblies by trine immersion," etc. *Ecclesiastical Researches, p. 72.* And Robinson further says that another council fifty-six years after the council of Nice, made provision to receive nine sorts of dissenters, and six of these were to be received without being rebaptized because they had been baptized in the name of the trinity. In saying that those dissenters had been baptized in the name of the trinity, he means that they had been baptized by a trine immersion, according to the manner of baptizing in the general church. Hence they were not required to be baptized.

The history of the early Church clearly and fully sustains the idea that both in the Catholic or general church, and in the bodies that dissented from it, trine immersion was the form of baptism practiced. And this being the case, this unanimity of sentiment both among dissenters, and those that constituted the Catholic Church, in regard to trine immersion, is a very strong argument for its correctness, or Divine origin. While the Dissenters and the general church differed on other points, they agreed with remarkable unanimity upon the form of baptism and believed that form to be trine immersion.

We give the following extract from Mr. Bowman's chapter of the pamphlet to which allusion has been made. It expresses pretty fully the main points against trine immersion contained in the work:

"1. Do those persons who refuse to submit to immersion (single immersion) practically do the same thing that the Corinthians did? The Corinthians denied in word the resurrection; those who refuse submission to the rite that God has set to symbolize it are in a sense chargeable with the same offense. They (the Corinthians) admitted the fact in *form* (baptism), and denied it in word. Those who believe the fact (resurrection) and deny the form (baptism—single immersion) are evidently culpable to the same extent.

"2. Does a tri-dipping teach a tri-theism? It does, because it teaches that there are three distinct names entered by so many distinct actions. This is unscriptural. There is only ONE GOD.

"3. Does tri-dipping teach that the Father and Spirit suffered in the redemptive work with Jesus? It does so teach, if it teaches Jesus' sufferings. Is such the fact? No. The Scriptures do not teach it.

"4. Does trine-immersion teach that the Father's

name is Father, and that Jesus' name is Son, and that the Holy Spirit's name is Holy Spirit? It does so teach, but the Scripture saith not so. Trine-immersionists should plainly state the Father, Son, and Holy Spirit's names since they profess to enter them in baptism; in the absence of such statement there is no name present to be entered. If the names are not pronounced, the candidate essaying to enter them is left in profound ignorance of the names. For instance, we will suppose the Father's name is JEHOVAH, the Son's JESUS, and the Holy Spirit's COMFORTER. Then Jehovah, Jesus, and Comforter, are the names to be entered, to be pronounced by the administrator.

"For a moment I will address myself to a trine-immersionist: Sir, you tell me that you have been baptized in (into) the name of the Father, and Son, and Holy Spirit; if so, you surely know those names; if you have entered them, you have heard them. Will you be so kind as to pronounce them? Can you write them? Make the effort to pronounce the Father's *name;* to write it. Remember father is not the name of the Father. Pronounce the name of the Son; write it; this we think you can do. Pronounce the name of the Holy Spirit. Remember Holy Spirit is not the Holy Spirit's *name.* *Write it.*

WRITE IT. WRITE IT. Now write again. Write the Father's *name*, and the Son's *name* by it or under it, then write the Holy Spirit's *name* by or under them, and after having thus done, see if these names are the names that the trine-immersionist administrator immerses into; and if they are not, you have either made a mistake in the names or he has, and in this case the names have never been entered and the party essaying to do so is yet standing without, having a form of entry, but has never entered. Does it not strike you, that if God had designed that believers in His Son should be dipped in His name and in the name of the Holy Ghost by distinct and separate acts, that He would have given those names in language sufficiently clear to enable us to understand them?

"Had He thus designed a dipping into three *names*, a trine-dipping, He would not have left us in ignorance of two of those names. If in our vain search for these names, we should discover appellations applied to the Father and Spirit, we must not hastily conclude that we have found their names, not take it for granted because we have found an appellation which describes their attributes or perfections, but prosecute the inquiry until we find Scriptural authority for a name, a NAME for EACH of the THREE.

It devolves upon trine-immersionists to show the three names, and not only to show them, but in their baptism to baptize in (into) those three names, and not take so much for granted in so solemn a matter as that of baptizing (*regenerating*). To profess to baptize in the name of the three in ignorance of those names, and virtually baptize in no names, is to thrice falsify, because to say *name* for *name*, when *name* is not the *name*, is evidently an untruth. This is self-evident. Therefore we may reasonably conclude that God does not require that of us which leads into such absurdities and difficulties. A *name* has been given, a glorious *name*, the name whereby we can be saved. Peter says of that name, 'for there is none other name under heaven given among men whereby we must be saved.' (Acts 4:12.) At the tenth verse of the same chapter you may learn who bore that name, 'that by the name of Jesus Christ of Nazareth.' ' Behold, a virgin shall conceive, and bear a son, and shall call his name IMMANUEL.' (Isa. 7:14.) 'And thou shalt call his name JESUS.' (Matt. 1:21.) "And when eight days were accomplished for the circumcising of the child, his name was called JESUS, which was so named of the angel before he was conceived in the womb.' (Luke 2:21.) Here we have the Son's name clearly stated, as the 'only name whereby we must be saved.' 'Immanuel'—God with us. Named before he was conceived. The mighty name, the complete name. Paul says, 'It pleased the Father that in him should all fullness dwell' (Col. 1:19), and that 'in him dwelleth all the fullness of the Godhead bodily.' (Col. 2:9.) If 'all fullness dwells' in Jesus, if 'the fullness of the Godhead bodily' reside in Him, He is the complete name, the ONE name, JEHOVAH, the LORD of LORDS. In HIM are hid the Father and Spirit's name, in Him dwells all authority. When, therefore, we enter by one faith Him in whom 'dwells the fullness of the Godhead bodily,' we enter the Godhead in all of its fullness, even the Father, Son, and Spirit. By one faith we enter the one ineffable name, Jesus, the Lord Jesus Christ, who by one death and one resurrection, procured our redemption, sanctification, and justification; whose complete redemption work we set forth in our one immersion for his one burial, and our one emersion for his one resurrection.

"We conclude that JESUS was once immersed for his burial, once emerged for his resurrection, which was in point of fact fulfillment of all 'righteousness,' of which fact his baptism was the type. And again, we conclude that believers are baptized for the same great fact, the burial and resurrection of JESUS—a monument of that fact. If this be true, the mode is clear. Nothing short of a single immersion, by a backward action, can teach in monumental form the great truth, *blessed truth.*"

1. As we have fully met the first inquiry in the fourteenth chapter of our work, we refer the reader to that.

2. To the second inquiry a very short reply will suffice for the candid. It is surely unjust and unfair to attribute to trine immersionists the doctrine of tri-theism. The doctrine of tri-theism is, that the Father, Son, and Holy Spirit are three distinct Gods. If any trine immersionists hold this doctrine, it is not a necessary consequence of trine immersion. Trine immersionists as a body, hold that there are three persons in the Godhead, but not three Gods. The three persons in the Godhead are the Father, the Son, and the Holy Spirit. Baptizing into each one of the three names, no more sanctions tri-theism, than does the naming of the three names in baptism as single immersionists do.

3. If there is any point in the third inquiry, it is like the second, an unjust and an unfair charge. Trine immersionists hold the commonly received

doctrine of the sufferings of Christ. "I have trodden the winepress alone." Isa. 63: 3. "Who his own self bare our sins in his own body on the tree, that we being dead to sin, should live unto righteousness: by whose stripes we were healed." 1 Peter 2: 24. How Mr. Bowman can with the least propriety, construe trine immersion more readily than he can single immersion to make it teach that the Father and the Spirit suffered, we cannot understand. In the baptismal formula there is nothing affirmed of the suffering of Christ, and indeed there is no direct allusion made to it. And it does seem to be a farfetched objection to trine immersion that it involves the suffering of the Father and of the Spirit, in the suffering of Christ.

4. The fourth inquiry demands a little more attentention, not because there is in reality anything in it against trine immersion, but its specious appearance may mislead the inconsiderate. Trine immersionists believe that the three personal manifestations of the Godhead, as we have them presented to us in the baptismal formula, are to be known and recognized by the three names, Father, Son, and Holy Spirit. They are known by other names in the Scriptures, but we are to look at them when baptiz-

ing, through the names they bear in the baptismal formula. We have seen in chapter fifth of our work, what "name" in the baptismal formula implies, and that it is into the persons themselves, and not simply into their names that we are to be baptized.

Mr. Bowman attempts to sustain a sufficient distinction between *"name"* and *"appellation,"* to make it improper to consider any appellation applied to either of the Divine Persons, as a name. We admit some distinction between the meaning of the two words, but that distinction is not generally or practically observed. We refer to Webster. He explains "Name" thus: "*To give an appellation to; to entitle; to style;*" etc. And he explains "Appellation" as follows: "*The word by which a thing is called and known; name; title.*" Then in his synonyms under "Appellation," he gives *name* and *title*, showing that he makes "Appellation" and "Name" synonymous. And in explaining the word Son, he gives the following explanation as a part of its meaning: "Jesus Christ, the Saviour;—called the *Son* of God, and the *Son* of man."

In the *Dictionary of Illustrations*, published by R. D. Dickinson, under the Art. Holy Spirit, there is a division under the head of *Names of the Holy*

Spirit. And in the list of names is, *Holy Spirit*, recognizing Holy Spirit to be the name of the third person in the Godhead.

In the *Cyclopædia of Illustrations of Moral and Religious Truths*, by John Bate, and under the explanation of the term Father, he says, "God is frequently called Father."

Cruden, in explaining the word Son, says, "This *name* is given to a male child considered in the relation he bears to his parents." And he closes his explanation thus: "Ezekiel is called Son of man about eighty-nine times: and Christ about eighty times in the evangelists."

Bishop Leighton says, "If you then call on the name of God, and particularly by this name, *Our Father*, depart from iniquity." And again: "By faith we are invested into a new sonship, and by virtue of that may call him *Father*, and move him by that name to help and answer us." *Leighton's Works*, p. 600.

The criticism then that Father, Son, and Holy Spirit, as they occur in the baptismal formula, are appellatives and not names, is incorrect. We surely are warranted by the phraseology of the baptismal formula, to call the three divine persons in the Godhead, by the three names, Father, Son, and Holy Spirit. These names are applied to them by our Lord, and they are recognized to be names by good literary authority. See a quotation from Prof. Curtis, page 113, and authorities for a plurality of names in the baptismal formula, Chap. IV, Sec. 3.

But to see the weakness of Mr. Bowman's argument against trine immersion, and the erroneous character of his theory, let his argument and theory be applied to his own practice. Let it be remembered that single immersionists use the same names that trine immersionists do. And as Mr. Bowman denies that Father, Son, and Holy Spirit are names, he proposes the names Jehovah, Jesus, and Comforter, as the names of the three persons in the Godhead. He says, "For instance, we will suppose the Father's name to be *Jehovah*, the Son's *Jesus*, and the Holy Spirit's Comforter. Then *Jehovah*, Jesus, and Comforter, are the names to be entered, to be pronounced by the administrator." Does Mr. Bowman use the names *Jehovah*, Jesus, and Comforter when he administers baptism? If he does not, his practice does not agree with his theory. If he does, he does not administer baptism according to the formula given by Christ, for that formula requires it to be administered "into the name of the Father, and of the Son, and of the Holy Spirit." Such is the dilemma that Mr. Bowman places himself in, by his course of illogical reasoning. And the attempt that he made in his zeal in opposing and repudiating trine immersion is powerless.

CHAPTER XX.

CONCLUSION.

THE discussion of the subject of trine immersion as far as we proposed to pursue it, is completed. And from the various lines of argument that we have used, trine immersion as the mode of immersion enjoined by Christ upon his disciples, has been established, and it surely cannot be regarded as destitute of all claims upon Christian belief as it has by many heretofore been through the strong prejudice that has been felt against it.

And it seems it has been looked upon by many as the form of baptism practiced by but a very small number of Christians. This, however, is a great mistake, as the facts brought to light in our discussion of the subject will prove. We are not to estimate the correctness of any Christian doctrine by the number of persons who accept it, but when the insinuation is made to prejudice the minds of people against any doctrine, that the adherents of that doctrine are few, it is right that it should be known that such an insinuation has no basis of truth, if it has none. And such is the case in regard to the insinuation above alluded to against trine immersion.

And if the decision of the question as to whether single or trine immersion is the correct form of Christian baptism were to be settled by numbers, it would be decided in favor of trine immersion, as it is very evident that the majority of all who have been immersed into the Christian faith, have been immersed by a trine immersion.

But trine immersion is not only the mode of immersion taught in the baptismal formula, but it is the mode of immersion that most fully and most clearly brings out the distinction in the Godhead that was designed to be brought out by the phraseology of the baptismal formula. It is a very generally recognized fact, that the baptismal formula is designed to teach a plurality and distinction in the Godhead. See sections 1 and 2 in Chap. IV. And when such a plurality and distinction are made sufficiently intelligible to be apprehended by the penitent and obedient believer, and he obtains clearly the idea that each of the divine persons named had his special office to fill, and his special work to do, in the work of redemption as well as in the work of creation, and that each has also his special work to do in the redemption of each individual, and that each baptized believer is brought by his baptism when he is properly prepared for it, not simply into the *name* of each of the divine persons in the Godhead, but into the persons themselves, and thus made partakers of the divine nature, he then has the view of the Godhead that the baptismal formula was designed to teach. And thus perceiving and appreciating his close relation to each, he has a basis for his faith, his love and his hope, that will sustain them in their full and complete development.

There is a vast amount of sweet, practical, and germinal truth contained in the expressive formula of Christian baptism, which trine immersion is admirably calculated to bring out in a fullness and completeness that no other form is. And we have tried to give some help to the Christian to bring out that truth for his edification and instruction. And we indulge the hope, that a careful and intelligent reading of our work, will give to at least some readers, a more clear and appreciative understanding of the import of the baptismal formula, *baptizing them into the Father, and into the Son, and into the Holy Spirit*, than they previously had.

And, lastly; we may say of trine immersion, as immersionists often say of immersion, when they say, in contending for immersion, that it is not the amount of water for which they contend, but obedience to the Saviour's command. So we say, it is not simply the three immersions we contend for, but it is the strict obedience to the Saviour's command, as we have seen that the command to baptize into the name of the Father, and of the Son, and of the Holy Spirit, requires a trine immersion, as there are three distinct persons into each of which the believer is to be baptized. A writer of the Baptist denomination, in referring to the parable of the two sons (Matt. 21:28), has the following remarks in regard to true obedience: "Now the 'doing the Father's will' is the one thing on which our Lord lays most stress as essential in the Christian life (Matt. 7: 23). He here plainly teaches that when that will is embodied in an explicit command, there is no obedience, whatever the intent, short of doing the specific thing commanded, in a 'pedantically literal' way." *The Mould of Doctrine*, by Dr. J. B. Thomas, p. 171. The words, "pedantically literal," are quoted by the author, and they were used derogatory to immersion.

The principle stated in the following words above quoted, "There is no obedience, whatever the intent, short of doing the specified thing commanded," being sound, the divine commands should be studied with candor, sincerity, and docility, that their true meaning may be ascertained, and when this is done, they should be strictly obeyed. *Be baptized*, is the command. *Be baptized into the name of the Father, and of the Son, and of the Holy Spirit*, is the form in which we are to be baptized. And this divinely given form requires, as we have seen in the discussion of our subject, a trine immersion. "Know ye not, that to whom ye present yourselves as servants unto obedience, his servants ye are whom ye obey; whether of sin unto death, or of obedience unto righteousness? But thanks be to God, that, whereas ye were servants of sin, ye became obedient from the heart to that form of teaching whereunto ye were delivered; and being made free from sin, ye became servants of righteousness." Rom. 6: 16-18 (*Revised Version*).

THE END.

INDEX.

Adamson Elder................................... 100
Adams's Robert, testimony to trine immersion........... 215
Alford Dean...................................... 21
Ambrose misquoted 273; the error corrected........... 274
Analogy, argument from............................ 164
Apostolic benediction............................. 107
Apostolic Constitutions.................... 10, 58, 83, 193
Argument 1.—Implied admission of single immersionists.. 152
   2.—Plurality of persons in the baptismal formula...... 155
   3.—The distinction of persons in the baptismal formula. 157
   4.—Analogy...................................... 164
   5.—Positive admission of single immersionists......... 172
   6.—History...................................... 212
   7.—Reformers, Theologians, and Literary men........ 214
   8.—Churches that have practiced trine immersion...... 223
Baptism, an act of worship, 255; backward action in, 260; bowing in, 259; in the cloud and in the sea, 165; not much controverted in the early centuries, 199; not changed in the third century, 205; not changed in the second century, 210; subverted,..................... 268
Baptismal formula, the, ordained by Christ, 1; practiced by the Apostles, 3; by the primitive Church, 6, 321; correct rendering of, 17; what there is in it, 33; not Trinitarian or anti-Trinitarian, 49, 50; in the possessive case 146
Baptisms, two, 167; plurality of..................... 240

364   INDEX.

Baptist churches in the early Ages, 246; were composed
    of dissenters, 252; practiced trine immersion 252
Basil, a witness to the plurality of names in the baptismal
    formula, 116; to trine immersion 294
Bate's Mr., explanation of name 55
Bengel 28
Barnabas 200
Bethune Dr 35, 40
Beveridge Bishop, ... 44, 221
Bingham 7, 8, 12
Braden-Hughy Debate 287, 297
Bryennios 10
Burges 45
Burrage Mr. H. T 188
Burial, baptism compared to a, 234; an English, 266;
    among pagans 261
Campbell's, Mr. Alexander, translation of Justin, 8; trans-
    lation of Tertullian 299
Campbell Dr 127
Cathcart's Dr. witnesses to trine immersion, 328; conces-
    sion to, 329; singular character of his work, 327; charg-
    es Jerome with unfaithfulness as a translator, 333; at-
    tempts to account for the prevalence of trine immersion
    in Western Europe by Jerome's faulty translation, 335;
    apparently overlooks the fact that the Greeks who use the
    Greek language practice trine immersion 336
Carson Dr 127, 238
Carthage, council of, ... 9, 275
Chambers's Cyclopædia, a witness to the divine origin of
    trine immersion 216
Christians, number of, in the second century 208
Christian Review 116
Christian Baptist 134
Church Advocate 245
Chrystal, his consistency vindicated 272

Chrysostom, his testimony to the Scriptural authority for trine immersion, 192; his testimony to his own practice of it.. 571
Clark, G. W.. 153, 173
Clarke, Dr. A... 39
Clarke, J. F.. 129
Conant, Dr... 103, 125
Concession to trine immersion............................ 198
Communion symbols, plurality in the.............. 78, 161
Council of Trent.. 87
Curtis, Dr.. 113
Cyril... 58
Dissenters, early, trine immersionists................... 344
Distinction in the Godhead, 37; in the body and blood of Christ... 78
Doddridge, Dr. on name, 57; makes reference to each person in the Godhead....................................... 159
Donatists, trine immersionists........................... 251
Duncan's Dr., translation of Tertullian............ 195, 298
Dwight Dr....................................... 21, 143, 150
Each, an explanation of................................. 160
Ellipsis explained, 122; occurs frequently in Scripture, 123; use of, 124; the words added, belong to the sentence, as much as if they were expressed, 123; occurs in the baptismal formula, 131; testimony adduced................. 139
Erret Mr.. 44, 259
Error, a common, refuted................................ 187
Essence of God.. 108
Eunomius charged with subverting the law of baptism..... 82
Fairbairns Dr................................... 27, 53, 55, 240
Father, Son, and Holy Spirit, their distinct work in creation and in redemption, 66; Christians are in them all....... 60
Father and God, both applied to the first person in the Godhead.. 107
Fathers, the primitive, misrepresented, 188; did not attrib-

ute trine immersion to tradition alone, but also to the Scripture, 192, 292; did not always use name before Father, Son, and Holy Spirit 57, 58
Figures explained.. 235
Ford Dr., says Tertullian joined the Montanists.......... 248
Forney Dr., his statement of the origin of trine immersion, 310; his misquotation of Ambrose 273; of Justin Martyr... 282
Ganse... 46
Gill Dr.. 102
Godhead, the three-fold manifestation of, 65; how known. 104
God and Father both applied to the first person in the Godhead... 107
Gospel Visitor.. 143
Grammatical equivalents................................. 145
Gregory and Ruter's Church History...................... 206
Horne... 29
Halley... 35
Hopson.. 45
Henry's Christian Antiquities........................... 84
Henry, Matthew... 98
Hart.. 124
Haynes, D. C... 248
Hinton, Dr... 265
Hermas... 200
Immersion, one, 237; plurality of immersions, 240; but little said about it before A. D., 200.................... 287
Injudicious language used against trine immersion....... 244
Jacobs.. 11
Jamieson... 128
Jerome... 239
Jews dipped three times in their solemn washings........ 225
Johnson, Eld. B. W..................................... 245
Jones... 314
Judson, Dr... 258

King, Dr. J. G 220
Kitto's Cyclopædia............................. 159
Knapp, Dr 320
Lange, Dr...................................... 20
Lard's Quarterly............................... 46
Latham Prof.................................... 121
Lock... 129
Luther 214
Manifestation of the Godhead 104
Marcion.................................. 311, 323
Martyr, Justin, misquoted, 282; the proper reading shown, 283; a witness to trine immersion 281
Milligan............................. 31, 59, 90, 93, 124
Meyer, Dr............................... 50, 178, 180
Monnulus................................... 9, 275
Montanus, the first dissenter 246
Montanists..................................... 247
Morrison 49
Name, written on the forehead, 77; referred to the divine essece, 87; to the essence of God.................. 89
Neander.. 309
Novatians, trine immersionists................. 250
Obedience, none where the specific thing commanded is not done...................................... 360
Olhausen, Dr................................... 89
"One immersion."............................... 237
Orchard, Mr.................................... 246
Pantaenas...................................... 309
Pelagius.................................. 83, 193
Pierce, Dr..................................... 150
Positive law, must be clearly expressed........ 93
Praxeas.................................. 194, 303
Princeton Review............................... 180
Proselytes, Jewish, were probably baptized by trine immersion.. 225

Purves, James.................................... 139
Ray Dr... 86
Reviews:
  1. Dr. Forney................................. 263
  2. Dr. Cathcart............................... 327
  3. Mr. F. M. Bowman........................... 342
Reeve's, translation of Justin.................... 284
Rice, Dr... 188
Riddle, Dr....................................... 29
Renunciation, in baptism......................... 298
Robinson... 246
Robertson. R. M.................................. 244
Ryle... 42
Sabellius.. 37
Selden... 225
Schaff's, Dr., implied admission that trine immersion can be traced to the apostolic age............ 289
Scott, Dr...................................... 15, 95
Shedd, Dr..................................... 11, 138
Sherlock, Bishop................................. 43
Sine, Eld. C..................................... 142
Single immersion, introduction of, 81; introduced by Eunomius, 82; not performed at first according to the baptismal formula, 82; performed in one name, in modern times... 89
Smith, Dr. Wm.,............................... 14. 319
Sozomon.. 266
Standard of correct speaking and writing......... 129
Stier, Dr.. 159
Strabo... 84
Sumner, Bishop................................... 96
"Teaching of the Twelve Apostles,"............... 288
Terry, Dr.. 123
Tertullian, assigns to trine immersion an apostolic origin, 194; misrepresented, 300, 302; the true meaning of the

misrepresented passage shown .. 304
Three, a sacred number........ 224
Theodoret.............................. 266
Tillotson, Bishop..................... 224
Tomline, Bishop....................... 139
Trent, council of...................... 87
Trine affusion......................... 230
Trine aspersion........................ 84
Trine Immersion, the prevalent practice of the church till the seventh century, 84; said to be "much the more fitting," 85; earlier in the Greek, than in the Latin church, 317; "undoubtedly the most primitive manner." 218, 220; practiced by both Trinitarians and Arians........ 52
Trinitarian controversy 102, 109
Tirtheism, unjustly charged to trine immersionists........ 351
Usage, the standard of correct speaking and writing.. 126, 159
Unity of the Godhead............................ 162
Versions, different, of the New Testament............. 23
Vossius 7, 8, 85, 217
Wall 202, 265
Waterland 37, 41, 239
Wardlaw, Dr,......................... 140
Wesley 215
Whately, Dr......................... 21
Whiston............................. 218
Wilkinson, Dr. W. C. 168, 171
Williams, W. R...................... 175

www.ingramcontent.com/pod-product-compliance
Lightning Source LLC
Chambersburg PA
CBHW030349230426
43664CB00007BB/583